Torn by God

A Family's Struggle with Polygamy

a novel

Zoe Murdock

H.O.T. Press

Published by
H.O.T. Press
Ojai, California 93023
www.hotpresspublishing.com

ISBN: 0-923178-06-6
ISBN - 13: 978-0-923178-06-2

Although this story is inspired by real events and is set in the
landscape of the author's youth, the characters are fictitious. They
should not be construed as real.

For Doc,

Without whom this book would not exist,

and without whom I would not exist.

∾∾

Dedicated to Momma and Daddy,

I've journeyed far, but memory keeps bringing

me home. I want to understand.

I love you. I miss you.

Z.

Acknowledgments

I am deeply indebted to all those who provided valuable feedback as I worked through the various drafts of this novel. Many thanks to Elio Zarmati, Susan Hart Hellman, Elizabeth Welles, and Nancy Decker who read with such enthusiasm and attention to detail I was inspired to continue improving the manuscript. Nancy Kurland was one of the first to read the entire manuscript from beginning to end. She had many valuable insights, as did Douglas Hill. Many thanks to Janet Marietta, Joanne Anderson, Dianne Woolley, Pam Kirkpatrick, Julie Albright, and Paul Van Dam who read and responded to the completed manuscript in a way that let me know how the story would be seen by different readers. David Kranes encouraged me from my earliest days of writing in the creative writing program at the University of Utah. I am forever grateful for his influence, his friendship, and his kind assistance in helping me see this story in a new way. And I can't forget Tricia Dunn with whom I shared writing in that little coffee shop beneath the freeway. Last, but not least, my sincere appreciation goes out to the writers in the weekly writing workshop that Doc and I have taught over the past eight years. That includes Jon Myhre, Jeff Guenther, Arthur Braverman, Wendell Jones, Jann Correll, Elizabeth Grumette, David Matzke, Jeff Lawson, Susan Justice, Sharon Hall, John Souchak, Gail Bellenger, Neal Ortenberg, Teresa Rooney, Lisa Snider, Rosalind Warfield-Brown, Philips Patton and the three hundred or so others who have joined us at one time or another. Much of what I know about writing has been garnered from these writers, not only from the comments they provide on my work, but from the complex and interesting stories they present each week for examination and discussion.

Torn by God

Chapter 1

. . . I saw a pillar of light exactly over my head, above the brightness of the sun, which descended gradually until it fell upon me.

Joseph Smith History 1:16

*T*he trouble started the day my dad saw God. It was a Saturday, a warm spring day in 1959. We'd just finished breakfast. Mom was doing the dishes, and Dad was reading his *Book of Mormon*. He'd been doing that a lot lately, and it was starting to get on Mom's nerves.

I was sitting across from Dad, playing solitaire, when Mikey popped up from under the kitchen table and grabbed one of my cards for the third time. I yelled, "Mom, tell Mikey to knock it off."

She threw her dishtowel on the counter and gave Dad an exasperated look. "Get your nose out of that book, Michael. Let's go for a drive or something."

Dad didn't even look up, but Mikey scrambled out from under the table and started jumping up and down. "Oh boy, oh boy. Let's go for a hike, Momma."

Twenty minutes later, we were bouncing down our dirt road. Once we turned at the mailbox onto the highway, we picked up speed, and I rolled down the window and hung my head out to feel the cool spring air on my cheeks.

Mikey got up on his knees and screamed, "Look, Bethy, look. There's little baby lamies."

He leaned out so far, Mom had to reach back and grab him by the seat of his pants. She laughed and said, "If you don't watch out, we'll find you bouncing down the road like a rubber ball."

She turned around and scooted a little closer to Dad. His window was open and the breeze sent her soft brown hair blowing out across the back of the seat. She looked so pretty.

Dad must have seen it too because he grinned and said, "What a beauty you are."

She laughed, but then turned away.

"Did I say something wrong?"

"Well, you've been spending so much time with your scriptures, I thought maybe you'd forgotten about me."

Dad's face darkened. "I'm just studying the gospel. We're supposed to do that, aren't we?"

"I know, but you're so preoccupied all the time."

He frowned, as if he thought she was criticizing him.

She hurried and patted him on the leg and said, "I'm sorry. I didn't mean anything."

After that, they stopped talking, and I went back to looking for signs of spring as we headed up into the canyon. The snow was almost gone by then. Even up on the side of the mountain there were only a few dirty patches in the shade and one long streak of slush running down the middle of the sleigh-riding hill. The trees up that high were still gray, with only a hint of a green halo that showed they were getting ready to bud. I gazed over towards the far side of the canyon. There were little misty patches of fog floating down into the tops of the cottonwood trees alongside the creek. The feathery whiteness of the fog against the stark blue of the sky gave me a feeling that something magical could happen down there.

Dad pulled off the highway at a little campground in a grove of tall pines where we sometimes went for picnics in the summer. We all got out, and I started to look around, but then Dad headed off on a muddy dirt road in the direction of the creek without saying a word. I ran to catch up and asked him why he didn't wait for Mom, but I guess he was too preoccupied to answer. He was walking fast and jumping the mud puddles, as if he was in a big hurry to get somewhere. I looked back to see if Mom and Mikey were coming, but they were still over by the car. I yelled, "Mom, hurry up."

She waved and yelled something, but I couldn't hear what it was.

Dad left the dirt road and took off across a big sagebrush field. I couldn't understand what was wrong with him. Why wouldn't he wait for me?

By the time I crossed the field and got to where the trail dipped down into the scrub oak, Dad was completely out of sight. It was kind of dark and eerie in the trees. With the fog sinking almost to the ground, it was hard to see more than a few feet ahead, and the air was so musty with the smell of last year's fallen leaves, I could hardly breathe.

When I came to a place where the trees were so thick I could barely get through, I began to think I was going the wrong way, but I couldn't see a sign of any other trail. I stopped and looked around, listening for Dad. But he wasn't there. It was as if he'd disappeared into thin air. I yelled, "Dad, Dad, where are you?" but there was no response.

I pushed my way further into the trees and heard a deep roaring sound that seemed to be coming from somewhere up ahead. At first, I couldn't figure out what it was, but then I realized it must be the creek. But why was it so loud?

I kept going, and the creek got louder and louder until I could almost feel it vibrating in my chest. I was feeling a little scared. I wondered if I should go back and find Mom, but I forced myself to go on. Finally, I broke out into a little clearing and saw the water. I couldn't believe that huge roaring river was the same little creek that went through the ravine behind our house. We always played in that creek in the summer, but now it was really deep and all churned up and full of mud and foam. The water had spilled over the banks and was swirling wildly around the trunks of the giant cottonwood trees. But the scariest thing was the sound. How could water make so much noise?

I wanted to get away from the deafening roar, but I couldn't leave without finding Dad. I was starting to worry that maybe he'd fallen in and been carried away. I didn't know what to do. Even if I found him, how would I be able to get him out of the water? I peered back through the trees and fog looking for Mom and Mikey, but they didn't seem to be coming. I'd have to find him myself.

I slowly worked my way downstream, climbing carefully over the rocks and scattered debris. Finally, I came around a bend and saw Dad. I couldn't believe my eyes. He was standing out in the middle of the creek without any clothes on. Had he gone crazy? The water was already over his knees, but he was wading in even deeper. He had something white in one hand, holding it high above his head, like he was trying to keep it from getting wet.

I hurried downstream, closer to where he was, and screamed for him to come out, but the water was so loud I didn't think he could hear me. He just kept going in deeper.

I scrambled over the rocks to the edge of the water, and that's when I saw his clothes lying in a heap on the ground. Everything was there except his church underwear. That must have been what he was holding over his head. But why would he take his sacred temple garments out there?

I couldn't do anything but stand and watch in horror as he continued out into the water. Pretty soon, it was all the way up to his chest. A huge branch came bouncing along the top of the rapids. I gasped when it crashed against his side and almost knocked him over. Somehow, he kept his balance and pushed it away.

Then, I thought I heard some kind of low rumbling sound, mixed in with the roar of the water. I realized it was rocks. They must be tumbling and crashing together on the bottom of the creek. I yelled, "Get out, Dad, quick before your feet get smashed."

I jumped up and down at the edge of the water, waving my arms and screaming, but I couldn't get his attention. Something seemed dreadfully wrong. Dad's face got all twisted up with fear and he started swatting at the air with his temple garments, as if something was attacking him. But there wasn't anything there. It really scared me to see him like that, and I was just about to go find Mom when a bright beam of light broke through the fog and shone right down on Dad's face. The light seemed to take away his fear and focus his attention on something high up in the top of the trees. He became so hypnotized, he didn't seem to notice how the water was buffeting him around.

I stood there holding my breath and praying that God would protect him. Gradually, the fog closed back in around him and the light began to melt away. I tried yelling at him again. This time, he turned and looked in my direction. Then, slowly, he started making his way out of the creek.

The icy cold water had turned his chest bright red. As he came out of the water, I tried not to notice his private parts. It was embarrassing to see him naked like that.

When he finally climbed up on the rocks, I started laughing and crying at the same time. He smiled at me, but it was an odd smile that made me feel like he was seeing right through me. His eyes were glossy and his face glowed, as if some of that strange light was still shining on him.

I looked at his feet and legs to see if they'd been hurt by the tumbling rocks. There was a little river of blood running down from his knee to his foot. I pointed and said, "Dad, you're hurt."

He seemed to notice me for the first time. He quickly held up his temple garments to cover himself, then turned away and pulled them on. When he turned back, I saw the blood had made a bright red stain on the white material of his sacred garments, but he didn't notice.

I grabbed his arm. "Why did you do that, Dad? You could've drowned."

He gave me a peculiar look and said, "Did you see what happened, Beth? Did you see it?"

"See what?"

"It was . . . I had . . . a vision."

For a minute, I wasn't sure what he meant. Then I realized that the beam of light was the same as the light that appeared to the prophet, Joseph Smith, when he had his vision. I'd seen paintings of his vision all my life, and they always showed the light coming down through the trees like that. Had Dad had that kind of vision? Did he see God like the prophet, Joseph Smith, did? Just thinking about it made me feel weird and kind of excited.

I wanted to ask him what God said, but I heard Mom calling to us over the roar of the water. Dad must have heard her too because he grabbed his pants and pulled them on real fast. He was still putting on his shirt when she and Mikey got down to where we were.

Mom took one look at Dad and said, "What in heaven's name have you been doing?"

I said, "He went out in the water, Mom. I was so scared. I thought he was going to drown."

She looked at the roaring river and then back at him and said, "That's crazy, Michael! Why would you do such a thing?"

He touched his finger to her lips. "Shhh, shhh, I'm okay."

She pushed his hand away and looked him over to see if he was all right. "Is that blood?"

The blood from his cut had soaked all the way through his pants, leaving a long red streak.

"It's nothing," he said. "Just a little cut." He wrapped his arms around her to calm her down. When she tried to push him away, he held her tighter, saying, "Shhh. Shhh."

The way Mom was acting must have scared Mikey, or maybe it was the roaring sound of the water, but he grabbed them both around the legs and started howling. That terrible howl and the roaring creek made me feel like the world was splitting apart, like the water was going to rise higher and higher until we all drowned. I yelled, "Come on, Dad. Let's get out of here."

Dad took Mom and Mikey by the hand and helped them back up the trail over the rocks, with me following behind. When we got away from the roaring sound of the water, the full impact of Dad's words hit me. Was it really possible he had a visit from God? Why would God talk to him?

When we got home, I stayed close to Dad. I wanted to ask him what it all meant, but he kept giving me a look that said to keep quiet. I decided he must be trying to figure out how to tell Mom what happened.

That night, I stayed awake until I heard them go to bed, then I sneaked down the hall to the laundry room and crawled into the dirty-clothes cupboard. It was tight and smelly in there with the dirty clothes, but it was a good place to listen through the wall to what they were saying in bed. I wiggled around until I was comfortable, and then I put my ear against the wall and heard Dad say, "Don't worry about that. Beth knows what happened. She was there. She saw everything."

"What did she see, Michael? The raging water? Her father about to be washed away?" Mom's voice was shrill.

Dad tried again. "None of that matters, honey. Something incredible happened to me today. I want to tell you about it."

There was silence behind the wall until Mom finally said, "All right, I'm sorry. I'm listening."

Dad told her about how he'd felt a strange excitement all day, but he didn't know what it was all about. Then, somehow, he'd ended up at the creek, almost without knowing how he got there. When he heard the roar of the water, he thought somebody was calling him to come in. "I know. It sounds crazy," he said, "but the thing that's really crazy is that I knew it was Satan that called me. Yet I still had to go in."

I couldn't believe what he'd said. Satan? Why would he listen to Satan? I thought it was God he was listening to. I pushed my ear even harder against the wall.

He told Mom how he'd been terrified to go in the water, but then he'd realized that his temple garments would protect him.

"Are you telling me Beth saw you without your clothes?"

"I didn't know she was there, Sharon. I really wasn't thinking about that."

Mom got all worked up about me seeing him naked and wouldn't let him go on. While they were arguing, I started thinking about how special it was that I was there when Dad had his vision, but I wondered why I hadn't seen God, or heard him speak. Maybe you had to have the priesthood to see God, and only boys had the priesthood. Or maybe you had to be more righteous than I was. I wondered if Mom would have been able to see God if she had been there.

I kept my ear to the wall. When Mom finally calmed down, Dad told her about the strange light and what an amazing experience it was. "When the light broke through the fog and fell upon me, everything changed. I was in the presence of . . . of God."

"Oh, Michael."

"No, listen, Sharon. It's true. You've got to believe me. That heavenly light filled me with such an amazing sense of peace and serenity. It's what I've been looking for all my life."

"I don't know what you're trying to say."

"I received the Lord and now I have to change my life."

"Are you telling me you talked to God?"

I couldn't believe it. He really had talked to God, and I knew God didn't talk to just anyone. The only problem was that Mom didn't seem to believe it.

Dad's voice got louder. "Something incredible happened today. I need you to understand that my life has changed forever. I have to fast and pray. I have to find out what the Lord wants me to do."

It was silent behind the wall, and then I heard the bed creak. Mom said, "I'm sorry, Michael. I don't know if I believe in . . . modern day visions. I'm not sure what happened to you today, but it frightens me. I don't think I can talk about it right now."

"Honey, please don't walk away."

"I'm sorry."

I heard the door close, and I knew Mom had left the bedroom. I stayed there on top of the dirty clothes for a long time, listening and waiting for her to come back, but she never did. Finally, I rolled onto my back and thought about their conversation. It disturbed me that Mom didn't believe Dad. If only she had been there, like I was. If she could have seen the beam of heavenly light and how it shone down on Dad, she would have known he was telling the truth.

Chapter 2

Yea, wo unto him that shall deny the revelations of the Lord,
and that shall say the Lord no longer worketh by revelation, or
by prophecy, or by gifts, or by tongues, or by healings, or by
the power of the Holy Ghost!

Book of Mormon
3 Nephi 29:6

*D*ad had a study down the hall from the kitchen. It was where he kept track of the accounts for his carpentry business, but he also had a big collection of Church books in there. After his visit from God, he stayed in his study reciting the scriptures and praying whenever he wasn't at work. It sounded like a ghost muttering behind the door. If he ever came out, the only thing he'd talk about was what God wanted him to do. He was fasting a lot and getting so thin, he could hardly keep his pants up. It worried me. I also worried about how upset Mikey was all the time. He couldn't understand why Dad wouldn't play with him anymore. There was no way I could explain it to him; I wasn't so sure I understood it myself.

One Saturday, Dad came out of his study and started wandering around the house, mumbling to himself. Mikey got right in behind him and marched along, lifting his knees real high, as if they were playing soldiers. When they got to the end of the hall, Dad turned around so fast he knocked Mikey down. He stared up at Dad with a bewildered look on his face and his chin quivering. Dad hardly noticed. He just went back to pacing.

A little later, I was in the living room helping Mom fold the laundry when Dad came down the hall, looking mad. He stopped in front of us and yelled, "What do you think happens if a man has a vision from God and denies it?"

Mom looked surprise. "Why . . . I don't know."

"Do you think God would ever forgive him?"

"Michael--"

"It's an unpardonable sin, Sharon! If I don't follow through on this, I'll be damned for all eternity."

That was the first time he'd ever yelled at Mom like that and it scared me. It was as if his vision, and all those scriptures he'd been reading, had taken over his mind and turned him mean. I didn't understand how God could let that happen. I started praying every night before I went to sleep that He would tell Dad what to do so we could get back to our normal lives. But I don't think God was listening to me.

I was surprised at how gentle and patient Mom was, regardless of how unreasonable Dad got. She didn't believe he'd seen God, but I guess she could see how important it was for him to believe it. Then one day, he got so agitated she decided she had to do something. She took his hands in hers and said, "Maybe you should go talk to the Bishop, Michael. Maybe he can help you understand what happened and what you should do."

He gave her a quick look. "I don't know. What if he thinks I'm . . .?"

"That's what the Bishop is there for, love. If you can't talk to him, who can you talk to?"

It was true. The Bishop was the head of the Church in our town. He was the person who was closest to the prophet and closest to God. He was the one who made all the important decisions in the Ward. He decided if you were righteous enough to be baptized, or to be married in the temple. He told you when you needed to pray for forgiveness, and he told the boys when it was time for them to go on their missions. Surely, he could help Dad.

The next day we stayed after Sunday School. I waited with Mikey and Mom on the wooden bench outside the Bishop's office while Dad went in to talk to him. It was strange being in the empty church with only the sound of murmuring voices coming out from under the door. The sunlight streamed down the hallways, reflecting off the polished white floors, reminding me of the heavenly light that shone down on Dad. I tried to imagine what the Bishop would say when Dad told him he had talked to God.

They were in there for so long, I got bored and went to look at the photographs hanging along the wall. They were pictures of all the men who had been Bishops in our town since those early days when Brigham Young first came to the Promised Land with the pioneers. I looked closely at their faces, wondering if any of them had seen God like Dad had, but there was no way to tell. I thought it was more likely to have happened to the old-time Bishops because they lived closer to Joseph Smith's time, and they had long hair and long beards like Brigham Young. Looking at those beards made me wonder why no one wore beards anymore. Then, I started wondering why there weren't any pictures of the woman and the children from the old pioneer days. I went back to the bench and asked Mom.

She shrugged. "I don't know. Maybe it's because they were all polygamists back then. The Bishops had so many wives. I guess the women and children kind of got lost."

I knew all about polygamists. The prophet, Joseph Smith, was one and so were Brigham Young and a lot of the other men in the early days when the Saints first came to Utah. There were even a few people in our town who were still polygamists, but they didn't belong to our Church. They'd been excommunicated and all the kids made fun of them and called them weirdoes and perverts.

I sat back down on the bench. "What would it be like to be a polygamist, Mom? Could you ever do it?"

"Heavens no. We'd have to hide from the law. I don't think that would be a very nice life. Do you?"

"No."

"But I guess the early settlers had to deal with it. Your father's grandfather was a polygamist. In fact, he was the one who hid Brigham Young when the U.S. army was coming to put everyone in jail for practicing polygamy. Did you know that?"

"Sure, Dad's told me about it lots of times. He's real proud of his grandfather. So what happened to all his wives?"

"I don't really know. I guess he had to stop living with them after the Church banned polygamy."

I tried to imagine my great grandfather in a big house with a bunch of wives and children. I thought it sounded kind of fun, but it wouldn't be fun going to jail, or getting excommunicated. The excommunication part was what confused me. Why was it okay with the Church for the early pioneers to be polygamists, if it was so bad now? I'd heard all my life that polygamy was one of God's Celestial laws. Somehow, it didn't make sense that God would change his mind about one of his divine laws.

I heard loud voices from under the Bishop's door. A few minutes later, they came out. The Bishop patted Dad on the shoulder and said, "Fast and pray about this, Michael. God will answer your questions."

Dad frowned and shook his head. "That's all well and good, Bishop, but if He does, I expect you won't believe that either."

"Now, Michael, you know I'm only--"

"Sure, sure, Bishop, you're only trying to help."

I couldn't believe it when Dad turned his back on the Bishop and walked away. Doing that to the Bishop was almost like doing it to God or Jesus. What was wrong with Dad?

The Bishop gave Mom a grim look and shook his head.

Mom seemed kind of ashamed. "I'm sorry, Bishop. He's having a hard time right now. Please forgive him." She turned and hurried after Dad.

I looked at the Bishop, wondering what he'd said that made Dad so mad. He obviously hadn't helped him, and if the Bishop couldn't help him, who could?

The Bishop went back in his office. I grabbed Mikey's hand and dragged him out to the car. Dad started up the engine and began yelling as he pulled out onto the road. "He didn't believe a word I said, Sharon. He went so far as to tell me not to talk about it to anyone."

Mom's mouth was tight, but she spoke gently. "I'm sure it's just because he wasn't there. That sort of thing doesn't happen everyday. Naturally, he's having trouble believing it."

"But that's the point, Sharon. There's never another person there when God appears to a man. No one was there when God appeared to Joseph Smith, but we believe it happened, don't we? We take it on faith."

I leaned over the front seat and said, "But I was there, Dad."

They both ignored me.

Mom said, "Well, yes. Of course, we believe in Joseph Smith's vision, but he was the prophet, and it happened a long time ago."

"No, no, he wasn't the prophet. He was just a young boy praying in a grove of trees. And it wasn't all that long ago."

Dad was driving too fast. I was afraid he was going to go off the road into the irrigation ditch. I'd never seen him drive like that, like he didn't care what happened to us.

Mom was focused on Dad and didn't seem to notice. "Yes, but God had a plan for Joseph Smith."

"Right. A plan. Are you saying he doesn't have a plan for me?"

"Well, maybe he does, but . . . Joseph Smith was told what he was supposed to do, wasn't he?"

He looked over at her, and it was as if he was seeing her for the first time in weeks. "Oh, I see. So, you don't believe me either."

"Yes, of course I believe you. It's just that…" She looked away.

"Just what?" He jerked the car towards the side of the road and we slid to a stop in a huge cloud of dust. He sat there glaring at her, but she wouldn't look back.

After what seemed like forever, she turned to him. "Look. I'm trying to believe you, Michael. But it's hard. You tell me God appeared to you. You say it as if it's the most natural thing in the world. Then you start comparing yourself to the prophet, Joseph Smith. What would you think if I told you something like that?"

"Sharon, I didn't make this up. You can't let the Bishop's opinion sway you." He grabbed her hands and held them to his chest. "We can't let this cause trouble between us, love. You have to believe me. We have to work together and try and understand what it means. Please, honey, don't turn against me."

"I'm not turning against you. I want to believe you, you know I do. It's just that . . . I wasn't there."

I leaned forward and tried again. "I was there, Mom. I saw it. It really did happen."

Neither of them even looked at me.

Dad held onto Mom's hands as if she was trying to get away. "I can't go on as if nothing happened," he said. "How can I do that?"

There were tears in Mom's eyes. "I wish I could have been with you, Michael. I feel like I'm standing in the dark. Like you've gone some place I can't follow."

Dad pleaded with her. "I wish you'd been there too, but you weren't. So, what should we do? We can't pretend it didn't happen."

Mikey started making little whimpering sounds, and rolling the window up and down. I tried to stop him, but he put his fingers in his mouth and whimpered even louder.

Mom finally noticed us and warned Dad. "We'll talk about this later, Michael. Let's get the kids home."

Dad reluctantly let go of her hands and pulled back out onto the road. When we got home, Mom told Mikey and me to go to our room and change and to stay there until she called us for lunch. I went upstairs feeling very confused. I'd never seen Mom and Dad fight like that before, and now, Dad was having trouble with the Bishop too. How could seeing God cause so much trouble?

I needed to talk to someone about it, but the Bishop had said Dad wasn't supposed to tell anyone about his vision, and I knew that meant I wasn't supposed to tell anyone either. I decided I didn't care. I had to talk to my friend, Tommy Atkins. He had a different way of thinking about things that sometimes helped me understand people. I desperately needed that right now.

Chapter 3

For behold, the Lord shall curse the land with much heat, and the barrenness thereof shall go forth forever; and there was a blackness came upon all the children of Canaan, that they were despised among all people.

Pearl of Great Price
Moses 7:8

*B*y the time Mikey and I got to school the next day, most of the kids were already in the classrooms. Tommy was waiting in the hall for me. I hurried up to him. Before I could say anything, the Bishop's daughter, Karen, came by. She glared at me and stuck her nose in the air, hurrying to the other side of the hall, as if she didn't want to get too close to us.

Tommy said, "What's with her?"

"I don't know. Just being her usual self, I guess." But it still made me wonder what she was thinking. I waited until she'd gone in the classroom, then I whispered, "I've got to talk to you, Tommy, but I can't talk here."

He grinned. "Well, I've got something to show you. How about we meet at the cemetery after school?"

Tommy was supposed to be in the seventh grade, but he'd sluffed so many times he'd been held back a year to my combined fifth and sixth grade class. I asked him once if he missed being with the kids his age, but he said it didn't make any difference because nobody talked to him anyway. It was because he wasn't a member of the Mormon Church like the rest of us. His father smoked cigarettes, and that got him labeled as bad because smoking was against the Word of Wisdom. Some kids were actually scared of Tommy's father. They'd cross to the other side of the road when they went past his house, afraid that he was the devil and he'd grab them if they got too close.

I'd always thought Tommy was cute. He had dark hair and shiny brown eyes that seemed to notice everything, but I'd never talked to him much either. Then one day, he'd grabbed my arm and pulled me into the trees behind the school playground. I was scared of what he was going to do, but he only wanted to show me a hummingbird nest. He'd found it and wanted to share it with someone and had decided on me. He told me it was very special to see the tiny eggs because hummingbirds always hid their nests where no one could find them. I liked how gentle he was with the eggs. It made me want to know him better. Over time, we became best friends, but we always met in secret places where we could talk freely away from the ridicule of the other kids.

When school was over that day, I made sure nobody was around, then snuck out the side door. I hurried across the playground, took the narrow trail through the scrub oak, and crossed the lumpy sagebrush field to the old pioneer cemetery where the original Mormon settlers had buried their dead. Tommy was already there, leaning back against a headstone, looking forlorn.

I plopped down into the wild grass beside him. "How come you look so sad?"

He shrugged. "Matt joined the Army yesterday."

"Your brother? Why'd he do that?"

He flipped a rock through the air and it pinged against another headstone. "He said it was his only ticket out of this stupid Mo-mo town. And besides, if he didn't go, he would've got drafted anyway."

"Really? I don't know any boys who've been drafted."

"That's because you only know Mormon boys."

"Don't they have to go in the army?"

He frowned and spoke in a whiny baby voice, "No, they've got to go on their missions instead."

I didn't understand why it made him so mad. If the Church called them on a mission, it wasn't their fault. It was a calling from God, and they had to do it. "Maybe they'll go in the Army when they get back."

"Maybe. I guess some of them do. Matt told me about one Mormon guy in the Army. They made fun of him because he was scared to go swimming. He had some crazy idea that Satan ruled the water. Finally, they made him go in, but he kept his magic underwear on for protection."

"Magic underwear?"

"You know. His church garments."

"Really? That's what my dad did."

"What?"

"He took his garments into the water for protection."

Tommy stared at me. "What are you talking about?"

I told him about Dad's vision. He rolled his eyes and said, "That's ridiculous. Why don't you tell me another one."

"No, really," I said. "He had a vision from God."

When I told him what had happened, he shook his head in disbelief. Then, he flopped back on the ground and put his arm over his eyes. He didn't say a word for a long time. I worried about what he was thinking. We'd been through some arguments about the Church before. Usually, he said it was all a bunch of religious crap.

This time, he didn't say anything about the Church, or the stupid Mos, and I wondered why. I lay down next to him and stared up at the wispy little clouds sailing across the pale blue sky. When he ignored me like that, it made me feel especially lonely and confused. Finally, I whispered, "Really, Tommy, don't you think people can have visions?" I rolled over onto my stomach and looked at him. "The scriptures say that God talks to people, so why wouldn't He talk to my dad?"

Tommy remained silent, and I thought maybe he'd gone to sleep. I nudged him once and he didn't move, so I nudged him again. He took away his arm and opened one eye. "Look, maybe God would talk to your dad. But I don't believe in that kind of stuff."

"Don't you believe in anything?"

"Sure, I believe in lots of things. But I don't believe what the Mormons say."

"But I'm a Mormon."

"You're different. The rest of them think they're better than everyone else. The only time they talk to you is if they're trying to convert you. What a bunch of crap." He sat up and started throwing rocks again. They bounced back at us and we had to duck to keep from getting hit, but Tommy didn't seem to care. I could tell he didn't want to talk about it anymore, but he was the only one I could talk to. Everyone else would tell the Bishop.

"I'm really worried, Tommy. What if nobody believes my dad had a vision, but he keeps believing it? What do you think they'll do?"

"They'll think he's crazy. But they're the crazy ones. Matt says that some people think Mormons are like cults that do voodoo."

"Voodoo?"

"You know, where you stick pins in a doll that looks like somebody, and it makes them sick."

"That's ridiculous. It's more likely we'd try to heal them."

"That's what I'm talking about. Mormons think they can heal people by rubbing magic oil in their hair."

"That's not magic. It's just a blessing. The Bishop gave Mikey a blessing like that when he was a baby. The doctor said he was going to go deaf from his ear infections, but the Bishop and my dad blessed him, and he got better."

"That's what I said, magic."

I shook my head in frustration and Tommy went silent again. He was obviously fed up with me. "Okay," I said, "we don't have to talk about that stuff anymore. I thought you had something to show me."

He frowned. "I don't think it's a good time. You'll just get mad."

"No, I won't. Come on." I reached under his shirt to tickle him and change the mood. That's when I felt something.

I tried to pull it out, but he pushed my hands away and laughed. "No, no, you can't see it. It belongs to Matt. I don't want you ruining it."

"Come on. You said you'd show me."

We wrestled over it a little longer and then he said, "Okay, okay."

He pulled out a picture, but before I could get a good look at it, he tucked it in the back of his pants. I tried to grab it, but he held my arms and grinned. "Poor little Mormon girl. Thinks her daddy had a vision."

It hurt my feelings and I jerked my arms away. "Why are you being so mean? I thought we were friends."

"'I'm not mean. I'm just telling you your head's full of manure." He put his hands over my ears and rocked my head from side-to-side.

I pushed him away. "You're just trying to get out of showing me the picture. Now, come on, you can trust me."

He frowned. "Okay, but it's not my fault if you get mad."

"I won't. I won't ever get mad at you. I promise."

He handed me the picture. It was such a shock it caused a kind of swirling sensation in my stomach. It was a photograph of a black woman. Her hair was pulled up on her head in smooth, shiny curls and she was wearing nothing but Church garments and sparkly red high-heeled shoes. She had bright red lipstick, and she was licking her little finger with a tongue so pink it almost didn't seem real. I couldn't stop staring at her.

When I finally looked at Tommy, he had a funny expression on his face. "Do you like her? How about those magic underwear?"

"Why would they take a picture like that? Are they making fun of Mormons? It's not very nice."

Tommy laughed. "What's wrong? She's all covered up from her neck to her knees."

"Maybe so, but you're not supposed to show your Church garments. Besides, I don't think black people are even supposed to be wearing them. They can't hold the priesthood, or go to the temple."

"Yeah, I know. And why don't you tell me why that is?"

"Because of God's curse on Cain. You know, he turned him black for killing his brother, Abel."

"You just believe whatever nonsense you're told, don't you? You never stop to think it might be a bunch of baloney."

"What do you mean? Everybody knows about that. It's in the Bible."

"More likely the Church just doesn't want black people around. They blame God so *they* won't be blamed for hating them."

"The Church doesn't hate people. They tell us to love everyone."

"Yeah, like they love me."

I had to stop and think about that. "It's only because you're not in the Church. People think you're going to hell if you're not a member of the Church. It's not because they don't like you. They're just . . . worried about you."

"Oh right. So, I guess it's okay for them to treat me like they do."

He wouldn't talk after that, and I didn't know what to say either. He was too upset to reason with. All I could say was, "I'm sorry people treat you bad. I wish they weren't like that."

"What in the hell do I care? I'm getting out of this stupid town as soon as I can. I'm going to join the Army, like Matt." He jumped to his feet. "Come on, let's get the hell out of here."

He hurried across the field with me trying to catch up. When we came out of the scrub oak into the schoolyard, I said, "Don't be mad at me, Tommy. It's not my fault what people do."

"I'm not mad. I'm just fed up with people telling me what to believe. Why don't they worry about themselves?"

"Do you think the Church is all wrong about everything?"

"What do I care? They can make up any dumb thing they want. I just wish they'd stop trying to convince everyone else to believe it." He squeezed my arm, trying to smile. "Look, I've gotta go." He hurried away without looking back.

The things Tommy said were spinning around in my head as I walked home. I hadn't ever questioned the Church before, but he'd got me thinking about things that scared me. Did people in other places really think Mormons did voodoo? Did they make fun of our temple garments and think the only reason black people couldn't hold the priesthood was because we didn't like them?

I closed my eyes, trying to escape the confusion, but I couldn't get away from that image of the black woman in her temple garments. I didn't know if I was more upset about someone taking that picture, or about the Church not allowing black people to hold the priesthood because of something that happened a long time ago.

I was still upset about it the next day after school as I walked to the church house for Primary. When I got there, I asked my teacher, Sister Andrews, why God wouldn't forgive the black people. She wrinkled up her nose, like she smelled something bad and said, "What on earth are you talking about, dear?"

"We're always talking about forgiveness, so why doesn't God forgive them so they can be full members of the Church?"

She frowned and plopped down into her chair. "Well, sweetie, maybe someday He will."

I should have let it go at that, but there were other things I wanted to know. "Why were they punished in the first place? They weren't the ones that killed Abel. And what about the Indians? Why were they cursed with red skin?"

"Oh, Beth. Where do you come up with all these questions?"

Then, I made the mistake of telling her about the picture of the black woman in temple garments. She grabbed my shoulders and shook me. "What picture? Where did you see it?"

I knew if she found out it was Tommy's he'd be in big trouble, so I didn't say anything, but then she threatened to tell my parents and the Bishop. That's the last thing I wanted her to do. It wouldn't only get Tommy in trouble, it would get me in trouble too, and maybe even Dad. Finally, I mumbled, "Tommy."

"Tommy? Tommy who?"

"You know. Tommy Atkins."

"That boy? What did he do, chase you down after school and make you look at it?"

I tried to keep from rolling my eyes. "Why would he do that? He's my friend."

She stood up. "Beth, I want you to stay away from that boy. Do you hear me? He's a bad influence."

"I thought we were supposed to be nice to people who aren't in the Church. I thought we were all supposed to be missionaries."

"I think you'd better let the real missionaries take care of people like that."

I wanted to tell her I wasn't going to stay away from Tommy no matter what she said, but that would have been another mistake, so I kept quiet.

She hadn't resolved any of my questions; she'd just proved that Tommy was right. I was beginning to wonder if maybe the Church really didn't like certain people. Maybe they didn't want us to have anything to do with them. But what about loving everybody? And what about trying to be a missionary?

I sat there going over it until I heard Sister Andrews say something about our annual daddy-daughter-date. Then, I perked up. It was a day we were supposed to spend with our fathers as a kind of training for how to act when we were old enough to go on a date. Maybe it would give me a chance to ask Dad some of the questions that were flying around in my head. And I thought, maybe, just maybe, if I got him alone, I could convince him to stop worrying about his vision all the time and let us get back to living a normal life.

That night, I planned to talk to Dad about our date, but I didn't have a chance. As soon as he got home from work, he stormed into the kitchen, threw his lunch sack on the table, and started pacing with a scowl on his face.

Mom came in and saw him. "What's wrong, Michael? Has something happened?"

"He goads me into talking. Then when I do, he tells me to get out." He pulled his sweatshirt over his head and threw it on the chair.

"What do you mean? Who told you to get out?"

"Brother Ellison. He said I couldn't work for him anymore."

Mom looked shocked. "Why would he do that?"

"He asked me outright. Put his arm around my shoulder, all buddy-buddy, and asked me to tell him what I saw, like he really wanted to know."

"He asked about the vision? How did he know about that?"

"I don't know. I guess the Bishop told him. I don't know who else it could have been, unless . . ." He spun around and glared at me. "Did you tell someone, Beth?"

"No, Dad." I felt bad saying that. I don't think I'd ever lied to him before, but I'd already been through the experience with Sister Andrews. I didn't want anyone else telling me to stay away from Tommy. Besides, I knew Tommy wouldn't have told anyone. Nobody ever even talked to him.

Mom must have believed me because she turned her attention back to Dad. "But why would the Bishop have told him?"

"I don't know, Sharon." Dad's face was grim and he was looking at Mom as if she was to blame.

"So, what did you say to Brother Ellison?"

"What do you think I said? I told him."

"You told him what, Michael?"

Mom's eyes took on that dark green shade that only happened when she was really upset. Dad must have seen it too, because he turned away and wouldn't answer her.

She stepped closer to him with her hands on her hips. "Oh, honey, you didn't tell him you had a visit from God, did you?"

"Why wouldn't I? Is it something I should be ashamed of?"

"No, Michael. I don't think it is, but if someone doesn't believe you, it's just going to get them riled up. What if he tells other people?"

Dad sank down into a chair and put his head in his hands.

Mom sat next to him and softened her voice. "Well, let's think about this. You just barely started framing his new study, didn't you? Is he going to leave it half finished? No, he wouldn't do that."

Dad just sat there with his hands over his face.

Mom scooted closer and put her arm around his shoulder. She told him he'd just have to call Brother Ellison in a few days when he'd had time to simmer down.

He looked at her in disbelief. "You're saying I should apologize?"

"No, no. Just give him a chance to say he's sorry. You know how he is. He gets all worked up about things. He's probably already feeling bad about it." She patted his arm. "Come on, Michael. Don't worry about it. Go take your shower. You'll feel better."

After a few minutes, he stood up and slowly went upstairs. Mom looked at me and let out a big sigh. She'd told Dad not to worry, but she looked worried. And I was worried too. Work always got kind of slow for Dad in the winter, so he needed all the jobs he could get when it was warm. Why were all these terrible things happening?

When Dad came back down for supper, he seemed to be feeling a little better. He even managed a smile when Mikey made a face on his hamburger patty with the ketchup. I decided to ask him about the daddy-daughter-date. At first he didn't seem interested, but I kept after him and he said we could go up to Pioneer Village on Saturday if I wanted to. It was kind of a kid place to go, but I thought maybe we could do something fun afterwards, maybe go for a hike in the mountains, or have a picnic at Liberty Park. At least it would give me a chance to talk to him.

Chapter 4

And they began to be divided into classes; and they began to build up churches unto themselves to get gain, and began to deny the true church of Christ.

Book of Mormon
4 Nephi 1:26

*J*ust as Dad and I were about to leave the house for our date on Saturday morning, the telephone rang. Dad answered it. He looked at Mom and shrugged, like he didn't know who he was talking to. Then he said, "Oh, yes, of course, I remember you. You haven't been gone from Church that long." He put his hand over the receiver and said, "Jacob Reuben."

Mom looked surprised. I was surprised too. He was Laura and Aaron Reuben's father, and they hadn't been in school for a long time. In fact, I thought they'd moved away until I heard the kids talking about how Brother Reuben had become a polygamist and didn't want his kids coming to school anymore. After that, if anyone talked about them, it was just to make fun of their weird clothes, or to joke about how many wives could get in Brother Reuben's bed before it would break.

Dad nodded. "Sure, Jacob. I'd be happy to discuss it with you. I'm just heading out for a day with my daughter, but I could stop by on the way. . . . Okay, I'll see you in a bit." He hung up the phone and looked at Mom.

She said, "Jacob Reuben? We haven't seen anything of him since he got excommunicated. What does he want?"

Dad shrugged. "He wants me to do some work."

"Really? That's strange. But come to think of it, he could use some help with that beat up old house of his. I've heard it's falling apart. Still, it surprises me. Those polygamists generally stick to themselves."

"Guess I'm the only carpenter he knows. I'll stop by and see what he needs done. I could use the work."

He frowned, and Mom said, "Now don't start thinking about Brother Ellison again. You'll find other work. Just go with Beth and have a good time."

We didn't talk much on the way up to the mouth of the canyon. Now that we were alone, I felt a little uncomfortable. Dad had been reading scriptures and praying and fasting for so long it seemed hard to have a regular conversation with him. And I wasn't so sure I should ask him my questions. If he found out about my conversation with Tommy, he might have the same reaction as Sister Andrews.

Dad turned up a steep dirt road on the side of the mountain. The truck bounced so hard from the ruts we both started laughing.

Dad said, "I think he needs a road builder as much as a carpenter."

"Yeah." I giggled. "I almost hit my head on that last one."

At the top of the hill, we pulled up in front of an old dilapidated house. There was nothing in the yard except a half-dead tree with a couple of squawking crows perched high up in the bare branches. There wasn't any grass, or flowers, or anything, just the bare dirt yard with an old brown car parked on the side of the house next to some kind of wooden pen. Before Dad had even turned off the engine, Mr. Reuben came out of the house, hurried down the rickety wooden stairs, and ran across the yard towards us. I was surprised by how different he looked from the last time I'd seen him. He'd grown a wild looking beard, and his hair had gotten long and seemed like it was full of knots. He reminded me of one of those old pioneer bishops on the wall at the church.

When we got out of the truck, Mr. Reuben grabbed Dads hand and started shaking it vigorously. "I'm very happy to see you, Brother Sterling. You don't know how glad I am that you've come." He kept shaking Dad's hand, like he was never going to let it go.

"Well, thank you. It's good to see you too, Jacob." Dad glanced over at me and raised an eyebrow.

That's when Mr. Reuben noticed I was there. "Well, now, who is this lovely young lady?"

Dad pulled me forward. "You remember Beth."

"Yes, I think I do. She was just a little bit of a thing when I last saw her. How do you do, Sister Elizabeth? You certainly have grown up."

He looked at me with such piercing eyes it made me nervous, but I thought I should try to be nice if he was going to give Dad work. I smiled, and he smiled back, still looking into my eyes, like he was trying to see deep inside me.

Finally, he stopped staring. He turned back to Dad and slapped him on the back. "Brother, you're probably wondering why I asked you to come up here. Well, I'll tell you. We want you to build us a church."

This time Dad raised both eyebrows. "A church?"

"Yes. I think it's time."

"Do you have enough people for that? I mean--"

Mister Reuben laughed and said, "Yes, well, we're still small, but the saints are gathering."

Dad leaned back against the hood of the truck to think about it, and Mr. Reuben glanced back at me and winked. I didn't understand why he kept looking at me like that. The way his eyes moved up and down my body made me feel like he could see through my clothes. No grownup had ever looked at me like that before. I stared at the ground, trying to get away from his eyes.

Dad didn't seem to notice what Mr. Reuben was doing. He said, "I don't know. A church is quite a big project. I generally do smaller things. You know remodels, cabinets, or maybe a room addition now and then. I'm really a carpenter more than a builder."

Mr. Reuben slapped him on the back again. "But that's exactly what we need. A carpenter. It's not going to be a big church, just a place for us to gather and give praise to the Lord. You can do it, Brother. I know you can. I've seen your work."

"But why me? Don't you have someone within your group?"

I wondered why Dad was resisting. Was he worried about working for the polygamists? Was he afraid of what people would say?

It was obvious Mr. Reuben didn't want to take no for an answer. He leaned closer and lowered his voice. "And there are other reasons we want you to help us." He looked around as if he thought someone might be listening and said, "I've heard things, Brother Michael. Maybe things I wasn't supposed to hear, but . . . let's just say it tells me there may be a place for you with us."

"I'm not sure what you mean, Jacob."

"Please. Call me Brother. Just because I'm not part of your church anymore, it doesn't mean we're not still brothers. Maybe I'm more of a brother to you than you think, more of a brother than the men in your church." He glanced back at me and winked again.

I watched as Dad and Mr. Reuben exchanged looks. It was like they were having some kind of silent conversation. I felt excluded and looked over at Mr. Reuben's rickety old house with its curtained windows. I wondered if his wives and kids were inside. Mom had told me polygamy was against the law, so maybe that was the reason he didn't invite us inside the house. Maybe he didn't want us to see them.

I couldn't remember having seen the original Mrs. Reuben at all since they became polygamists. I wondered if she still lived in that house, and if the other wives lived there too. And what about their kids, Laura and Aaron? Were they stuck inside that little house all the time, unable to attend school? If so, how were they ever going to learn anything about the world? I felt sorry for them and knew I'd never want to live like that.

By the time I turned my attention back to Dad and Mr. Reuben, they were shaking hands, as if they had come to some kind of agreement. Dad smiled and said, "Okay. I'll call you in a few days."

Mr. Reuben patted him on the shoulder, like they were old friends. "Good. We're not quite ready to start the church, but we can get started on the planning process."

Dad opened the truck door for me, and Mr. Reuben leaned down close to my face and said, "See you later, little sister."

I felt so uncomfortable with his closeness, I just turned away, but Dad gave me a nudge, so I said, "Goodbye, Mr. Reuben."

He quickly grabbed my hand and held it tight against his chest. "Please, little sister, call me Brother. We are all brothers and sisters under God."

I jerked my hand away and got in the car, but Mr. Reuben didn't want to let us go. He held onto Dad's arm and gave him that same piercing look. "Don't let them convince you that God has turned silent, Brother. They can't take that away from you."

Dad didn't respond for a second, and when he did, his voice cracked. "Thank you, Brother. Thank you for that."

Dad's eyes glistened with tears as we bumped back down the dirt road to the highway. At first, I didn't understand why he was crying, but then, I realized they were tears of joy because Mr. Rueben believed in his vision. That must have been what Mr. Reuben meant when he said, "they can't take that away from you." I was relieved to see Dad happy for a change, but I was nervous about what people would think if he started spending time with the polygamists. It wasn't something people did in our town. Still, it would give him some work and he needed to make money. I tried to be optimistic. "I'm glad you're going to build their church, Dad. I'm sure you'll do a good job."

He shook his head. "I don't know. I may be biting off more than I can chew."

"But Mister . . . I mean Brother Reuben thinks you can do it."

"That's good of him. He's very kind."

I wasn't so sure Brother Reuben was kind. His smile seemed kind of phony to me, like it wasn't really coming from his heart. But I couldn't tell Dad that. I didn't want to take away his happiness. "I'm glad somebody finally believes in your vision."

He looked at me. "You believe, don't you, Beth? You were there."

"Yes. Of course I do." I said the words, but I was becoming less sure about it. If God really did talk to Dad, why didn't He reveal his plan for him, like He did with Joseph Smith?

"Now if only your mother could believe." The happiness drained from his eyes when he thought about Mom.

I hurried and said, "I'm sure she wants to believe, Dad. It's just that she wasn't there. It must be hard to imagine that kind of thing, if you didn't see it for yourself."

"A person has to have faith in those situations."

"Maybe you should tell her what God said and what He looks like, then she'd know you saw Him."

"It wouldn't help, honey. It's not the kind of thing you can describe with words."

"Why not?"

"Our human eyes are not used to seeing heavenly beings. The light was blinding."

"But you heard His voice, didn't you?"

"Yes, yes, I did. I heard it clearly."

"What did He say, Dad?" It was something I'd wanted to ask for a long time. I held my breath waiting for his answer.

He shook his head. "It's sacred, Beth. It's not something I want to speak of."

"But you've told Mom what He said, haven't you?"

"I'm telling you, she needs to fast and pray. Then God will tell her what He wants her to know."

"Are you saying God would speak to her too?"

"You know what I'm talking about, Beth. The Holy Ghost. The scriptures say, 'I would exhort you that ye would ask God, the Eternal Father, in the name of Christ, if these things are not true; and if ye shall ask with a sincere heart, with real intent, having faith in Christ, He will manifest the truth of it unto you, by the power of the Holy Ghost.'"

He was right, I did know about the Holy Ghost. I received the Holy Ghost when I was baptized and confirmed a member of the Church, when I turned eight. The Holy Ghost was supposed to be the comforter, the one who whispered in your ear, telling you the answer to your questions. But why wouldn't Dad tell me what God said? I was there. Surely it would be okay with God for me to know.

Dad grew silent, and I started thinking about Brother Reuben and wondering what made him decide to become a polygamist. Why was he willing to get excommunicated when everybody knew that was the worse thing that could happen to you? I touched Dad's arm to bring him back from his thoughts. "Dad," I said, "do you think Brother Reuben stopped believing in the gospel? Is that why he was willing to be excommunicated?"

"Oh, no. I'm certain he still believes what we believe, but he thinks the Church has changed too much. He thinks we should be living the original doctrine, the Celestial Laws that were practiced during the time of Joseph Smith and Brigham Young."

"You mean doctrine like polygamy?"

"Yes, that, and other things."

"Like what else?"

"Like the Law of Consecration. And it's obvious from what Brother Reuben said that they still believe in personal revelation."

"What's the Law of Consecration?"

Dad looked over at me in surprise. "Aren't they teaching you anything in Sunday School?"

"It's where everybody pools their money, and then the Bishops give back what the people need. It makes everyone equal. Right?"

"That's right. That's what the scriptures say we should do."

"So, why did we stop doing it?"

"I guess the saints weren't willing to give up their hard earned dollars even for a place with God in the Celestial Kingdom. When the Lord saw the people weren't able to do it, He rescinded the law until a future time. We pay tithing now, and make fast offerings, and we give money to build new churches."

"Do you think God's mad about it? I mean, when the people won't do what he wants them to do?"

He shook his head. "I don't know. Sometimes I wonder." He got a far away look in his eyes and went back inside his head.

I looked out the window and realized we were halfway to Pioneer Village. The day was going by and all we were doing was thinking and talking about church things, like always. I tried to find something that might attract Dad's attention, but I didn't think he'd care much about the sunlight shimmering in the trees alongside the road, or the piles of amazingly white clouds towering high over the mountains. It made me feel sad that we never got to focus on that kind of thing anymore. We hadn't really had any fun since Dad had his vision.

I noticed a falling-down barn beside the road with an old organ sitting outside it. I thought it was funny. "Look, Dad, there's an old organ. Do you think the farmer keeps it out there so he can play music for his chickens?"

He just mumbled, "Chickens?" and didn't even look where I was pointing. He was too absorbed with something in his mind to pay attention to anything in the real world.

As we pulled into the parking lot at Pioneer Village, I said, "Come on, Dad, it's too boring thinking about church stuff all the time. Let's go have some fun for a change."

He shook his head, as if he was trying to clear it. "Life is not all fun and games, Beth. There are things a man must do on earth if he's to become a god, things I must do to make sure we can all be together as an eternal family."

I wondered what he meant by becoming a god. How could a person become a god?

Chapter 5

I understand the law of celestial marriage to mean that every man in the Church, who has the ability to obey and practice it in righteousness and will not, shall be damned.

Joseph F. Smith (1878)
Journal of Discourses

Inasmuch as laws have been enacted by Congress forbidding plural marriages . . . I hereby declare my intention to submit to those laws, and to use my influence with the members of the Church over which I preside to have them do likewise.

Wilford Woodruff, President
October 6, 1890

*T*he next day was the first Sunday of the month, which meant it was Fast Sunday. Mikey and I hated Fast Sunday because we had to be in church all day, and we were always starving by the time we got to eat anything.

I dressed for church, and had just gotten downstairs, when I heard someone at the front door. It was the deacons collecting the fast offerings for the poor. I took the stiff brown envelope from Scott and ran to get the money from Dad. He was in his study furiously writing something in his notebook. He didn't even look up when I came in.

I waved the envelope. "Dad, the deacons are waiting."

"Oh, right." He got out his wallet, gave me ten dollars, and went back to writing.

I took the money back to the deacons, thinking there was something odd about the way Dad acted. What was he writing that was so important?

When we got to church, we all went our separate ways, me and Mikey to our Sunday School classes, Mom to Relief Society, and Dad to Priesthood meeting. Later, we met up in the chapel for Fast and Testimony Meeting. Like always, we sat in the back row where we could see everyone when they stood up to bare their testimonies.

After we partook of the sacrament, the Bishop went up to the microphone and said he hoped our hearts would be filled with the spirit of the Holy Ghost while we bore our testimonies. He sat down, and it was just like always: one person after the next stood up, everybody saying the same thing about how they knew Jesus Christ was the son of God, and Joseph Smith was the true prophet, and how our church was the one and only true church in the whole world. It almost put me to sleep. But then, Sister Bradford stood up. I knew it was going to get interesting. The boys down the row from us knew it too; they started giggling and poking each other in the ribs.

The thing that was so funny about Sister Bradford was that she always put her hand down inside her dress and rubbed the top of her breast while she bore her testimony. It was like she couldn't talk unless she was doing that. I don't know why she didn't realize everybody was laughing at her. She always talked in a booming voice, but the most interesting thing was that she'd talk about things nobody else dared talk about in church.

She started by giving us all a big frown. Then she said, "Now I know Jesus said, 'Ask and it shall be given you; seek and ye shall find it; knock and it shall be opened,' but I've been knocking and seeking and asking for months, and my car's still broke down, and yesterday the washing machine overflowed and ruined the carpet, and God still hasn't stopped Sister Nielson's dog from doing his business on our front lawn, even though I've prayed about it a thousand times."

She turned around and glared at Sister Nielson who was sitting a few rows behind her. Sister Nielson looked the other way, and Sister Bradford shook her head and continued. "And another thing, I've let it be known for quite some time that I wouldn't mind being called to teach a Sunday School class now and then. I like children, even though

God's never blessed me with any of my own. It's not my fault, and I'm not saying it's my husband's either, but . . ." She stopped and glanced around at everybody, looking confused. "Uhh . . . what was I saying?"

Brother Bradford was sitting on the bench next to his wife. He stared straight ahead, as if he didn't know who she was. The Bishop cleared his throat, but Sister Bradford didn't notice. She pulled a little white hanky out of the top of her dress and started patting her forehead and her neck. "I thought the Sisters of the Relief Society might think about me for once, but no, they--"

"Sister, please." The Bishop was back up at the microphone. "I'm sure there are others who want to bare their testimony. Maybe you could share the floor."

She got all flustered and red in the face. "Well, Bishop, I thought this was a chance for us to tell the truth about things. But if you don't want to hear it . . ." She plopped down on the bench beside her husband and started fanning herself furiously with a big flowered fan. Her husband put his hand over his eyes and shook his head.

After that, it didn't seem like anyone else wanted to bare their testimony. We sat there for a long time, waiting, and looking around at each other. Then, all of a sudden, Dad stood up. He coughed several times, and people twisted around in their seats to look at him.

He took out the papers I'd seen him writing on in his study and unfolded them. He cleared his throat and started reading. "In the Doctrine and Covenants, section ninety-three, verse one, it says, 'Verily, thus saith the Lord: It shall come to pass that every soul who forsaketh his sins and cometh unto me, and calleth on my name, and obeyeth my voice, and keepeth my commandments, shall see my face and know that I am.'" He looked up. "What does this scripture mean? Doesn't it mean that any righteous man can see God? I mean, I don't see how we can take it any other way."

It scared me to hear him ask about that scripture. Was he going to tell them about his vision too, even though the Bishop said he shouldn't talk about it?

The Bishop jumped up and hurried to the microphone. "Yes, Brother Sterling. We'll think about that."

But Dad wasn't finished. "In his teachings, the prophet, Joseph Smith, said, if we pay attention to the flow of pure intelligence from the Holy Spirit, we will grow in our understanding of the principle of revelation. In that way, we can become perfect in Christ. Isn't that the same thing that Alma was saying in section twelve, verse ten of the Book of Mormon? 'And therefore, he that will harden his heart, the same receiveth the lesser portion of the word; and he that will not harden his heart, to him is given the greater portion of the word, until it is given unto him to know the mysteries of God until he knows them in full.'"

I looked around. Some people were smiling, but it seemed like others didn't know what Dad was talking about, except maybe, Brother Ellison. His face was all red, and he was jerking his head at the Bishop, like he wanted him to make Dad stop. Mom pulled on Dad's arm to try to get him to sit down, but he hardly noticed her.

Dad's voice grew louder, as if he was getting more confident in what he was saying. "Brothers and Sisters. I'm here to tell you that a man can commune with God, even as the prophets of old communed with Him. And I am not talking about the still small voice of the Holy Ghost, but the voice of the Lord Himself. It happened to me, and though some choose not to believe, it does not change the fact of it."

Some people shook their heads, looking confused. Others started whispering. Dad just stood there staring straight ahead with his pupils so big it made his eyes look black. I glanced towards the benches on the other side of the aisle to see what Brother Ellison was doing, but he wasn't there. I turned around and saw him and his family just heading out the door.

The Bishop tapped on the microphone to get everybody's attention. "I don't know what you think you're doing, Brother Sterling. But I think you've said more than enough." He turned to Sister Henderson in the front row. "Please, Sister, would you lead us in the closing hymn."

Everybody started singing, and Dad sat down. After the closing prayer, we stayed seated until everyone had left the chapel. Then, Mom stood up and said, "Come on, Michael, let's go."

It was embarrassing the way everybody stared at us on our way out. They'd be talking all excited, then stop as we went by. I don't think Dad even noticed. His eyes still had that same look, like they were made out of glass.

When we got in the car with the doors closed, Mom said, "How could you do that, Michael, after the Bishop told you not to? Did you really expect people to believe you?"

He squeezed the steering wheel and looked straight ahead. "And they that will harden their hearts, they will know nothing concerning his mysteries. They will be taken captive by the devil, and led down to destruction."

"Stop it, Michael! You're driving me crazy with those scriptures." Her face softened. "It worries me, honey."

Dad still wouldn't look at her. He started the car and drove out of the church parking lot. When we came to our road, instead of turning, he continued straight ahead. "I think we'll go see Brother Reuben."

Mom yelled, "What?"

"He invited me to drop by today. He wants to talk to me more about building his church."

"I don't want to go up there. Especially, not now."

He glanced over at Mom. "I have to talk to him, Sharon. He knows I'm telling the truth. He may be the only one who doesn't think I'm crazy . . . including you, I guess." He glanced at her again.

"I didn't say you were crazy. I just . . ." She didn't finish her sentence. Instead, she turned and stared out the window.

When he headed up the dirt road to Brother Reuben's house, Dad didn't even try to miss the potholes. I had to hold onto the door handle for dear life, and Mikey yelped every time we hit a bump and he flew up off the seat.

Mom was disgusted. "Slow down, Michael. You're going to ruin the car."

We pulled up in front of Brother Reuben's house in a cloud of dust. It didn't look like Mom was going to get out. She just sat there with her arms folded tightly across her chest. Then Mikey yelled, "Look, Bethy, little baby goats." He jumped out of the car and ran toward the pen at the side of the house.

I got out and followed him. Inside the old wooden pen, there was a big momma goat with nipples and two little baby goats. Mikey started squealing. He poked his hands through the gaps in the boards. The baby goats came over and licked his fingers with their little pink tongues. He started giggling and that got me giggling too. I reached in and rubbed the head of the little black goat with a white patch on his face. It was strange; he had two small bumps on his head that felt like horns, only they were soft and fuzzy like they were made out of fur.

I heard Dad come up behind us. "This is no time for shenanigans. Now, come along, you two."

I was surprised to see Mom was there too. I guess she'd decided to go in with Dad after all.

Just then, Brother Reuben came hurrying around the side of the house, smiling through his wild beard. "Oh, there you are. I thought I saw you out front, but then you disappeared." He came over and grabbed Dad's hand and started shaking it vigorously, just like the last time we were there. "Thank you for coming, Brother Sterling. And thank you for bringing your lovely family along."

"We're only here for a short visit. The children are hungry after fasting all day."

Brother Reuben looked over at me and winked. "That won't hurt them. It lightens the body and grows the spirit."

Dad took Mom's arm and pulled her alongside him. "You remember Sharon?"

"Of course, I do. It hasn't been that long. How do you do, Sister?"

Mom mumbled, "Fine."

Brother Reuben gathered us all up and herded us toward the front of the house, keeping his arms out, as if he was herding sheep and he thought one or the other of us would try to escape. I was the last in line, and as I went through the door, he squeezed my shoulders and whispered, "It's very nice to see you again, little sister."

The feel of his hot breath on my ear gave me the chills and a feeling of disgust. I shrugged off his hands and hurried inside.

It was a beautiful sunny day outside, but inside, the house was cold and dreary. When my eyes finally adjusted to the darkness, I saw a woman sitting on an old worn-out couch with a baby on her lap and another little girl hanging onto her leg. The woman's mousy brown hair was pulled up into a tight bun, but I could tell it was really long because the baby was pulling on a loose strand that hung almost to the woman's waist. I thought she must be Brother Reuben's first wife, the one we knew from before when they were attending our church, but she looked so different from the last time I'd seen her, I wasn't sure if it was really her. I didn't know how she could have gotten that old in such a short time. And why did she look so sad and worried? Was something wrong?

Brother Reuben's voice broke through my thoughts. "Brother and Sister Sterling, you remember my wife, Sister Ella?"

So, it *was* the wife we knew. It was Laura and Aaron's mother, and she seemed to have two new kids. But how could she have had them that fast? And where were Laura and Aaron and the other wives?

Mom went over and sat down on the couch next to her and patted her leg. "Of course, I remember you, Ella. How are you?"

Sister Reuben tried to push her loose hair back up into the bun, but it just fell down again. "I'm fine, I guess. These two keep me busy."

Mom stroked the baby's cheek with the back of her finger. "She's a real sweetheart, isn't she? How old?"

"Three and a half months."

"And the little one there looks like she's just learning to walk."

"She's two. Old enough to get into things. You know that stage?"

"I sure do." She looked over at me and Mikey and smiled.

Mikey pulled on my arm and whispered, "Bethy, I'm starving."

I knew we weren't going to get to eat anytime soon, so I just shook my head at him.

Brother Reuben was talking quietly to Dad in the corner of the room when, all of a sudden, he spun around and yelled at his wife. "Where are the children? I told you to get them in here."

Sister Reuben looked all flustered. She jumped up and the little girl hanging onto her leg fell backward and started to cry. Brother Reuben gave his wife a mean look that made me feel really bad for her.

Mom said, "Here, let me hold the little one, Ella."

Sister Reuben put the baby in Mom's arms. She scooped the little girl up onto her hip and hurried into what looked like a small bedroom. A minute later, she came back with Aaron and Laura. I was shocked when I saw Laura. We had been in the same grade at school, but now she seemed older, almost like she wasn't a kid anymore. Her hair was as long as her mother's, but she just had it pulled back with a ribbon. She was wearing a long, plain blue dress with long sleeves and thick white stockings, and old scruffy brown shoes. Her outfit was really old-fashioned and way too hot for such a warm spring day.

Laura and Aaron stood next to each other by the bedroom door, looking awkward, until Brother Reuben said, "Say hello to your guests, children."

Laura stepped forward and mumbled, "Hello."

I said, "Hi, Laura. We've missed you at school. How come you don't come anymore?"

She glanced over at her father and then down at the floor. "It's better learning at home. You don't get confused by all the sinful things."

Brother Reuben smiled and nodded. "That's right. She's learning what a girl needs to know and that's enough. Aaron, say hello to your young friend, Brother Michael."

Aaron came over and grabbed Mikey's hand and shook it like he was a grown man. I expected Mikey to giggle, but instead he faked a serious look and shook Aaron's hand real hard. Brother Reuben seemed satisfied. He took Dad's arm, pulled him into another small bedroom, and closed the door behind them.

Sister Reuben seemed to relax a little when he was gone. She put the little girl back on the floor and said, "Sister Sterling, would you and the children like something to drink?"

Mom shook her head. "Oh, no, don't bother with that. You've got your hands full."

"It's not a problem, if you don't mind holding the baby for a minute more." She looked at Laura and said, "Watch your sister."

Laura came and took her little sister to a chair in the corner while her mother hurried into the kitchen. Mikey sat with Aaron on the floor, and I just stood there next to the couch, feeling out of place.

After a few minutes, Sister Reuben came back with a big pitcher of something red that looked like Hawaiian Punch. She set it down on a lamp table, hurried back in the kitchen for glasses, and then poured us all a drink. She plopped back down on the couch, as if she was exhausted, and took the baby from Mom.

While we were drinking our punch, I noticed how Sister Reuben kept glancing nervously at the closed door where Dad had gone with Brother Reuben. Mom must have noticed too, because she kept smiling at her like she was trying to make her feel more comfortable. She said, "The punch is very good, Ella."

"Oh, I'm sorry. It's all I had."

"It's quite refreshing." Mom sat quietly for a minute. She looked around the room and then over in the corner at Laura and the little girl. "So, you're schooling the children at home?"

Sister Reuben glanced at the door to the other room again. "I'm not sure I'm doing it right. I've never done that sort of thing before."

"Don't you have any help?" Mom turned to me. "Beth, don't just stand there. Why don't you go talk to Laura?"

I didn't know what I would say to Laura, so I just stayed where I was.

Sister Reuben put the baby up to her shoulder and patted its little back. "I'm sorry. What did you say, Sister Sterling?"

"Please, call me Sharon. I asked if you have any help teaching the children."

Sister Ella frowned. "Sometimes my Sisters help, but they--"

"Mother!" Laura had jumped up, as if to warn her mother.

Mom ignored Laura. "Oh, you have sisters. Do they live close by?"

Sister Reuben glanced back at Laura and then at the closed door. She just shrugged and looked at the floor without answering.

At first, I didn't get it. Then I figured out what was going on. She must be talking about Brother Reuben's other wives. But I didn't know why she would try to keep it a secret; everybody in town knew they were polygamists.

After that, Sister Reuben stopped talking and Mom did too. It got so uncomfortable, I was glad when Dad and Brother Reuben finally came out of the other room. They were smiling and looking happy with each other. Brother Reuben said, "Well, I'd like to get together again to continue this conversation. It was most enlightening."

He turned to the rest of us, still smiling. "I hope you all enjoyed your little visit. I'm sure we all feel very blessed to have the chance to get to know each other better." He put his arm around Dad's shoulder. "Maybe you could come over again, Brother, and we can talk in depth. I have something to tell you that I'm sure will interest you a great deal. If you don't mind, I'd like some of my Brethren to join us as well. They need to hear your story."

Dad seemed a little embarrassed. "Really? Do you think so?"

"I know so."

"Well, I wouldn't mind talking to them, if you want me to."

"Of course. We'd like that very much. How about tomorrow?"

Dad glanced over at Mom and then back at Brother Reuben. "Sure. I can do that. I'll come by after work, if you don't mind me coming in my work clothes."

"That's fine. A man has to work, doesn't he?"

We went to the door and when we were outside Brother Reuben took Mom's hand and held it real tight, giving her his penetrating look. "We hope to see you again real soon, Sister Sharon. I'm sure Sister Ella enjoyed chatting with you. I'm sure you'll get to know each other a lot better over time."

As we walked to the car, Brother Reuben called out, "Goodbye, Sister Elizabeth. Remember, there's always a place here for you."

I looked back. He was smiling and waving, but I didn't say a word. I didn't like the way he always paid special attention to me. There was something disturbing about it. I would've liked to ask Mom what she thought he was doing, but she had other things on her mind.

As soon as Dad had maneuvered the car down though the bumps to the main road, she turned to him and said, "Do you really think it's wise to spend time with him? What will the Bishop think?"

"What concern is it of his?"

"They're polygamists, Michael."

"It's not right to judge people, Sharon. Brother Reuben is a spiritual man. He reads the scriptures. He prays. He raises his family according to the gospel."

"But look at that poor wife of his. One baby after the next. She looks worn out. And you should have seen how she acted. She was scared to death to say anything, even when he wasn't in the room."

I leaned over the front seat. "She's right, Dad. Laura wouldn't let her talk about the other wives. She called them her sisters. Where are they anyway? If they're polygamists, why aren't they around somewhere?"

He looked at me in the rearview mirror. "That's none of your business, Beth."

Mom wouldn't let it go. "That's right, Michael. Where are his other wives? I don't see how he can afford to keep a separate house for each of them. How many does he have anyway?"

Dad gave her a critical look. "I don't know and I don't care."

"But maybe you should care. What if people find out you're talking to him, and they start thinking you're interested in joining his group?"

"What do I care what people think? This is a man who truly understands visions."

"Is that right? Has he had a vision too?" There was a sharpness in her voice that surprised me.

Dad frowned. "I didn't say that."

"Well, has he?"

"No. I don't believe he has. But he's a righteous man, and he wants to speak with God. It just hasn't happened yet."

"Maybe he wants to take lessons from you." I'd never heard Mom be sarcastic like that. It made me realize she was really disturbed about something.

"You can insult me if you want, but I'm telling you there are things I know now that I didn't know before. I've tried to explain it to you, but you act as if nothing has changed. You seem to think we can go along like we did before, living a superficial version of the gospel."

"Superficial?" She turned away from him and stared out the window.

Dad reached for her hand. "Don't do this, Sharon. The Lord did appear to me. It must have been for a reason. I think Brother Reuben can help me find out what that reason is."

"Oh, Michael. Are you sure you know what you're getting yourself into?"

"If Brother Reuben and his followers are willing to open themselves to the truth, I think I should meet with them. Maybe it's the Lord's will and it's He who has brought us together."

Mom shook her head and rubbed her forehead as we drove the rest of the way home in silence. My mind was going a mile a minute, thinking about Brother Reuben and the polygamists and what kind of life they had. Dad seemed to be very interested in Brother Reuben, but I could see it worried Mom and made her agitated. Where was it all going to lead?

Chapter 6

A person may profit by noticing the first intimation of the
spirit of revelation . . . when you feel pure intelligence flowing
into you, it may give you sudden strokes of ideas . . .

Teachings of the
Prophet Joseph Smith (1838-39)

*T*hat first night Dad went up to Brother Reuben's by himself, Mom
pretended like it didn't bother her. But she kept dropping things while
we were fixing dinner, and she kept hunching up her shoulders and
pressing them back down, like she was trying to relieve the tension.
And then, even though it was a school night, she let Mikey and me
stay up a lot later than usual. I'm sure it was to keep from being alone
while she waited for him to come home.

It was well after ten when we finally heard Dad's truck in the
driveway. We all ran outside in our stocking feet. Mom got to him
before he could even get out of the truck. "I thought you got lost."

Dad looked surprised. "It's not that late, is it?"

"Isn't it? I guess I'm just not used to you being out at night." She
gave him a little kiss on the cheek. "How was it?"

He didn't answer her until we were back in the house and we were
all sitting on the couch with Dad in the big chair across from us. His
face was glowing and he seemed all excited about something. "It was
wonderful, Sharon. Those people truly believe in revelation. They
even have a special class to prepare themselves and a book that
teaches them how to put their minds in a heightened state of
awareness in which a vision can occur. It's amazing."

Mom didn't seem interested. "Are you hungry?"

"No. I couldn't eat a thing. I'm . . . I'm filled with the spirit of the Lord."

Mom gave him a skeptical look. He jumped up and went into the kitchen for a glass of water. She followed him and so did Mikey and I.

"Who was there? Was it just the men or was it the whole group?" Mom acted nonchalant, as if she was just making polite conversation, but I knew she really wanted to know what had happened up there, just like I did.

"Just the men this time. But Brother Reuben wants us all to get together real soon."

Mom didn't like that. She cornered Dad by the sink and said, "I'm not sure we should start meeting with those people, Michael. I mean . . . I don't see the point. It's not like we're going to join them, so what's this all about?"

Dad slipped around her and went to the other side of the table. "It can't hurt to talk. If I'm going to build their church, I need to get to know them better. Besides, I want to learn more about the Law of Consecration and other early doctrine of the Church. You know, they actually practice the Law of Consecration. I've always wanted to know how that kind of communal living would work."

He went back in the living room, while Mom stayed by the kitchen door and continued asking her questions. "What other doctrine?"

"You know, things related to the early teachings of the Church. Things we're taught, but we never think about all that much."

"You mean, like polygamy?"

"It's called Celestial Marriage, Sharon."

She raised her eyebrows. "You're not getting interested, are you?"

He sat on the couch, stretched his arms up, and yawned. "Boy, I guess it is getting kind of late. I'm tired. It's been a long day."

Mom sat down next to him. "Well, are you?"

"Am I what?"

"Getting interested in polygamy?"

"Oh, come on, Sharon. I'm just talking to them. Mostly, I just want to hear what they have to say about revelation. I think they can help me understand what happened to me, and maybe it will be revealed what the Lord has in mind for me."

"I thought you said Brother Reuben had never had a vision."

"That's right, I don't believe he has."

"So, you know more about it than he does."

"So? What's your point?"

Mom shook her head. "I don't understand. It seems like they have more to learn from you on that subject than you have to learn from them."

Dad's eyes lit up. "That's right, and that's why they want me to teach them. As part of their weekly lessons."

Mom frowned and looked at the floor. "And when do these lessons take place?"

"Every Tuesday night."

"I see. So, now you're saying you'll be gone every Tuesday?"

"It's only for a short time."

"And I don't suppose I'm invited."

"Well, no. It's just the Brethren. You know, those of us who hold the priesthood."

"What about Ella? Wasn't she there?"

"Well, I guess she was. She made us something to eat, but she wasn't in on the meeting, and neither were any of Brother Reuben's other wives, or the wives of any of the Brethren."

"So, I guess that's why you're not hungry."

Mom spun around to me and Mikey and yelled, "Why aren't you in bed?" The force of her anger almost took my breath away.

"You didn't tell us to."

"Well, I'm telling you now. Hurry up." She put one hand on Mikey's back and the other on mine and pushed us across the living room to the foot of the stairs. Then, she went back towards Dad for another round.

After I was in bed, I could hear them arguing downstairs long into the night. I couldn't hear exactly what they were saying, but it made my stomach ache to hear them being that way with each other. Why couldn't they talk like they used to, like they were best friends, instead of enemies?

It turned out that Tuesdays weren't the only day that Dad was gone. There were lots of other times when he didn't come home after work. Sometimes when he did, he brought Brother Reuben with him.

They'd go into the study and wouldn't come out until after the rest of us were in bed.

At first, Mom would knock on the door and try to get him to eat something, but he always said he wasn't hungry. I thought maybe he was eating out at a restaurant, or at Brother Reuben's house, but more likely he was fasting. He was loosing even more weight, and his face was becoming pale and sunken.

Mom kept asking me, "What in the world are they doing in there?"

I'd go and put my ear up against the study door, trying to figure out the answer to her question. Mostly, it seemed like they were reading scriptures and praying. Then one day, I heard Brother Reuben say, "Heed this, Brother. Satan is in every corner waiting to sway you from the Lord's work. Follow the path of righteousness, or ye shall surely be punished."

Dad's reply was too low for me to understand, but Brother Reuben responded with, "That above all else. You must steel yourself against the persuasions of the gentle sex. They are weak and need our guidance. Their emotions carry them away with longings for frivolous things that will only do them harm. We must use our strength in the priesthood to dissuade them from their corruptions. We must teach them to be sparing in all things. And obedient, above all."

I couldn't believe it. It sounded like Brother Reuben was giving Dad instructions for controlling Mom. Dad should have thrown him out of the house and locked the door. But he didn't. It was as if he'd fallen under Brother Reuben's spell, a spell that worked even when Brother Rueben wasn't around. It made Dad act strange. If he talked to us at all, he talked in words that sounded like scriptures, warning us about what God wanted us to do. I felt I was losing him. Like I couldn't talk to him in a regular way. It made me sad and lonely and a little scared.

One day, he came out of the bathroom and whispered, "Woe unto the child who hears her friends but doth not hear the voice of God."

I said, "What are you talking about?"

"I'm saying you better pay attention if you want to hear the voice of God."

"I didn't think God talked to girls."

He frowned. "You never know, Beth. You never know."

What was that supposed to mean? Did it mean God might talk to me? I tried to think what I'd ask him if he did, but my mind went blank. Then I started thinking of how much trouble it caused when Dad talked to God, and I wasn't so sure I wanted it to happen.

Not long after that, Dad came home from work with a truck full of groceries. I couldn't believe it when he kept going out and bringing in more and more sacks. Instead of putting everything in the cupboards, or the refrigerator, he cleaned out the closet under the stairs and put the food in there. I watched while he arranged it all. There were things like canned vegetables and chip beef and big bags of sugar and flour and rice and beans and several large bottles of oil. I asked him what it was all for, and he said, "It's our three year's supply. We've got to be prepared."

I knew from church that we were supposed to keep a three years supply of food, but we'd never really done it. "What are we preparing for, Dad?"

He glanced up at me and went back to arranging the stuff in neat rows. "You never know what might happen."

I said, "It doesn't really look like enough food to last us three years."

"Well, no. But it's a start."

"Won't it get old and nasty?"

"We have to replenish it, Beth. If it starts to get old, we'll use it and buy more to replace what we eat." It was just another example of how Brother Rueben was influencing him.

Mom was going crazy with the whole situation. Sometimes she'd cry, and sometimes she'd get so angry I thought she was going to knock down the study door, but it was usually when no one was in there. Then one day, she came out of the laundry room with a long piece of drywall tape with blue handwriting on both sides. It was all bent from being folded up, but I knew it was the stuff Dad used for taping over the corners when he remodeled a house. She was holding the tape out in front of her, like it was something bad that she didn't want touching her.

"What's wrong, Mom?"

"I found this in your father's pocket."

"What is it?"

She shook her head and tears came to her eyes. "Oh, Beth. I never thought it would go this far."

"What?"

She didn't answer me.

"What is it, Mom? What's he doing now?"

She wiped her eyes and folded up the tape and put it in the pocket of her apron.

That night when Dad got home, Mom met him at the door. "I thought you weren't interested in polygamy."

He tried to dodge her. "What are you talking about?"

"I found your notes, Michael."

"What notes?"

"These." She pulled the drywall tape out of her pocket and held it up in front of him.

"What are you doing with that?" He tried to grab it, but she folded it up and put it back in her pocket.

"It's obvious what you're doing, Michael. You're searching the scriptures, trying to justify polygamy. Is that what you're talking about on Tuesday nights with Brother Reuben and his crew?"

"We talk about a lot of things."

He started to go upstairs, but Mom grabbed his arm and held it. "If you can talk to them about it, why can't you talk to me? Please, Michael. What's happening to you?"

"You wouldn't understand, Sharon. You want me to be the man I used to be, but I've changed. These people understand that. They understand that God has a plan for me and they respect me. They're interested in what I have to say."

He tried to pull away, but she wouldn't let him go. "But, Michael. I need to know what's going on. You have to talk to me."

Dad pried her hand from his arm. "I've got a meeting in a few minutes. I've got to take a shower."

He hurried upstairs. Mom watched him go and then burst into tears. She went into the kitchen and sat down and cried so hard it scared me.

I tried to comfort her. "Maybe he's just talking to them because they believe in his vision. Maybe, if you believed him, he wouldn't go over there all the time."

She put her head down on her arms and sobbed even louder.

After Dad left that night, she didn't seem to know what to do. She wandered around the house looking miserable, every once in a while stopping to cry. I tried to talk to her, but she told me she wanted to be left alone. I don't know what time Dad got home, or if he ever came home at all; he wasn't there when I got up the next morning.

I kept thinking about Mom all the next day at school, hating for her to be alone when she was so upset. Then, when I got home, she was on the phone with somebody laughing. I was glad she was feeling better, but a few minutes later she was crying. "I don't know what I'm going to do. I hardly ever see him anymore. I'm afraid I'm losing him."

That really scared me. Maybe Dad hadn't come home last night. Is that why she thought she was losing him? Was he going to go away with the polygamists? I sat on the stairs and listened to see if I could figure out who she was talking to.

Suddenly, she was laughing again. "Oh, dear, do you really think that would work? He doesn't have much of a sense of humor these days. I don't know if he's even interested in that anymore." She listened for a minute. "Maybe you're right. Maybe that's what he needs." She laughed again. "I'll have to think about it. Maybe I'll come for a visit and you can show me what to do. I'll call you later."

After she hung up the phone, I followed her into the kitchen. "Who was that?"

"Linda."

"Your old high school friend?"

"That's right."

"I didn't think you talked to her anymore."

She smiled sadly. "I could use a friend right now."

"Yeah. We all could."

Her eyes got misty, and she came over and put her arm around me. "It's a little lonely for me right now."

"I know, Mom. I wish it didn't have to be like that." I stood in front of her, wondering if I should ask her the question that was on my mind. I started to ask and then put my hand over my mouth as tears came to my eyes.

"What is it, honey?"

"You said something on the phone."

"What?"

"Do you really think we're going to lose Dad?"

She touched my cheek. "I was just talking. Don't you start worrying about that. Everything will be fine. I feel a lot better since I talked to Linda."

"Are you sure?"

She didn't answer me.

"Are you going to go see Linda, like you said?"

"I've been thinking about it."

"Why don't you have her come here instead? No one ever comes to see us anymore, except Brother Reuben."

"Maybe. We'll see."

We went into the living room. Mom opened the drapes. The sky was full of heavy clouds with dark edges. She said, "Oh, dear. Looks like a rainstorm's coming. We better get the clothes off the line."

I ran upstairs for the clothesbasket. When we got outside, the clouds were racing across the sky towards us. I saw a bolt of lightening and could only count to three before I heard the clap of thunder. I yelled, "Hurry, Mom. It's going to get us."

The wind was flipping Mom and Dad's temple garments around on the clothesline in a way that made it look like they were socking and kicking each other. The sight of it was so real it made my heart flutter. I grabbed the legs to keep them apart. Mom took the clothespins off the top and they fell down into the dirt before I could get them in the basket. "I'm sorry, Mom."

She laughed. "Oh, never mind. It's clean dirt."

She grabbed my hand and we ran towards the house just as the raindrops began to fly.

Chapter 7

For the husband is the head of the wife, even as Christ is the head of the church. . .

Holy Bible
Ephesians 5:23

*T*hat Friday, after Mom talked to Linda, Dad came home from work and for once he didn't have Brother Reuben with him. He headed for his study, but before he could close the door, Mom intercepted him. "Given that you don't want to do anything with me anymore, I'm going to go see Linda. I expect you to watch the kids."

"Since when have you been talking to Linda? I didn't think you'd seen her since her divorce."

"I haven't, but now that I've lost my husband to the polygamists, I think I'll get to know her again."

"I don't want you associating with . . . that woman."

Mom glared at him. "What do you mean, that woman? She's my friend."

"She's divorced, Sharon. She's not a good influence."

"That's ridiculous. She's the same person she's always been."

"I'm telling you, I don't want you to go."

"Well, that's too bad, because I *am* going."

I guess Dad realized he couldn't stop her because he went in his study and slammed the door. Mom ran upstairs. I followed her and watched while she changed her clothes. "Can I come with you?"

"No, Beth. I'm going alone."

"But what am I supposed to do while you're not here?"

She looked surprised. "What do you mean? You'll do what you always do. And besides, your father will be here."

"I know, but he'll just be in his study the whole time."

"It's not a big deal, Beth. I'm just going to visit a friend."

"What are you and Linda going to do?"

"I don't know." She smiled a little. "Maybe she'll tell me about the secret lives of her customers. She's a beautician, you know."

"Is she going to fix your hair?"

"Maybe."

"Are you going to tell her your secrets?"

She gave me a sideways glance. "What secrets?"

"I mean, are you going to tell her what Dad's been doing?"

"She already knows."

"Why can't I go with you, Mom? It's too boring around here. We haven't done anything fun for so long."

"Stop it, Beth. I told you, I need to get away by myself for awhile."

After I watched the car disappear down the road, I sat on the edge of the porch and stared into the apple orchard for a long time. For some reason, I had a bad feeling about her leaving. What if something happened to her? I knew it was a dumb thing to worry about, but with all the trouble we'd been having at home, I couldn't control my mind.

After awhile, I went inside and tried to read, but I was so restless I couldn't concentrate. I wandered upstairs and found Mikey on his side of the bedroom. He was watching his hamster spin around in its wheel. I stood behind him and watched too. I said, "I wonder why Petey doesn't get bored running around in circles all the time."

Mikey whispered, "Shhh. He thinks he's in the forest."

"How do you know that?"

"Because he told me." He opened the cage door and stuck his hand in the wheel to stop the spinning. Then, he gently brought the hamster out of the cage. He held it up next to his ear and made little whispering sounds.

"Mikey, hamsters can't talk."

"They can too." He made the little whispering sounds again.

"That wasn't the hamster, it was you."

He giggled. "I know, but sometimes he talks in my dreams."

"Oh, yeah? What does he say?"

Mikey's eyes got real big. "He doesn't like the cage, Bethy. He only stays in there because he loves me. Do you think I should let him go outside?"

"You better not. What if he can't find any food out there?"

"Yeah. He might starve. I better keep him."

He put the hamster back in the cage, and we went downstairs. I got his fairy tale coloring book and the big box of crayons out of the closet and took them to the kitchen. While Mikey was coloring, I tried to think of something to keep myself occupied, but I was too agitated. I went in the living room and looked out the window to see if Mom might be coming back, but I couldn't see anything in the darkness.

I went upstairs again and ended up in Mom and Dad's bedroom. I turned on the light and slid the closet door open until I could see the long black bag that held Mom's wedding dress. I hadn't looked at the dress for a long time, and I wanted to see it again. I unzipped the bag just far enough to reveal the lace and the little white beads sewn onto the satin bodice. I put my face against the material and smelled the perfume that still clung to it. It made me wonder why Mom had stopped wearing perfume. Didn't she care if she smelled good anymore?

I zipped the bag back up, and was just about to close the closet door, when I noticed Mom's notebook stuck back behind her shoeboxes. Why had she hidden it there? She'd never done that before.

I sat on the floor and pulled the notebook out to see what she'd been writing about. The first pages were all about happy times with Dad, like the story of how they went down to the creek and kissed in the old tunnel beneath the road, and how they laughed and went "skinny dipping" in the pond. It was one of my favorite stories about their life before I was born.

As I turned to the last pages of the notebook, the writing got more and more sad. It broke my heart to see how lonely and afraid she was and how much she hated Brother Reuben for taking Dad away. In some places the ink was blurry, and I knew she'd been crying. It made me cry too. Why couldn't she talk to Dad about how she felt, instead of hiding her feelings in the back of the closet? And why couldn't he see what was happening to her? He hardly ever even looked at her anymore. Had he stopped loving her?

I left their bedroom feeling depressed. When I got back downstairs, Mikey was still in the kitchen coloring. He'd scribbled all over the face of Rumpelstitlskin with a horrible green color, and the stacks of coins were purple instead of gold. It looked like he'd gone through the whole book and scribbled on just about every picture. I said, "Why'd you do that, Mikey? Now what are you going to color next time?"

"Momma will get me a new book."

I shook my head and left him to his coloring.

I went and peeked into Dad's study to see what he was doing. It was dark. For a minute, I didn't think he was in there, but then I heard him praying, ". . . Lead her not into temptation and deliver her from evil, for thine is the kingdom and the power and the glory, forever . . . He sobbed, and then he said, "Please, Lord, bring her home safe to me."

I tiptoed inside the room, went over to where he was kneeling by the window, and put my hand on his shoulder. "Don't worry. She'll come home."

"Oh, Beth. I just wish . . ."

"What, Dad?"

"That your mother and I could join together in body and spirit."

"But you're the one who's always gone, and you're the one who never wants to talk to her. She's lonely, Dad."

He stood up quickly and went back to his desk. "It does no good to talk. It only leads to argument. I can't bear it."

"But Mom just wants things to be like they used to be."

"It can't be that way! Don't you understand? Things have changed."

"No. I'm not sure I do understand. Why do you want to ruin everything? At least we were happy before."

"We've got to live the gospel now."

"But we've always done that. We go to church, and we try to be good, don't we?"

"No, Beth. That's not enough. I'm talking about the real gospel. The gospel that was given to Joseph Smith, the gospel that came directly from God."

"You mean like Brother Reuben talks about. How does he know what's right?"

His voice got softer. "I can see I've got to teach you what the Lord wants. It's my duty as your father to teach you. But your mother doesn't want to learn. She doesn't believe in me. I think she's afraid to hear the truth."

"Why would she be afraid of the truth?"

He walked back towards the window waving his hands in the air. "She's afraid of . . . being different, I guess. Afraid of what people will say. Look, I think it's time for you to go to bed. It's late."

"Can't I wait until Mom gets home?"

"No, Beth. Do what I say. Find Mikey and get him to bed."

"We've got to take our baths first."

"Okay, do it. Then go to bed." He pushed me out of the study and closed the door.

I took Mikey upstairs, and was just getting ready to give him his bath, when I heard the front door open and close. It had to be Mom. A few seconds later, Dad yelled, "Oh my dear God. What have you done to yourself?"

I heard a little laugh from Mom. "Oh, sorry, Michael, Linda fixed me up a bit. We thought it might get you interested in something besides your scriptures and prayers."

"You look like . . . like a whore."

"A whore? Well, I guess that means it's not going to work, huh?"

I peeked out from behind the bathroom door as they got to the top of the stairs. I almost gasped when I saw Mom. She was wearing a slinky dark green dress, with smoke-colored nylons, and high-heeled shoes. She had on mascara and lipstick and she had pale green shadows above her eyes. But the thing that took my breath away was her hair. It was dyed red, and it was all pulled up on top of her head, with soft curls falling down around her face. I could hardly believe it was Mom. I didn't know she could look that . . . glamorous.

Mikey pushed his way underneath my arm. When he saw Mom he started giggling. Luckily, Dad didn't hear him. He didn't look like he thought it was funny at all. In fact, he looked furious. He grabbed Mom's arm and pulled her towards the bathroom. I whispered, "Quick, Mikey. Let's hide." We hopped into the bathtub and I closed the shower curtain and put my finger over my lips to tell Mikey to be quiet.

Dad pushed Mom into the bathroom. He got hold of one arm and started wiping her face off with a washcloth. She slapped at him with her other hand and yelled for him to stop, but he yanked both her arms down and held her wrists together. He rubbed harder and harder, but it only made black and green and red smears all over her face. I wanted to yell for him to leave her alone, but I was too scared.

He seemed furious that the makeup wouldn't come off. He put soap and water on the washcloth and scrubbed her face harder. She just stood there with her arms straight down at her sides, not even trying to stop him anymore. Mikey started to whimper. I put my hand over his mouth, hoping they hadn't heard him. But they didn't seem to be noticing anything. They were both crying by then.

When he finished scrubbing her face, Dad threw down the washcloth in disgust and hurried out of the bathroom, slamming the door behind him. Mom just stood there crying and staring at her hurt face in the mirror. I got out of the bathtub and went to hug her, but she pushed me away. "Please, just leave me alone."

It hurt my feelings, but I got Mikey and took him to our room and put him to bed. Neither one of us could sleep. After awhile, he came around the screen that divided our room and whispered, "Can I sleep with you, Bethy?"

He crawled in next to me and pulled the covers over his head. I heard him snuffling under there for a long time before he finally went to sleep. I lay there listening to the whistling sound in Mikey's nose and the sound of Mom's crying coming through the wall. I couldn't understand why I hadn't helped her. I should have made Dad stop, but his fury had terrified me. It was as if he'd turned into a different person. Mom hadn't done anything except try to make herself pretty, so why did he act like she'd committed the worse sin in the world. I didn't understand how he could treat her so bad.

Finally, Mom stopped crying and left the bathroom. I could hear her wandering around the house. I heard the front door open and close and my heart raced with fear, thinking she was leaving again. I sat up, and was about to go down and check, when I heard the stairs creak. I knew she'd come back in the house. Dad never once came out of the bedroom, but I could hear him in there coughing and making muffled choking sounds, like he was trying to hide his crying in the pillow. He should have gone and asked Mom to forgive him. He should have done it right then, before things got worse.

I must have finally fallen asleep because I woke the next morning to the sound of Dad yelling. I ran downstairs to the kitchen and found Mom backed into the corner. Dad was so mad he was shaking. "What in the hell did you think you were doing? Dressing up like a harlot. I can't believe you'd let the children see you like that."

"I thought they'd be in bed, Michael. I thought you and I could be together."

"Is that right? And you thought I'd be interested in that?"

"Linda thought . . ."

He looked at her in disgust. "I see. You two sat over there scheming about how to get to me. That's just great."

"No, Michael. I was just trying to--"

"Do you really think that's the way to my heart?"

"I don't know. I had to do something. I can't take this anymore." She put her hands over her face and started sobbing.

"I'll tell you what you can do. You can take those clothes out and burn them. And you can tell Linda you're never going to see her again. And you can do something about that . . . wicked hair." He pushed in even closer, trapping her in the corner.

She burst forward and pushed him away. "Who put you in charge of the world, Michael? You think I have to listen to what you say?"

Dad seemed surprised by her strength. "It's a wife's duty to listen to her husband."

"Is that right? Says who? Brother Reuben?"

"It's what the scriptures say, and you know it. I'm the one with the priesthood. It's my duty to lead my family in righteousness. What kind of man would I be if I didn't?"

"Yes, indeed. What kind of a man would allow his wife to be involved in decisions that affect her life and the life of her children?"

"Our first duty is to God, Sharon. Can't you get that through your head?"

"You think He wants you to destroy your family?"

"Destroy it? You're the one who's destroying it. I feel shame just looking at you. You'd better get down on your knees and beg God to forgive you before He brings his fury down upon this house." He turned his back on Mom and ran from the kitchen. I heard the front door slam, and a few seconds later I heard him drive away.

Mom didn't seem to be able to move from that corner of the kitchen. Her mouth was all twisted, and she was gasping for breath, as if her tears had backed up in her throat. She looked wild and strange with her long red hair. Then, she started hitting herself in the head with her fists, crying, "Why did I listen to her? I should have known it was a crazy idea." She sobbed and hit herself again and again.

I ran to her. "Mom, please. You're going to hurt yourself."

"I just wanted him to notice me. To realize I'm still here. That I'm still alive."

I grabbed her hands and held them to my heart. "Please, Mom. You're scaring me."

"I've made a big mistake, Beth. I don't know how I'm ever going to prove to him I'm not really like that."

"Like what?"

"A whore, Beth. A whore."

"You're not a whore. You were just trying to look pretty."

"I made a mistake. I didn't understand what he wanted. How could I think he'd be interested in that?"

It was terrifying to see her like that, but I didn't know how to convince her that it wasn't her fault.

All the rest of the day, she wandered around the house muttering to herself. Every time she got something out of the cupboard she'd slam it closed. She washed the same spoon over and over again, and then she turned and threw it across the room. I tried to talk to her but she just said, "Shush, I'm trying to think."

Mikey came downstairs. He was so afraid of Mom, he hid behind me. I hugged him. "It's okay, Mikey. She just needs time to think."

By the afternoon, I was worn out from watching her go around and around. I took Mikey up to our room. He sat on the floor and played with his Mister Potato Head, while I tried to read Alice in Wonderland. It was no use. I couldn't concentrate. It seemed like our house was just as crazy as the place in the book. I couldn't stop thinking about how mad Dad got. Would he ever forgive her? Or maybe, it was Mom that would never forgive him for scrubbing her face like that. I thought Dad was the one who was wrong.

Late that afternoon, I was going down the hall when I heard a sound coming from the bathroom. I put my ear up against the door. It was scissors. What was Mom doing with scissors? Was she cutting her hair, trying to get rid of it like Dad said?

I hurried to the bedroom and put my ear up against Mikey's wall so I could hear better what was going on in the bathroom.

Mikey said, "What are you doing, Bethy?"

"Shush. Mom's in the bathroom. I think she's cutting her hair."

Finally, I couldn't hear the scissors anymore. I was amazed at how quiet the house was without that sound. I could hear a crow squawking outside and a breeze scratching the tree branches against the window. For some reason, I was afraid. I wanted to run outside with the crows, someplace where there was more air to breathe.

Then I heard another sound. Mom had the clippers going, the clippers that Dad always used to give Mikey his short hair cut for the summer. Mikey must have heard it too because his eyes got real big. Oh, no. Now what was she doing? I hurried to the bathroom and tried to get in, but she had locked the door. I knocked loudly and said, "Mom, stop! What are you doing in there?"

She didn't answer.

I was trying to figure out what to do when I heard Dad come home. Oh, please God, don't let Brother Reuben be with him. I hurried out into the upstairs hall. I could hear Dad walking around downstairs, but I didn't hear any voices. I decided he was probably alone.

I heard him coming up the stairs. It scared me, and I ran back inside the bedroom and closed the door. He called out, "Sharon, where are you? Where are the kids? Isn't anybody home?" He stuck his head in the bedroom and said, "Beth, where's your mother?"

I was scared to look at him, but I said, "I think she's in the bathroom."

A second later, I heard him rattling the handle of the bathroom door. Then he knocked and said, "Sharon, are you in there? What are you doing? Come out, I want to talk to you."

Mikey came over and pulled on my arm. He wiggled back and forth, making little whiny sounds. He was squeezing himself between his legs. I knew what that meant, but I didn't know what I was supposed to do about it. Mom was in the bathroom and she wasn't coming out.

Dad started beating on the bathroom door, and Mikey pulled on my arm even harder. I whispered, "You're going to have to wait, Mikey."

He squeezed himself even tighter. I could see by his face that he was about to start crying. He pulled me towards the bedroom door. "I gotta go now, Bethy."

Out in the hall, Dad was kneeling on the floor with his head pressed up against the bathroom door. He was talking to Mom real soft. "Please, honey. I'm sorry for what I did. It's just that you . . . frightened me. I thought Satan had sent you to tempt me. But you were just trying to tell me you were lonely. I know that now. Please, honey, please come out."

I could see he was feeling bad about what he'd done, and it hurt me to see him sitting like that with his head up against the door. He was so forlorn, he didn't even notice Mikey and me.

Just when I was about to give up and take Mikey outside to pee, I saw the bathroom door move. It moved just a little. I wasn't sure if I'd really seen it, but Dad must have felt it on his head, because he scooted back. When she didn't come out, he scooted in closer again. He was looking through the crack of the door when it started to get wider. Mikey and I moved closer too. It was like there was a magnet pulling us all towards the bathroom door and we couldn't resist it.

Suddenly, the door swung open, and Mom came out. Mikey and Dad and I all made the same sound at the same time, a whooshing sound, like we were sinking beneath water, and we were trying to get our last breath of air. Mom's hair was all gone. Her head was completely bald. It was all white and glistening, and I could see the bones of her skull under the skin. It was terrible to see, but I couldn't stop staring at it.

Dad grabbed her around the legs and started sobbing. She patted his head, but she wasn't really looking at him. And she wasn't looking at me or Mikey either.

Then Mikey let go of the grip he had on my hand. I looked at him. He was staring at the floor, holding his arms stiff against his sides. There was a big puddle around his feet.

There was nothing I could do about it. We were all stuck, like statues that couldn't move. Finally, after what seemed like an eternity, Dad stood up. He put his arm around Mom and brought her down the hall past Mikey and me to their bedroom. Just before he closed the door, he looked back at us. He didn't say a word, but I knew he was telling me I had to be strong and take care of Mikey for a while. I took Mikey to our bedroom and helped him change his underpants. He was quiet and pale and sleepy. I said, "Maybe you should take a nap, Mikey. When you wake up everything will be okay."

He didn't speak. He just crawled into bed and pulled the covers over his head.

I got a rag from downstairs and cleaned up the puddle in the hall. Then I went in the bathroom and closed the door. Mom's long red locks were all over the floor. I picked up a few wisps of hair and let them float back down to the floor. They were like angel wings falling from heaven. At first, I was going to sweep everything up and put it in the wastebasket, but I couldn't bear to think of her hair being in there with the trash. I went and got a little box I'd been saving and carefully put it inside. I stood there for a long time, holding the box and looking at myself in the mirror. I tried to imagine how it would feel to be bald like Mom. Why had she done it? What was she trying to say?

Chapter 8

Let the woman learn in silence with all subjection.

Holy Bible
1 Timothy 2:11

*A*fter Mom shaved her head, everything changed. The red hair had made her look like a different person, but when she cut it all off, she really did change. By the next day, it was as if we were living with a stranger.

It was nine o'clock, and Mom still hadn't come downstairs. Dad and I went ahead and made breakfast, and then, he went up to get her. She came down with him, but it was obvious she didn't want to. He put his arm around her and led her to the chair. "Now we're all going to sit here and be a family again."

When he sat down, he kept his hand on her arm, as if he thought she'd try to get away if he didn't keep a hold on her. He said, "Michael, say the blessing."

Mikey squirmed around and wouldn't do it. I think Mom's bald head scared him so much he couldn't speak. Finally, after Dad told him again, he squeezed his eyes shut and said his prayer real quick. "Bless God for the food and make it nourish us. Make everything nice and don't let bad things happen ever again. Please, Jesus, amen."

Mom kept her eyes closed. After Dad watched her for a minute, he said, "Sharon, are you with us?"

She slowly opened her eyes, but kept them fixed on her plate.

Dad said, "I made you some nice scrambled eggs. Won't you at least try them?"

She shook her head and just sat there. I tried not to look at her, but it was hard. I kept noticing different things, like how her ears stuck out, and how not having any hair made her face look long and sad.

Nobody talked the whole time we were eating, but when we finished, Dad said, "I have something I want to say." He cleared his throat. "I hope you'll forgive me for what I did to you, Sharon. I know now that you were just trying to show me you were lonely. You thought I was leaving you behind. But that's not true. It's only that I've felt such a lack of cooperation. I didn't know how to talk to you. Well, from now on, I'm going to tell you exactly what's going on. That way, we can work together. There will be no more loneliness, no more . . . going away . . . no more taking counsel with others outside this room. Do you understand?"

Mom looked up for the first time and glared at him.

"Why do you look at me like that? I'm trying to work with you. I'm the patriarch of this family. It's my duty to help you understand."

She shook her head, first slowly, and then harder and faster.

Dad looked desperate. "I know you didn't mean to turn against me. You just got some fool idea in your head from Linda, but you just can't do that, honey. It broke my heart to see you like that."

But it was Mom who was holding her heart. She had tears in her eyes, and she looked like she was just about to get up and run.

Dad grabbed her arm. "I'm sorry. I shouldn't have brought that up again. I don't know how to do this very well."

I think he really was sorry. It looked like he wanted to cry too. Instead, he cleared his throat and tried again. "The thing is we all need to work together. The Lord has given us a wonderful blessing. He has chosen me for some special purpose. I want to share this blessing with you, honey. I want to share it with all of you, if you'll just let me." He reached out towards Mikey and me.

Mom stood up and held onto the back of her chair. Her lips were quivering, and her eyes had turned a dark green. "You act like some kind of holy prophet, and I'm supposed to just sit here and do whatever you tell me to do."

Dad jumped out of his chair. "Don't you understand? It's the Celestial Kingdom that's at stake here. I'm just trying to guide you and the children to our eternal life. That's all. If you can't accept that, I--"

Mom screamed, "I can't take this! You were never like this before. We shared in the decisions. We always talked about everything. You used to say you loved that about our relationship. Why are you ruining everything?" She fell back down in her chair, sobbing.

Dad dragged his chair next to hers and put his arm around her. "Listen, Sharon. A woman's role is different from a man's. The scriptures say that. The divine plan for a man is that he will be a god one day, the ruler of his own kingdom. He has to understand all things and follow all of God's divine laws. He must guide the woman. She is his helpmate, and she will be the vessel of his children, the mother of the spirits that will inhabit his kingdom in the next world. That's a divine calling in itself, honey. You should be joyful."

She pushed her chair away from him. "Oh, Michael. First you said you didn't even know what God said to you and now you've made up all this . . . this meaning. It's got to be Brother Reuben's influence. He's trying to convince you to live like him. Don't you see he's taking over your mind? By convincing you that you're someone special, he's slowly but surely leading you away from us. Away from the Church. Away from the Lord. Can't you see it?" She rubbed the sides of her head, leaving long red streak marks on the white skin where her hair used to be.

He shook his head. "No, Sharon, it's not Brother Reuben's influence. It's the divine gospel of the Lord, Jesus Christ. You know that the doctrine of polygamy came directly from God. It's not Brother Reuben's idea. It's written in the Doctrine and Covenants, you know that. What Brother Reuben teaches is nothing but what we've learned in church all our lives."

"That's not true. The Church doesn't condone polygamy anymore. You know that."

"But it's true that we will live that doctrine in the next world. It's required if a man is to become a god."

"Being a god? Is that what this is all about?"

"It's the highest goal, Sharon. It's the reason we've been sent to earth where we can carry out our earthly ordinances in preparation for that glorious day."

"But where is all this going to leave me and the children?"

"Beside me, Sharon, right beside me, in the Celestial Kingdom."

"I don't know if I want to be there."

Dad looked shocked. "What do you mean? How can you say that?"

"Because I don't know who you are anymore," she screamed. Her hands were clenched, and I could see she was shaking.

Mikey started whimpering. When nobody paid any attention, he started beating the table with the end of his knife. Mom grabbed the knife away from him and shook it at Dad. "See. See what you're doing to us?"

"Oh forget it. I might as well save my breath. I thought we could have a civilized conversation, but I can see you're not interested. I knew it. I just knew I couldn't count on you to understand anything." He picked up his glass, slammed it down on the table, and stormed out of the room. A second later, I heard the study door slam.

Mom and Mikey and I just sat there. Nobody said anything and none of us looked at each other for a long time. I felt like something had broken, something that none of us could fix. I wanted to run after Dad, but I was afraid if he came back they'd start yelling at each other again. I sat there, frozen, unable to decide what to do.

After what seemed like an eternity, Mom got up and slowly cleared the table. Then, without a word, she started washing the dishes. I took Mikey upstairs and told him to find something to do while I sat on my bed trying to think. Pretty soon, I heard Mom come up and go into the bedroom. She didn't come out the rest of the day.

That night, Dad got a spare blanket and pillow from the hall closet and put them on the couch. Then, he took Mikey and me upstairs to our room and said, "Let's pray for your mother."

He had us kneel on the floor by Mikey's bed while he said the prayer. "Our Father in Heaven. There is conflict in our home. Help us find peace and love. Bless my wife that she may find the faith and strength to do Thy will so that we may come to dwell in Thy Celestial Kingdom someday. And give me the strength to withstand her persuasions to turn away from Thy work. I am weak in my love for her and need your help. I ask that you be with us, to guide us according to your will, and I ask these things in the name of Jesus Christ, our Savior. Amen."

After I got in bed, I thought about Dad's prayer. More than anything else, I wanted the peace and love he asked God for. And I was pretty sure I still wanted to go to the Celestial Kingdom, even if Mom said she didn't want to go there. Getting to the Celestial Kingdom was the reason for everything we did at church, the reason we tried to be good. I started thinking again about what would have happened if Mom had just believed in Dad's vision in the first place. Would he have felt like he had to go talk to Brother Reuben? What if she told him she believed him now? Could things get back to normal? I didn't know if it was possible, after all that had happened.

The next day, Mom got up and fixed breakfast, but she wouldn't look at any of us, and she wouldn't say a word. I couldn't get used to how strange she looked with her bald head, and I guess Mikey couldn't either. He looked like he wanted to cry. He pulled me into the corner and whispered, "I want Momma back."

I hugged him. "Me too, Mikey, me too."

Dad watched every move she made. At first, he tried to talk to her, but it was as if someone had come in the night and taken her voice away. It was terrible to be ignored like that. And when she didn't talk, none of the rest of us wanted to talk either. The house got so quiet you could hear the crows cawing outside the window.

Dad went upstairs after breakfast. When he came down a while later, his face was all red and swollen. He followed Mom around the house, and finally, he stopped her in the hallway and put his arms around her. "Please, honey. Can't we talk about this?"

She pulled away and went upstairs to the bedroom.

That's when he gave up. He turned to me and said, "I don't think she wants anything to do with me. I might as well go to work."

"Don't go. Please, Dad. She's too upset."

"I don't want to. But it's not doing any good for me to stay here. Maybe she'll come out of it if I leave for awhile."

Mikey grabbed his arm. "I wanna go too, Daddy. Please take me."

"No, Michael. You and Beth stay here. Keep an eye on your mother. Tell her I won't be gone long, if you can get her to listen."

Later, when Mom came downstairs and found out Dad wasn't there she looked scared.

I hurried and said, "He's just gone to work. He'll be back soon."

She sat on the couch with her head in her hands and rocked back and forth making little moaning sounds. I was going to tell her things would be okay, but before I could get it out, she clamped her hand over her mouth and ran for the stairs. She moved so fast, I knew something was wrong. I followed her up to the bathroom where she started throwing up.

When it was finally over, she flushed the toilet, but stayed on her knees staring down at the water for a long time. She was shaking and I said, "Maybe you ought to lie down, Mom. Maybe it would make you feel better."

She let me help her up, and I took her to the bedroom, but she still wouldn't talk to me. She just motioned with her hand for me to leave her alone. I kept going in to check on her, but she never responded when I asked if she was okay. She just stared at the ceiling, acting like she didn't hear me. It was a terrible, long day.

When Dad finally got home that afternoon, I told him what had happened. He ran upstairs to the bedroom. I watched from the door as he knelt beside the bed and took Mom's hand in his. "What's wrong, honey?"

She didn't respond.

"Please, Sharon. I can't stand to see you so unhappy. I've been thinking about it. You tell me what you want me to do, and I'll do it."

Mom just stared into the air, like he wasn't even there.

He kissed her hand and then kissed it again and held it against his cheek. "Look, if you want me stop seeing Brother Reuben, I will. I'll stay here with you, and we'll find our way together."

At first she didn't move. Then she lifted her hand and brought it down to where it almost touched his hair, but she quickly took it away. I don't think he knew she'd almost touched him, almost forgiven him. When she wouldn't talk to him, he eventually got up and came out of the room. He looked at me sadly and said, "It's hopeless."

After that, Dad did what he said he was going to do; he stopped seeing Brother Reuben. He came home every night after work and focused all his attention on Mom, but she still didn't recover. She wandered around the house all day when he was at work, and she was constantly throwing up, whether she ate anything or not. I tried to imagine what was going on in her head, but I didn't know if she was punishing Dad for what he'd done, or if she was just so depressed she'd given up on trying to be happy. Maybe what she was really thinking was that, sooner or later, he'd go back to seeing Brother Reuben.

Chapter 9

No power or influence can or ought to be maintained by virtue of the priesthood, only by persuasion, by long-suffering, by gentleness and meekness, and by love unfeigned.

Doctrine and Covenants
Section 121:41

*S*chool was out for the summer, and I really missed Tommy. We hadn't seen anyone else since we stopped going to church when Mom got sick. Then one night, someone knocked on the front door. I was so excited to think we finally had a visitor, I raced down to see who it was. When I opened the door, Brother Reuben was standing there. He winked and whispered, "Hello, pretty little sister. It's good to see you."

I got an immediate stomachache. He looked scary, with the shadows from the porch light distorting his nose and his eyes glowing like little sparks of light beneath his thick eyebrows. I couldn't even see his lips beneath the wild hair of his mustache.

When I didn't say anything, he changed his tone. "Is your father home?"

"Stay here."

I shut the door in his face and ran to find Dad. He was lying on the bed next to Mom with his face pressed up against her arm. I didn't want her to know Brother Reuben was there, so I said, "Dad, can you come downstairs? I need to show you something."

He lifted his head. "Can't you see I'm resting with your mother?"

"It'll only take a minute. I promise." I pulled on his arm.

When I wouldn't let him alone and he said, "Okay, okay."

We got downstairs, and I whispered, "Brother Reuben's outside."

"Why didn't you let him in?"

"I didn't want Mom to know."

He glanced up the stairs. "Okay. I'll go outside and talk to him."

He left the door open a crack and I could hear him say, "I'm afraid I can't talk with you, Brother. My wife is not doing very well. She needs my attention."

Brother Reuben didn't seem to care about that. "We need your attention too, Brother. You've been gone too long."

"I'm sorry. But there's nothing I can do about that right now."

"You've made a commitment to us. And you've made a commitment to the Lord. You can't turn away from that."

I wanted to push back the door and scream for him to go away. If Mom found out he was there, I didn't know what she'd do.

Dad said, "I'm not turning away. I'm telling you, my wife is not doing well at all."

"I see." Brother Reuben was quiet for a minute, then he spoke in a low voice. "You know it's her duty to obey you. You're the patriarch of this family, are you not? How can you let her pull you around by her apron strings?"

"You know that's not true. There are things I must teach her, but now is not the time to do it. She's been sick. I've got to go slowly."

It sounded like Dad was irritated, but he wasn't telling Brother Reuben to go away. He was just telling him to be patient, and that made my stomach ache even more.

"Well, we all know that women will take whatever they can get and by whatever means. But you've been called by God to do His work, Brother Michael. I don't think you should forget that. I expect to hear from you soon."

When Dad came back in the house and found me behind the door, he frowned. "We don't need to tell your mother about this."

"I know that. But why does he have to keep coming around? I don't like him."

"Don't say that, Beth. There's nothing wrong with Brother Reuben. It's just that I should have found a way to bring your mother into our discussions."

"Why didn't you, Dad? You should've found a way to talk to her."

"I know, honey. I feel bad about that. It seemed like . . . well, we don't need to go into it now."

He started up the stairs, but I pulled him back. "But what if she never gets better? What if she never talks to us again?"

"We've got to help her. We've got to be gentle and give her time."

"Okay. But I don't think it's going to help if you start seeing Brother Reuben again." I was giving him a warning, and I hoped he was listening.

He put his arm around me and we went upstairs together.

I was almost getting used to Mom's silence and depression. Then one day, I watched her go down the hall, and out of the blue, she pushed open the back door and went outside for the first time in ages. For a minute, she just stood on the porch, shading her eyes with her hand, as if the sun was too bright. I thought she might come back in, but she didn't; she stepped off the porch and went out across the grass.

I watched her wander around the yard, absently rubbing her hand through the short bristle of hair that had grown back on her head. She examined the flowers in the garden, stopping to pinch off some of the dead blooms on the chrysanthemums, then she went and sat in the old wooden chair next to the apple tree.

I sat down on the porch and watched her. After a few minutes, Mikey came out and sat next to me. "What are you doing, Bethy?"

"I'm watching, Mom."

"Why?"

"I just want to make sure she's okay."

He watched with me for a few minutes, but then, he got restless. "It's too boring. Why don't we run through the sprinklers? I want to do something fun for a change."

"You can if you want to."

He ran in the house and came out a few minutes later in his swimming trunks. I helped him drag the sprinkler to the middle of the lawn and turned on the tap. He ran toward the water until it was just barely hitting him in the face, and then he squealed and ran away from it. He did it again and again, every time getting a little braver and squealing a little louder. I looked at Mom to see if the noise was bothering her. She was watching him and smiling. It was the first time I'd seen her smile in ages, so I dared Mikey to go all the way into the center.

He ran through the middle, squealing all the way through to the other side, but when I looked, Mom wasn't watching anymore. She'd turned back to the garden.

I went and stood behind her chair to see what she was looking at. The garden had grown wild without her caring for it, but it still had a strange beauty about it. The flowers were all growing together with their different colors, and there were two monarch butterflies fluttering up and down, and honeybees diving, and spiders dancing in their shimmering webs. I saw a hummingbird hanging in the air, drinking sugar from the morning glories, and I whispered, "Look, Mom, a hummingbird. Isn't it pretty? How does it stay in one place so long?"

She didn't answer me, but she still had a bit of a smile on her face, which made me think she was listening, and that she was seeing the hummingbird, and the butterflies, and the flowers. She looked softer and more peaceful than she'd been in months.

Seeing Mom out in the garden like that, gave me hope that things would get better, but when it got to be late afternoon and Dad still wasn't home, I got worried again. He'd said he was just going to the grocery store, and now, it was getting dark and he wasn't there. I got a sick feeling in my stomach. Had Brother Reuben intercepted him somewhere?

Even though Mom hadn't noticed what anyone was doing for a long time, she also seemed worried about where Dad was. She kept going in the kitchen to look at the clock and then into the living room to look out the window. Finally, she stopped in front of Mikey and me and said, "Where's your father?" She said it as if she'd been speaking all along.

I couldn't believe my ears. Had she really said something? I had to force myself to calm down before I could answer. "I don't know, Mom. He said he was just going to the grocery store."

Mikey's eyes were huge, like he'd seen a ghost or something. He kept looking at me and then looking back at Mom, but she just kept talking. "It's pretty late. Maybe we should call someone."

"Uh . . . who would we call?"

"I don't know." She stood there, looking like she was trying to decide what to do. Then she said, "Should we fix dinner? Maybe he's just late. Won't he be hungry when he gets home?"

I hoped that she was right about Dad, that he was just late. It would be terrible if he was with Brother Reuben on the exact day she started to talk again.

Mikey went to her, looking real shy. "Let's do it, Momma. Let's all fix dinner."

We were standing in front of the open refrigerator, trying to decide what to fix, when we heard the truck in the driveway. We ran to the front door. As Dad got out of the truck, Mom called out, "Oh, there you are."

He looked over and laughed a little nervously. "Boy, you must all be really glad to see me, or else I'm in big trouble."

Mom said, "You were gone a long time. Is everything okay?"

"I'm sorry. There was something I had to do." He looked at me and raised his eyebrows. I just shrugged. I didn't know any better than he did why Mom had decided to talk.

He carried the groceries into the kitchen and set them on the counter. Then he said, "Hold on. I'll be right back."

He hurried outside and came back in with a box under his arm. When I saw it, I got all excited. I thought maybe he'd remembered my birthday that was coming up pretty soon. I grabbed his arm and said, "What's in the box, Dad?"

He looked at me and winked. "We'll see about that later. We should probably have something to eat first." He set the box on the table in the living room. He glanced at me again, and then he put his arm around Mom's waist and led her to the kitchen.

We decided on hamburgers, and Mom took charge of everything. It felt wonderful to have her in the kitchen again, with all of us moving around, bumping into each other, and laughing. It seemed like a hundred years since anything felt that good at our house. I wondered if maybe we were waking up from a bad dream we'd been living in.

When we'd finished eating, we did the dishes, and then I said, "Okay, Dad. Now do we get to see what's inside the box?"

"What do you think, Sharon? Are you ready for your surprise?"

So the present wasn't for me, it was for Mom. For a minute, I was disappointed, but then I realized she needed a present a lot more than I did.

Dad waited until we were all in the living room and sitting down, then he picked up the box and put it on Mom's lap. It wasn't wrapped or anything. It was just a plain white box like the ones they put clothes in at the ZCMI department store. Mom pulled the top off, spread the paper that was inside, and let out a little gasp of surprise. It was a soft blue dress, just the color of her eyes when she was happy.

Dad said, "Hold it up, honey. Show us how it looks on you."

Mom put the box on the table and stood up with the dress in front of her. She moved slowly back and forth, showing it off, the material floating as if a breeze was blowing through it. She looked at Dad and tears rolled down her cheeks. I felt a chill of joy in my spine when she went over behind his chair and put her arms around his neck and whispered something. He squeezed his eyes shut and let out a deep sigh. When he opened them, there were tears in his eyes too, but there was also a hopeful smile on his face.

Chapter 10

In sorrow thou shalt bring forth children, and thy desire shall be to thy husband, and he shall rule over thee.

Pearl of Great Price
Moses 4:22

*L*ife seemed almost normal for a while. Dad brought home a soft brown wig for Mom to wear, and the next Sunday we went back to church for the first time in months. It was strange that nobody asked where we'd been for all that time. And even though you could easily tell the wig wasn't her real hair, no one asked Mom why she was wearing it. Maybe they already knew the answer. Maybe it was like what Tommy said once, people in a small town always know what's going on, no matter how hard you try to keep it secret.

It felt good being back at church and around the other kids again, but then I noticed they were always watching me, and it started to get on my nerves. The worst one was the Bishop's daughter, Karen. She'd whisper to the other girls behind her hand, and then they'd all start laughing. She must have told them how Dad had been spending time with the polygamists. I wondered how long it would take them to forget about that and start treating me normal.

I started worrying about what Dad had said to Brother Reuben about being patient. Just in case he was still thinking that way, I kept my eye on him, and whenever the telephone rang, my heart jumped. Luckily, it didn't ring very often, and Brother Reuben never called or came to the house. After a while, I began to feel a little more relaxed, and I started to think about other things, like seeing Tommy.

Tommy must have read my mind, because one morning he showed up, saying he wanted to talk. I was still nervous about leaving Mom home alone with just Mikey, but I decided to take a chance. I told Mom I'd be back soon, and Tommy and I headed down to the creek. On the way, I told him about my dad and Brother Reuben, and how Mom had cut off her hair, and how she got depressed and wouldn't talk to anyone.

He stopped and said, "Oh, man. That's terrible."

"I wish I could have talked to you, Tommy. It was really lonely."

"Why didn't you come over?"

"I didn't dare leave my mom alone."

We came to where the trail dipped into the scrub oak and something really eerie happened. Crows started flying in from all directions, landing on the tops of the trees, until the branches were all speckled with their coal black bodies. Then, two or three at a time, the birds would swoop down to a place just ahead on the trail. They'd hop around for a bit, then fly back up to the top of the trees again. They were squawking and making so much noise we could hardly hear each other talk. Tommy waved his hands in the air and yelled, "Hey. What's all the racket?"

They just squawked louder.

It disturbed me to see the crows swoop down like that, as if they wanted to scare us away. I started to back up, but Tommy said we should try to make our way through them. As we got closer to where they were landing, we saw what all the commotion was about: there was a crow lying on its side with its feet sticking straight out. Its eyes were wide open and staring. It was obviously dead.

Tommy said, "Oh, I get it. It's a crow funeral. That's why they're acting so strange."

"Really? Crows have funerals?"

"Yeah. They come from all over to say goodbye to their dead friend."

"Do you think we should bury it?"

"Naw. They might not like that."

"How long will they stay?"

"Not very long. Probably just long enough to say goodbye. Come on, we should leave them alone."

I was still feeling bad about the dead crow when we came out into the clearing by the dam. It was the first time I'd been to the creek since Dad had his vision. That made me sad. We usually spent a lot of time at the creek in the summertime, swimming and exploring the trails, but we hadn't been there once since school got out.

The creek wasn't roaring like it was that day with Dad, but it still gave me goose bumps when we jumped off the cement wall next to the pool that was created by the dam. But then, we sat down on a large flat rock that had been soaking up the warmth of the sun all day, and I started to relax. I took off my shoes and dangled my bare feet into the cool water. "Try it, Tommy. It feels good."

"Naw. I don't feel like it." He gave me a sideways look. "Did you hear what happened down here last Saturday?"

"No. I haven't heard much of anything about anything."

"Well, you know Leslie Ingham, don't you?"

"Sure. She's a year older than me. About the same age as you, right?"

"Yeah. Well, she has this cousin named, Wendy, from somewhere else. She was in town visiting Leslie last Saturday, and they came down here. I guess Wendy hadn't ever been to the creek before, and she got all excited. They started wading. Right over there." He pointed to the shallow end of the pool where the rocks were poking out. "Somehow Wendy's glasses fell off. Leslie and her started dunking down under the water trying to get the glasses, but the dam was open on the bottom, and it kept pulling the glasses further away. The girls went in deeper and deeper, trying to get them."

"They shouldn't have been doing that. My dad says you have to be really careful when the dam's open."

"He's right. Leslie said she knew they were getting too close to the dam. She tried to tell Wendy that, but Wendy said her mother would be really mad if she lost her glasses. Leslie said she tried to stop her, but she went down underneath the water one more time. That's when it pulled her in."

"Oh no. What happened?"

"The water going under the dam acted like a vacuum. It pulled her all the way down to the bottom. It was like it was trying to suck her through to the other side, but the hole wasn't big enough. When she didn't come up, Leslie went under and saw that Wendy's face was stuck up against the opening at the bottom of the dam. She says she tried to pull Wendy loose, but she couldn't get her unstuck. I wondered why Leslie didn't get stuck too, but when I thought about it, I decided Wendy's body must have filled up the hole and that took away most of the vacuum."

It was terrible to think of Wendy stuck down there with her face smashed up against the metal of the dam. What would it be like if you could never come up? You'd have to hold your breath and hold your breath until you couldn't do it anymore. You wouldn't be able to cough the water out because the rest of the water would be there, and you'd just breathe in more and more of it until you were all filled up with water. I was getting really upset thinking about it. I stood up. "I don't want to be here anymore, Tommy."

As we were walking back up the trail, I said, "I wish you hadn't told me that story. It's just another terrible thing. I've had enough terrible things in my life."

"I'm sorry. I guess I needed to tell someone, but after you told me what's been happening to you, I should've realized--"

"No, it's okay. It just makes me think of what could have happened to my dad. I can't stop seeing that girl's face stuck down there at the bottom of the dam."

"Maybe, it's not so bad to drown. Matt told me once that it's really scary at first, but it doesn't last very long. Once you breathe the water, it's all over, and you don't know anything anymore."

I wasn't so sure about that. After seeing the dead crow, and then hearing about Leslie's cousin drowning, it felt like death was all around me. I started thinking that something bad might have happened at home. I told Tommy to hurry.

He tried to convince me it was all in my mind, that I was just feeling nervous because things had been rough for so long, but I couldn't get over that bad feeling.

When we got to the house, I threw open the back door and found Mom standing there waiting for me. She looked upset.

"What's wrong, Mom? What happened?"

"Where've you been? I've been looking all over for you."

"I told you I was going with Tommy. We went down to the creek."

"I'm sorry, honey. I forgot what you said."

I saw that she was dressed up and had her purse under her arm. "Where are you going?"

"That's why I've been looking for you. I've got to go down and see Doctor Wilson."

"Oh no? Are you sick again?"

"Nobody's sick. I just have to talk to him about something. Now hurry upstairs and change your clothes, if you want to go with us."

I said goodbye to Tommy and went to change my clothes. When I came back downstairs, Mom and Mikey were already waiting in the car.

On the way to the doctor's office, I kept seeing Wendy's face pressed up against the dam with all the weight of the water pushing her down. It made me feel like I couldn't breathe. I was feeling kind of panicky, and I wanted to tell Mom about it, but I thought it would upset her. That was the last thing I wanted to do. Instead, I shook my head hard and tried to make the image disappear.

When we got to the doctor's office, Mom got in to see him almost immediately. The nurse brought out a coloring book and a big box of colored pencils and put them on the table for Mikey. She gave me a cardboard doll with a box of paper clothes. "Here, sweetie, this is kind of fun. If you press the clothes against the doll with the magic wand, they'll stick."

What did she think I was, eight or something? I put the doll on the table, sat back and watched Mikey draw with the colored pencils. I guess it was supposed to be a picture of our family. We were standing in front of a house with apple trees all around. He was coloring the picture in a crazy way. Dad was lime green and Mom was pink with bright red hair, with little snips of it on the ground. He colored me blue, himself purple, and we were holding hands. All of us were frowning. The house was two-storied, like ours, but he'd colored the windows orange, red, and black, almost like the house was on fire and the flames were blazing out. I realized that was the way he saw it. Even now, when things were a little better, he was still scared, and I guess I was too. Sometimes I wondered if we'd ever recover.

I looked up and saw Mom over by the door talking with the doctor. I strained to hear what he was saying.

"I still wish you would have come in sooner. It's not good to wait this long. You must have known what was happening."

"I guess I did, but I had other things on my mind." She put her hand up to her hair, then quickly put it back down again.

The doctor looked worried. "Are you sure everything's alright at home?"

"I don't know. I hope so."

"What about Michael?"

"Oh, I expect he'll be happy. You know how the Lord said, 'Go forth and multiply.'"

The doctor put his hand on her shoulder. "Let me know if there's anything I can do. Make another appointment in about a month, but call me sooner if you run into any problems. I'm concerned about your weight."

He started to walk away but turned back. "And try to stay relaxed. That's the best thing for the . . . you know."

"I'll try. Thank you."

On the way out to the car, I asked Mom why she had to come back in a month.

"Oh, it's nothing. He just wants to do a regular checkup."

"But why did he say there might be a problem?"

"Beth, I really don't want to talk about this right now!"

"I'm sorry. I didn't mean to make you mad."

"Honey, I'm not mad. I just have some thinking to do. I'll talk to you about it later. Okay?"

"Okay, Mom." I didn't ask her any more questions.

When we got back in the car, I thought about what she'd said to the doctor about going forth to multiple. Those were the words they used in church to mean you should have babies. Was that what she meant? Was she going to have a baby? Maybe that's why she said Dad would be happy. But if that's what it was, why wouldn't she tell me? Why would she want to keep it a secret? And how come the doctor said there could be problems? I wished she'd tell me what was going on so I'd know if I should be worried or not.

Instead of going straight home, Mom drove to the Five and Dime store. I could hardly remember the last time we'd been there. "You didn't say we were coming here. Do we get to buy something?"

She smiled. "I thought it would cheer us up to have a treat."

We went inside and Mom led us over to the snack bar. "How about ice cream?"

Mikey started chanting, "I scream, you scream, we all scream for ice cream."

We both got a double cone and Mom got a big glass of milk. When we finished eating, and we were walking back through the aisles of the store, she stopped and picked up a tiny pair of shoes inside a plastic box. "Look, at these, Beth. Aren't they adorable?"

That really made me think she was going to have a baby, but I tried to hide my excitement. "I can't believe even a baby could have feet that small."

"Don't you remember when Mikey was a baby?"

"I remember when he had an earache and he cried all night. Didn't Dad and the Bishop give him a blessing?"

"Really? You remember that? You were so young."

"I think so. Did it happen?"

She smiled sadly. "Yes, it did. I guess it just shows how we remember the hard times."

"It wasn't so bad. He got better, didn't he?"

She brightened. "That's right. He did."

While we were driving home, I couldn't stop thinking that Mom was going to have a baby. I wanted to ask her, but I was afraid she'd say no and spoil my excitement. I thought a baby was exactly what we needed for a fresh start.

When Dad got home from work that night, I expected Mom to tell him about the baby right away, but it wasn't until after supper and they were alone in the kitchen that I heard her bring up the subject. When she told him she'd been to the doctor, he said, "Oh, dear. Is something wrong?"

"Not exactly. He says we're going to have a baby."

"What? Are you sure?"

"That's what the test says. Doctor Wilson was upset that I hadn't come in to see him sooner."

"But everything's okay? The baby's alright?"

"As far as I know. He says I need to put on some weight."

"That's wonderful, honey. I'm thrilled. I've been praying for this."

Mom frowned. "Have you? You didn't tell me that."

"We'll have to get ready. When is it due?"

I could tell by Dad's voice that he was so excited he could hardly contain himself. I was having the same problem, but Mom's voice was flat, as if she didn't really care. "The doctor says late December."

"Christmas time? Oh, that's special. What a blessing."

When I heard that, I couldn't keep from running into the kitchen. I threw my arms around Mom and said, "I knew we were going to have a baby. I knew it. That's really wonderful, Mom."

She smiled a little. "It's not nice to eavesdrop, Beth. But yes, it's true."

"Can I tell Mikey?"

"I guess you'd better. We don't want him to be the only one left in the dark."

When I told Mikey the baby was coming in December, at Christmas time, he got all excited and yelled, "Oh, boy. Oh, boy. A little baby Jesus boy."

"Well, it might be a girl," I suggested.

Mikey started screaming. "I don't want a girl. I want a boy. I want a boy."

I didn't know what to do with him. I was afraid he was going to have a tantrum. "Okay, Mikey. Don't get crazy. It probably will be a boy."

I heard a noise, and I turned around and saw Mom and Dad standing in the doorway. He had his arm around Mom's shoulders, and there was a big smile on his face. Mom was smiling too, but there was something sad about her smile. It made me wonder why she wasn't as happy as the rest of us. What was she thinking? Was she worried about something?

Chapter 11

For God doth know that in the day ye eat thereof, then your eyes shall be opened, and ye shall be as gods, knowing good and evil.

Holy Bible
Genesis 3:5

$\mathcal{M}$om and I were in the kitchen one day doing the breakfast dishes. I'd been thinking a lot about the baby and wondering how it all worked. I said, "Mom, how does the baby breathe when he's inside you?"

"It doesn't have to breathe. I do the breathing for both of us."

"Really?"

"Yes, the baby gets its oxygen from my blood."

"How does that work?"

"I think maybe it's a little too complicated to explain. By the way, Beth, you keep calling the baby, he. We don't know that it's going to be a boy."

"I know. I keep forgetting. Mikey wants a boy really bad. He calls it his little baby Jesus Christmas boy."

"Well, it might not come on Christmas. You can't always pin it down to a specific day."

"Why not?"

"Babies seem to have a mind of their own. They come when they're good and ready. For example, you were eager. You came two weeks early."

"What about Mikey?"

"He didn't want to come. Even when I went into labor, it took twenty hours."

"Labor? What's that?"

She laughed. "Oh, you don't want to know about that, believe me."

"Sure I do. Come on, tell me. Please." I pulled on her arm.

"Well, let's just say it's when the baby tells you he's about to make his entrance into the world." She didn't seem to want to say anything more about it.

We finished the dishes, and I followed her upstairs to the laundry room and watched while she ironed Dad's shirts.

"So, how did you get pregnant anyway?"

She laughed. "You sure ask a lot of questions."

"How am I supposed to know, if you don't tell me? What if it happens to me?"

She gave me sharp look. "Hopefully, that won't happen for a long time, and not until you're married."

"But what if it does? Some of the girls say it can happen if a boy pees on the toilet seat and you sit on it accidentally. That sounds pretty dumb. Is it true?"

She laughed. "Don't get yourself all worked up, Beth. You can't get a baby like that."

"Well, then, how does it work?"

"You'll learn about it next year in school. It's not something you need to think about until then."

I wanted to know the answer now. Not knowing, made me feel stupid, especially now that I'd graduated from Primary into Mutual. My new teacher, Sister Stringham, was always talking about how babies were the most important thing in a girl's life, the thing that we were made for. If that was true, why was it such a big secret how it happened? I was going to have to figure out some way to find out.

A few days later, Tommy showed up at the house, and I realized he'd know the answer to my question. I hurried him outside and said, "I've got to ask you something, Tommy. Do you know some place where we can talk in private?"

"Sure. Come on."

He led me along the irrigation ditch up towards Johnson's mink ranch. When we got to where the ditch turned west, Tommy grabbed my hand. He pulled me through the tall stalks of the pussy willows until we came to an overgrown trail I'd never seen before. Pretty soon, we came to a wooden hut. You couldn't see it from the main trail, and most people wouldn't even know it was there. I knew it must be his brother's secret place.

"What about Matt?" I said, "Won't you get in trouble for bringing me here?"

"Naw. He won't be using it anymore. He said it's my hut now that he's gone in the Army."

I followed him inside. It was dark, but there were streams of glittery sunlight coming in through the holes between the boards in the ceiling. There was a small hole for a window, but it was on the shady side, and not much light was coming in there. For some reason, being in Matt's hut with Tommy made me nervous.

I stood awkwardly by the door, while Tommy went over to the corner and got a blanket from inside a box. He sat down cross-legged, and I went over and sat next to him. He said, "Okay, what do you want to talk about?"

"I'm not so sure now."

"Why not?"

"Well, maybe you don't know the answer anyway."

"You'll never know unless you ask."

I thought about it for a minute and tried to convince myself that it was just a question. But if it was just a question, why was I feeling so nervous? Maybe it was because it was a girl thing, or because I knew Sister Stringham would be mad at me for asking. Tommy would probably think I was stupid anyway, but he was my best friend; if I couldn't ask him, who could I ask? Finally, after debating with myself for several minutes, I blurted it out. "How does a person get pregnant?"

"What?"

"I asked my mom, but she wouldn't tell me. She said to wait until I learn about it in school next year, but I want to know now. Can you explain it?"

"Maybe you should ask one of your girlfriends."

"They don't know anything. They think it happens when you sit on a toilet that some boy's peed on. When I told my mom that, she just laughed. And besides those girls aren't talking to me much these days."

Tommy squinted at me through the dim light. He had a weird look on his face, like he thought what I'd said was amusing, but he seemed embarrassed too.

"So, do you know how it happens, or not?"

"Sure I do. I'm not stupid."

"Well, if you're so smart, tell me."

He sat there looking at me with that weird expression, then he finally said, "I think I'd have to show you some things instead of telling you."

"What do you mean?"

"Well, it's kind of hard to explain with words."

I said, "Okay, then, show me." I moved a little closer to him. I felt daring, like I was about to learn something I wasn't supposed to know. But it must be all right to know it, because Mom said I'd learn about it in school. If I went ahead and learned it now, I'd be able to tell the other girls the truth, and maybe they'd get interested in talking to me again. I grabbed his arm. "Come on, show me."

"If I do, you better not tell anyone."

"Why would I do that?"

"I don't know. You'll probably just end up being mad at me."

Suddenly, I wasn't so sure I wanted to know. "What would I have to do?"

He reached over and yanked on the bottom of my shorts. "You have to take these off."

"Why?"

"So I can show you."

"No. I don't want to do that."

"Okay, then, forget it." He lay back on the blanket and put his arm over his eyes, his usual sign that he didn't want to talk about it anymore.

I lay on my side next to him and ran my finger along the blue stripe of his shirt. "Why can't you just tell me about it, Tommy?"

"I don't want to. You wouldn't understand anyway."

"How do you know?"

He just clicked his tongue.

"Well, how do you know so much about it anyway?"

He let out an impatient breath. "Matt told me a long time ago."

It seemed like he was trying to be a big shot, like he knew everything, and I was the dumb one. I didn't like that feeling. I got up my nerve and said, "Okay, I'll do it."

He sat up quickly, waiting for me to pull down my shorts.

"Don't look."

"What do you mean, don't look? How can I show you, if I don't look?"

"Okay, but wait until I'm ready."

He gave me another exasperated look, then closed his eyes.

I slipped my shorts down over my knees and said, "All right. They're off."

When he opened his eyes, he shook his head. "You've got to take them all the way off, and your panties too."

"I'm not going to do that."

"Okay, don't. It's okay with me. Let's go." He stood up and started to leave. When I didn't come, he looked back.

I sat there on the blanket trying to decide what to do. There was something in me that wanted to do it. I didn't completely understand why, but thinking about it made me tingle down there, and in my stomach too. I made up my mind and slowly pulled my panties down.

Tommy just stood there staring at me, like he was frozen and couldn't move.

I said, "Well, come on. I don't want to freeze to death."

He sat back down, whispering, "It's not cold."

"Well, then, why am I shivering?"

He touched my leg and the shivering got even worse. "Come on. Hurry up and show me."

He told me to open my legs, and when I did, he put his hand down between them. His fingers were warm. It felt like he was touching a place right in the center of me.

"There's a hole here." His voice cracked, and I felt a shiver come through his finger. "That's where the baby gets in."

"But how? I whispered. "Where does it come from?"

"From here." He put his hand on the front of his pants.

"Really? Show me."

"I don't know, Beth. Maybe we shouldn't."

"Come on, Tommy. I showed you."

"But--"

"Please."

Tommy was breathing hard. He looked all flustered as he got up on his knees and undid his belt. He pulled off his pants and there it was, his private part. I'd never seen a boy naked like that, except for Mikey, and Dad, that one time up at the creek. I felt like I was being bad, but I was excited too.

I tried not to look at Tommy, but I could tell he was looking at me. He lay down beside me with his hot mouth against my neck. His nakedness was touching my leg, and it felt all warm and soft. He put his hand back between my legs, and then I felt a change in the feeling against my leg. Tommy moaned, and I sat up real quick. "What's wrong?"

He grabbed his pants and went into the corner, facing away from me. As soon as he started getting dressed, it made me feel naked. I grabbed my panties and shorts and put them back on as fast as I could. I felt all wet between my legs, and I was embarrassed because I thought I'd let some pee leak out. I thought maybe the quivery feeling made that happen.

After I was dressed, I started worrying about what Tommy would think of me. He was standing at the door looking out. I didn't know what to say because I wasn't sure what had happened. I wasn't even exactly sure if he'd answered my question.

Then, I remembered what Sister Stringham had said about girls being like roses and how we'd be spoiled if someone touched us. Was I spoiled now? Tommy had touched me, but he'd just barely touched me. People touched each other all the time, didn't they? What was so bad about that? Deep down inside, I knew this kind of touching was different. I knew it was the kind of touching that spoiled a girl. I got so scared, I started crying.

Tommy came back from the door and reached down to pull me up from the blanket. He looked serious, and he seemed somehow different than he was before. "Let's go."

All the way back to the house, I wanted to say something, but I couldn't think what to say. I guess Tommy couldn't either. He'd look at me, and I'd look at him, and then we'd both look away. It felt like things had changed between us. Would we still be friends? I really needed him to be my friend. He was the only one I could talk to, but now it seemed like there was something in the way that made it difficult. I was mad at myself for asking him the question in the first place. Why was I so stupid? Why didn't I just wait to learn about babies in school, like Mom said?

That night in bed, I couldn't stop thinking about what we'd done in Matt's hut. It took hours for me to get to sleep, and then I woke up all covered with sweat. I'd been dreaming that something was chasing me. I couldn't see what it was, but it was coming at me from all sides. From up above and down below. No matter which way I turned, it was waiting for me.

It left me shaking, and I was having trouble getting my breath. Then, suddenly, I was freezing. I took off my wet nightgown and moved over to the dry side of the bed to try to get warm, but I still couldn't stop shivering. I looked around and noticed the moon. It was shining clear across my bed, making my skin a ghostly white. The light was blue and shimmery. I could almost feel it dancing on my skin. I tilted my head back and looked out into the night. That's when I saw a dark shadow fly into the tree outside the window.

I got up on my knees and pressed my nose against the glass to see what it was. That's when I heard the cry, "Whoo. Whoo."

It was a huge owl. At first, I could only see its silhouette, but then it turned its head around and flashed its yellow eyes at me. We stared at each other for a long time, and then it flew away. It was such a strange thing. It almost felt as if the owl was trying to tell me something. After the bad dream, I wasn't sure it was something I wanted to hear.

Chapter 12

*And when he shall manifest himself unto you in the flesh, the
things which he shall say unto you shall ye observe to do.*

Book of Mormon
2 Nephi 32:6

*O*ne afternoon, not too long after my experience with Tommy,
Brother Reuben showed up at our house again. When I opened the
door, all he said was, "Is your father home?"

I glared at him. "No, he's at work."

He pushed me aside, went into the living room, and plopped down
on the couch with his long legs stretched out in front of him. "I'll just
wait for him here."

I couldn't believe it. He acted like he owned the house, like he was
Dad's best friend, or something, and we wouldn't mind if he just came
in and took over the living room. I was standing there trying to think
of some way to get rid of him when Mom came downstairs.

Brother Reuben sat upright and smiled at her sweetly. "Oh, there
you are, Sister. I was wondering if we could have a little talk before
your husband gets home."

Mom wouldn't go near him. She stayed by the bottom of the stairs,
with her hand on the rail, ready to run. "I don't have anything to say
to you, Mr. Reuben."

"Well, maybe you could just listen. I understand you have some
reservations about Brother Michael spending time with us."

Mom's eyes narrowed. "That's between Michael and me. It's none
of your--"

"Come now, Sister, I know you've been having trouble, and I know that's why Brother Michael has been staying at home with you. But what happened to him is not going away. He is a special person to God. And in that light, you are special too."

She came into the living room with her hands in fists beneath her armpits. "I'm sorry. I don't care to listen to this."

Brother Reuben sighed and shook his head, as if it was just so frustrating that Mom couldn't understand what he was saying. "Now, Sister, I'm sure you'll agree that if the prophet, Joseph Smith, had listened to his wife's objections, we wouldn't have the Church."

"As I recall, she only had a problem with the doctrine of plural marriage."

Brother Reuben nodded. "Just my point, Sister. Joseph Smith received a revelation concerning the divine law of Celestial Marriage. There was nothing he could do but follow God's mandate."

Mom didn't respond.

"I'm sure you're thinking to yourself that the Lord rescinded polygamy, at least for the time being . . . that is, until we are in the next world."

"That's right. We're not supposed to be doing it now." She sat down hard on the arm of the chair, and I went to stand beside her to give her my support.

"Now why would the Lord have given us a law and then, just when it was most convenient in terms of what the federal government wanted, take it away. It doesn't make sense, does it?"

"That's not for me to say. It's up to the Prophet and the Lord."

Brother Rueben crossed his legs and cocked his head to one side. "Let me ask you something, Sister. Are you aware there were prophecies given to certain leaders in the early Church, prophecies that told of how later prophets would lead the Church astray? What if the Lord never meant for us to give up plural marriage? What if that was Lucifer's work? And what if it's now your husband who God has chosen to lead us back to the true path of righteousness? If that's so, what do you think will happen to you if you stand in the way?"

She stood up. "I think it's time for you to leave."

"Now, now, open your mind, Sister. You're too quick to voice your objections. You're not really thinking about what I'm saying."

She sank down into the chair again and put her hands over her face. "Why can't you just leave us alone?"

Brother Reuben leaned forward and touched her knee. "Sister Sharon, listen to me. I understand you're carrying a child in your womb. Don't you realize that child is a gift from God? A confirmation of His love for you. As a mother, you're responsible to teach your children the true gospel. Isn't that right? But you can only teach them the true gospel if you know what that is. And you do know. You've heard it all your life. It's the original gospel, the gospel as it was given to the prophet, Joseph Smith. That is what you must teach your children."

She stood up quickly and went around behind the chair, holding onto the back for support. "Who do you think you are, telling me what I must do? And how do you know about the baby? Did Michael tell you?"

He ignored her question. "Sister, do you remember what Jesus said to His mother, Mary, when she tried to dissuade Him from His work? 'How is it that ye sought me? Wist ye not that I must be about my Father's business?' The Lord does not look kindly upon your interference with Michael. Submit yourself to the Lord, woman. Claim your blessings and be redeemed."

Mom leaned forward and shouted at him, "I don't intend to ruin my children's lives. I won't make them outcasts like your children."

Brother Reuben didn't say anything. He was looking at her as if he was waiting for her to calm down and be reasonable. Then, his eyes got that piercing look. "'Blessed are ye when men shall revile you and persecute, and shall say all manner of evil against you falsely, for my sake. For ye shall have great joy and be exceedingly glad, for great shall be your reward in heaven.'" He spoke in a deep booming voice that almost rattled the walls.

Mom put her hands over her ears and started moving her head back and forth with her eyes clenched shut, as if she was trying to make him disappear. But Brother Reuben just seemed to get bigger and louder. "Be ye not selfish, woman. Turn thyself away from evil. Do it now, before it's too late."

Mom's face contorted with pain, and she clenched her stomach. Brother Reuben shot up from the couch and reached out, but he couldn't catch her as she turned and ran for the stairs. A few seconds later, we could hear her in the bathroom, throwing up.

I couldn't stop myself. I ran over and started punching Brother Reuben in the stomach with all my strength. I yelled, "Go away. Leave us alone."

He just laughed. He grabbed my arms and pulled me so close I almost gagged on the dirty smell of his shirt. I struggled to get free, but he held me tight and whispered, "Someday you'll understand the importance of all this, sweet Elizabeth. Someday it will become perfectly clear."

I felt like I was suffocating, but there was nothing I could do to escape. He had my arms held with one hand and he was pressing on the back of my head with the other one. I thought I was going to throw up too. Then, I heard the sound of Dad's truck. Brother Reuben must have heard it too because he quickly let go of me. I ran and threw open the door and yelled, "Come quick, Dad. Brother Reuben's here. You've got to make him leave."

When Dad came in, Brother Reuben was sitting on the couch with his legs crossed, as if nothing had happened. He jumped up and hurried toward Dad. "Brother Michael, there you are."

He shook Dad's hand and patted him on the shoulder. "Your wife and I have had a nice little chat. I think we understand each other better now."

Dad looked at me. "Where is she, Beth?"

"Upstairs . . . throwing up."

He ran up to the bathroom with me on his heels. "Sharon, what's going on? What's wrong?"

She started to cry.

When he tried to comfort her, she pushed him aside. She hurried to their bedroom and closed the door in his face. Dad tried to get in, but she must have been pushing against the door on the other side.

He knocked and begged her to let him in, but she yelled, "Go away! Just leave me alone."

We ran back downstairs where Brother Reuben was still sitting nonchalantly on the couch. Dad yelled, "What did you say to her?"

"The truth, Brother. I told her God's truth, something you should have done a long time ago."

"It's not your place to speak to her. Now, I think you'd better leave." Dad grabbed his arm and tried to pull him up.

But Brother Reuben wasn't finished. He shook off Dad's hand and stood up on his own. "You let your wife guide your actions when you should be the one guiding her. If you turn away from God's work you shall not go unpunished."

"We'll talk about this another time. Please, Brother, I think you should go."

Brother Reuben shook his head in disgust. "I see you're a weak man, Brother Michael. I'm sorry to see that. I can't imagine how the Lord could have chosen you for his blessing. Why not a man like me, someone who's willing and able to meet the challenge?"

He looked into Dad's eyes. "Still, he must have seen something in you. You're a spiritual man. I know by our studies that you understand many things. You just don't have the strength to deal with your wife."

Brother Reuben's words seemed to be getting to Dad. He stood there staring at the floor with his arms hanging down at his side. Finally, he looked up. "I don't think you should say those things to me, Brother."

"I'm just telling you the truth. Someone's got to do it. You should thank me."

"Why can't you understand?" Dad pleaded. "I can't do this without Sharon. I can't bear her unhappiness."

"She made a covenant to obey you when you were married in the temple, did she not? Remind her of that. If you show her your strength, she'll listen."

He clapped Dad on the arm and smiled, as if everything had been decided. "Now then, I think you should be at our studies group meeting this Tuesday."

"I . . . I don't know."

I wanted to kick Dad in the shins and make him say no, but Brother Reuben had taken away all his strength, just like he had taken Mom's. He seemed to want to be in charge of everybody, and he didn't care what harm it did.

He clapped Dad on the shoulder again and said, "Okay, then, we'll see you on Tuesday."

Dad looked shrunken and weak as we stood at the door and watched Brother Reuben drive away. I tried to imagine what he was thinking. Was he afraid of Brother Reuben, or did he believe what he said about how Mom should be treated? Why didn't he stand up to Brother Reuben? Why didn't he tell him, once and for all, to go away and leave us alone?

Chapter 13

*And now I ask of you, my brethren, how will any of you feel if
ye shall stand before the bar of God, having your garments
stained with blood and all manner of filthiness? Behold, what
will these things testify against you?*

Book of Mormon
Alma 5:22

*B*rother Reuben's visit brought back all the old trouble. The
excitement we'd felt about the baby coming completely disappeared. I
don't know how Brother Reuben knew about the baby, but it made
Mom suspicious that Dad had been seeing him on the sly. Dad flatly
denied it, but Mom couldn't bring herself to believe him. When she
stopped talking to him, he disappeared into his study again and
turned back to his fasting and prayers.

Then, late one night, Dad woke me up. "Hurry, Beth, you've got to
get up."

I was still half asleep, but I could see Dad was really scared.
"What's wrong?" I said.

"We've got to take your mother to the hospital."

"Why? What happened?"

"There's no time for questions. Get Michael dressed and come
downstairs as fast as you can."

While I was trying to get Mikey awake, Dad yelled, "Quick, Beth.
Get a clean towel from the bathroom."

I told Mikey to hurry and ran to the bathroom for the towel. When
I got downstairs, I saw Mom lying on the couch in her bathrobe. Her

face was pale and covered with little beads of sweat. I ran to her and said, "What's wrong, Mom?"

Dad pulled me away. "There's no time for that. Take a blanket and pillow out to the car. Put it in the back seat and leave the door open."

I did what he said. When I got back in the house, he was helping Mom off the couch. I got really scared when she stood up. There was bright red blood all over the couch and on the back of her robe. A towel, wrapped around a bag of ice, fell out of her robe. It had blood on it too, but I couldn't tell where the blood was coming from.

I gave Mikey the clean towel, put Mom's arm over my shoulder, and helped Dad carry her out to the car. It was hard for her to get in the back seat because of being pregnant, and I think whatever was bleeding hurt her a lot. When she was finally lying down, she started to cry.

Dad took the clean towel from Mikey and wrapped it around the bag of ice, then he opened Mom's robe and helped her put it between her legs. He told me to get in the back seat and keep an eye on her, but there wasn't any room on the seat, so I straddled the hump in the middle of the floor. Mikey got in front with Dad and we headed for the hospital.

I held Mom's hand the whole way, talking to her softly, trying to give her some comfort, but she kept moaning. It just about broke my heart. If only I knew what was wrong.

It took us a long time to get to the hospital. Mom's pain seemed to get worse and worse. She kept holding her belly and squeezing her eyes closed every few minutes, as if the pain was coming in waves and it was almost more than she could bear. When we finally arrived, Dad jumped out of the car and ran inside. He came back a few minutes later with two men in long white coats. They lifted Mom gently out of the car. They put her on a bed with wheels and pushed her inside. Dad went with them, leaving us outside alone.

I stood there with Mikey, looking at the car with all its doors wide open under the bright red emergency sign. I didn't know what to do. I just knew Mom and Dad were gone, and I was supposed to take care of Mikey.

After a minute, I decided we might as well get back in the car to wait. Mikey didn't want to get in the back seat where the bloody blanket was, so we got in front. He hadn't said a word the whole time everybody was taking care of Mom. When we were back inside the car, he looked at me with big sad eyes and said, "Bethy, is Momma going to die like my little chicky did?" Before I could answer, he started crying real hard.

I shouted, "Don't even think about that! Nobody's going to die."

He sniffed and said, "Then what's wrong with her?"

"I don't know. We'll just have to wait until somebody comes and tells us."

We had to wait for a long time, and I didn't know if it was getting cold, or if I was just shivering from fear. I hadn't even considered that Mom might die, but after Mikey said it, I started wondering if it really could happen. I felt a darkness swoop down on me that was so thick and heavy it felt like black water filling my lungs. I tried to think of something else, but my mind kept coming back to the same question again and again. Was Mom going to die?

Finally, Dad came out of the hospital. He got in the car, and without saying a word, he started up the engine.

I said, "Where are we going? We can't leave Mom here alone."

He looked over at us. "I'm just parking the car. We've got to go back inside."

He pulled over under a street lamp and sat there with his hands on the steering wheel, as if he couldn't move.

"Is she going to be okay?"

The look on his face was so full of fear it made my heart race. "I don't know. I don't know. She's lost all that blood. If only . . ." He stopped talking and starting rubbing his forehead.

"If only what, Dad?"

"It's all my fault."

"How could it be your fault? What did you do?" I thought he was saying he'd hurt her, that it was his fault she was bleeding.

Tears streamed down his face. "It's not what I did. It's what I didn't do." He covered his eyes with his hands and whispered, "Please, Lord. Don't take your anger out on her. I can't bear it." He started sobbing.

I touched his shoulder. "Dad, don't cry. I'm sure God's not mad at her. How could he be?"

He turned and looked at me. "Don't you understand? He's punishing me. I thought I was doing what He wanted, but the truth is I'm weak. I don't deserve His trust." He covered his whole face with his hands and cried even louder.

Suddenly, I was confused about everything. Could it be true? Could Mom be sick because God was punishing Dad for not bringing us back to the original gospel like Brother Reuben said? Or was He punishing her? Maybe He was punishing all of us. Maybe it was because of what I did with Tommy in Matt's hut. I'd been worrying about that ever since it happened. I'd been feeling dirty and sinful and now the full weight of it came down on me.

I grabbed Dad's arm. "Do you really think God would punish her for somebody else's sin?"

He nodded sadly and whispered, "'The sins of the father shall be visited upon the children.' The sins of the husband shall be visited upon the wife."

All my life I thought I knew what I was supposed to do. I wasn't always perfect, but at least I knew what was right and wrong and I tried to do my best. Now, I had this sin inside me and I couldn't escape the feeling that Mom's bleeding was all my fault. It wasn't Dad, it was me. I closed my eyes and whispered, "Please, God, if you have to punish somebody, punish me, not Mom."

Dad blew his nose and I opened my eyes. He said, "I've got to get back inside."

"Can we come too? Please, Dad. "

He looked a little confused. "Well, I guess you better. You can't sit out here all night."

We followed him into the hospital, and he took us to a big waiting room and told us to sit in the corner. "I'll go see if they'll let me be with your mother."

He stopped at the counter, and I saw a blond-headed lady look over at us and nod her head. After he left the room, she came over and gave Mikey and me each a small carton of chocolate milk. She pointed to a table. "There're some books there if you want to look at them, sweetie. If you or your little brother need to go to the bathroom, or anything, the restrooms are down the hall." She pointed in that direction.

I was too upset and worried to read, but I found a book for Mikey. While he looked at it, I tried to calm myself by watching all the people in the waiting room.

After a few minutes, Mikey yanked on my arm and pointed at a picture of an owl in his book. "What does it say about the owl, Bethy?"

I took the book and read for a minute. "It says that the Indians believe that when an owl cries, it means somebody's going to die."

I should have thought about what I was saying before I said it, because Mikey grabbed my arm and said, "Oh no. Does that mean Momma's going to die? I don't want her to die, Bethy. Don't let her die."

I said, "Shhh," and hugged him. "Don't worry, Mikey. I don't think it's really true."

But I wasn't so sure. The book said the owl was a bad omen, and I'd seen an owl that night after I'd been with Tommy in Matt's hut. The one in the tree outside my window had those same piercing yellow eyes as the one in the book, and the same head turned around backwards, looking at me, accusing me of my sin. I couldn't stop staring at those eyes.

I was still worrying about the owl's warning when Dad showed up with Mom's doctor. The doctor seemed concerned. He sat down next to me and patted my leg. "Your mother's lost a lot of blood, Beth. We need to give her some while we wait for a new supply. Do you think you could do that?"

"You mean, give her some of my blood?"

"Yes. I think it would help her."

Mikey jumped out of his chair. "Give her mine. I wanna do it."

Dad pulled him back to his seat. "You're too young, Michael."

The doctor smiled a little at Mikey and looked back at me. "It might make you a little dizzy, but it won't hurt much."

"I don't care if it hurts. I'll do anything if it will make Mom better."

"We should get started then. Will you come with me?"

I followed the doctor through the swinging doors into the emergency room. He took me into a small room with windows on all sides, at the end of the larger room. Mom was lying there on a tall bed. I couldn't tell if she was breathing. Her skin was so pale and translucent I thought that maybe she was already dead. The doctor must have realized what I was thinking because he patted me on the shoulder and said, "She'll be all right. She just needs a little blood to bring back her color."

A large friendly nurse came in and stood next to me. She smiled and touched my shoulder.

The doctor said, "I'll check back in with you later, Beth. Don't worry. You'll be just fine."

Before he could go, I said, "What about the baby, will the baby be all right?"

He and the nurse glanced at each other, and then he patted me on top of the head. "Don't worry about that. Just do what the nurse says."

When the doctor left, the nurse helped me out of my clothes and into a hospital nightgown. Then she lifted me up on a bed that was even taller than Mom's and got me hooked up to the tube that was going to carry my blood to Mom.

I said, "Can I talk to her?"

"I don't think she can hear you right now, honey. She's very tired. There'll be plenty of time for talking later."

The nurse turned the lights down and pulled a curtain around us, then she sat in a chair at the side of the room. I closed my eyes and listened to the soft murmurs of the people in the outer room. After a few minutes, I started to feel sleepy.

I must have fallen asleep, because all of a sudden, something made me jerk, and I woke up. I felt kind of woozy and closed my eyes again trying to remember my dream. There was a tube going between Mom and me, just like in real life, but in the dream, the blood was flowing in both directions. Mom's blood was getting mixed with mine, and my blood was getting mixed with hers, so that we were becoming the same person. Her blood made me feel sad, and it made me hurt so bad down between my legs, I didn't know if I could stand it.

In the dream, I talked. I said, "Mom, why do we have to hurt so much? Why do we have to bleed?" She whispered back, "I'm sorry, darling. I don't know how to save you. I don't even know how to save myself." Then Dad's voice boomed down from up above, like he was God, and Mom and I were the children who had to listen. I looked for him, but I couldn't find him anywhere. I grabbed Mom's hand and tried to run, but she couldn't go. Somebody was holding her by the other hand, and they were stronger than I was. I screamed, "Momma, Momma. Come with me. Hurry." Then her hand was gone, and I was running away by myself. I turned back and saw her, but her face was getting dim. I wanted to go get her, but I couldn't, and I didn't know why. I fell down on the road and cried, "Please, God. Help her." But even in the dream, I knew God wasn't listening.

When I opened my eyes again, Dad was standing between me and Mom. He had one hand on my head the other one on Mom's. He looked like he'd been crying. When he saw I was awake, he leaned over and kissed me on the forehead and whispered, "My precious girl." Then he kissed Mom and said, "My two precious girls. Please, dear God, keep them safe."

I wanted to say, I don't want God's blessing. I just want Mom back like she used to be. I just want us to laugh again sometimes, and play tag on the back lawn on summer nights, and make hamburgers on the outside grill. I want to go to Liberty Park on Sunday afternoons, and have watermelon, and feed the ducks. But I didn't say any of that. Just like God couldn't hear me in the dream, I knew Dad couldn't hear me either.

Chapter 14

And I also beheld that all children who die before they arrive at the years of accountability are saved in the celestial kingdom of heaven.

Doctrine and Covenants
Section 137:10

*I*t was hard to leave Mom at the hospital, but we had no choice. The doctors said they wanted to watch her for a few days to make sure the bleeding didn't start again. When Dad started up the car to take us home, Mikey started sobbing. "Why can't we take Momma with us? What if the owl comes and we're not there to protect her?" It was the same thought I was having; who was going to watch her and keep her safe?

The phone was ringing as we came in the door at home. Dad hesitated. He looked like he thought it was someone from the hospital calling with bad news. He picked up the phone, listened for a minute and, said, "I'm sorry, but I have other things to worry about right now. Sharon was bleeding. I had to take her to the hospital."

He listened again and said, "That's right. It's gone now." Then he yelled, "Don't you think I know it's my fault? But she's still in the hospital, and I have the children to look after, so there's nothing I can do." He slammed down the phone and stood there staring at it with his face burning red.

I said, "Who was that?"

He hurried to his study and closed the door without even looking at me.

I knew it had to be Brother Reuben. Nobody else could affect him that way. He must have been blaming Dad for what happened to Mom. I wondered what he'd say if he knew about my sin. Whose fault would he think it was then?

I kept thinking it was my fault the whole time Mom was in the hospital. I tried to make up for it by taking care of Dad and Mikey as best I could, but I didn't know if it would make any difference to God. I had always thought God was gentle and loving, but now it seemed like He just wanted to punish everyone, and I didn't know exactly what you had to do to be forgiven.

Dad was distraught without Mom. He cried a lot, and sometimes I heard him in his study yelling. Most the time he was yelling at himself, but sometimes it sounded like he was yelling at God. He still had to go to work to pay the hospital bills, which meant I'd end up home alone with Mikey. That wasn't easy. Almost everything I did either made Mikey mad or made him cry.

One afternoon, when Mikey was feeling especially lonely for Mom, I went and got one of his picture books. I took him to the couch and flipped through the pages until I came to a story called *The Lad with the Goat-Skin*. I asked Mikey if he wanted to hear it.

"Oh that's good. I like goats. Brother Reuben has goats."

"I know, but let's not think about him."

I started reading about the poor old woman and how she put her son, Tom, in the fireplace ashes to keep him warm.

Mikey said, "Wouldn't he get burned up?"

"I guess if she put him in the ashes, it means the fire was already out."

"But wouldn't he get dirty?"

"Gosh, Mikey, I haven't even gotten past the first page and you're already asking questions. How will we ever find out what happens?"

He was quiet until I got to the part where Tom had to fight the Devil. Mikey got all excited and started pointing at the picture. "Look, Bethy. The Devil's got horns. Does the Devil really have horns?"

"I don't think so."

"But why would they put it in the picture, if it wasn't true?"

"Maybe they just wanted to make it more interesting."

He grabbed my arm and squeezed it. "It's got to be true."

I tried to finish the story, but Mikey kept interrupting until I finally gave up.

When Dad got home a few hours later, Mikey met him at the door, yelling, "Daddy, Daddy, does the Devil have horns?"

"Wait a minute. Let me get in the house."

After he took off his work shoes and put them in the closet, Mikey said, "Well, does he?"

"Does who, what?"

"Does the Devil have horns?"

"Let me wash up. Then I'll tell you all about it."

He went upstairs, and a few minutes later, he came down with his clothes changed. We went back in the living room, and he sat Mikey and me down on the couch. "So, you want me to tell you about the Devil. Let's see . . . where should I start?" Dad thought for a minute and then he said, "When we were in the spirit world--"

Mikey interrupted. "What's the spirit world?"

"It's the place we were before we were born. We were there with our Heavenly Father, our Heavenly Mother, and all their spirit children."

"But where is it?"

"That doesn't matter. What's important is that our Heavenly Father told us that if we were going to progress and become like Him, we'd have to go to earth and get a mortal body and pass certain tests."

Mikey said, "What's a mordal body?"

"Mikey, let him tell the story."

"It's okay, Beth." He patted Mikey on the chest. "This is a mortal body. It's made of flesh and blood. Unlike the spirit body, it can die."

Mikey frowned. "Does that mean I'm going to die, like Momma?"

Dad looked alarmed. "Now that's not true. Your mother is not going to die. She'll be home before you know it." He put his arm around Mikey and continued. "The reason God wanted us to have bodies is so we could learn important lessons and eventually become like Him. You see, God was a man once. He had a body like ours. Then, when He died and was resurrected, He was exalted and became our Heavenly Father. We're all His spirit children, everyone who's ever lived on earth and everyone who's still waiting in the spirit world to be born."

I remembered how on our daddy-daughter date Dad said he had to do certain things if he was to become a god. That must have been what he was talking about. So, it *was* possible for a person to be a god, but what kind of things did you have to do to make that happen? Could I be one too? I wanted to ask Dad, but Mikey had a different question.

"What about the Devil, Daddy? What about him? Are you sure he doesn't have horns?"

"I'll get to that in a minute, son. What you need to know is that God told His spirit children that most of us would never make it back to the Celestial Kingdom because of the sins we'd commit while we were in our mortal bodies. We were scared, and our older brother, Lucifer, said he would be the Savior and come to earth and make sure that none of us did anything wrong. That way, we could all make it back to our Heavenly Father. But our oldest brother, Jesus, knew that our Heavenly Father wanted us to have free will. That way we could decide for ourselves what we would do. Jesus said, 'Thy will be done.' He promised He'd come to earth as our Savior and teach us how to get back home, but He wouldn't force us to do what He said, like Lucifer wanted to do."

Mikey just stared at him. I don't think he understood a word of what Dad was saying. He screwed up his face and whined, "But you still didn't tell us about the Devil."

"Okay, okay. After Jesus gave his plan for our salvation, our Heavenly Father decided to let us all vote on which way it would be. Did we want to follow Lucifer, or did we want to follow Jesus? One third of the spirits decided to follow Lucifer, and the rest of us went with Jesus. The ones that went with Lucifer got angry and said they were going to do it their way. He and his followers were cast out of heaven. That's when Lucifer became known as Satan. His followers never got their bodies, like we did. Instead, they became devils, and now they spend all their time trying to tempt us. They're jealous, and they don't want us to reach the Celestial Kingdom because they'll never be able to go there."

Dad stopped and put his hand over his eyes for a minute, then rubbed his forehead. I wondered if the story was making him think about Mom and all the issues of temptation and punishment that we'd been living with. Was he still feeling like it was his sin that made Mom sick, like I was?

He put his arms around us and pulled us close to him. "I should spend more time teaching you these things. I don't know why I haven't done it. I'm sorry." There were tears of regret in his eyes.

I said, "But we learn things in Church and Sunday School. You don't have to teach us everything."

"I know. But you have to understand how important it is that you never listen to Satan. Listen to the Lord and obey Him in all things, or we won't be together in the next world."

I said, "I know, Dad. We will."

The phone rang and Dad jumped up to answer it. While he was gone, Mikey turned to me with a confused look on his face. "So, do devils have horns or not?"

"I don't know, Mikey. I guess that's not the important part of the story."

I went upstairs to think about becoming a god and all the things a person could do if they were a god. Then, I remembered how Dad had told Mom that she would be the mother of the spirit children who lived in his kingdom. Was that the only role a girl could have? To be a mother?

After Mom had been in the hospital five days, Dad went to pick her up. When they got home, and he was helping her in the door, I noticed how flat her stomach was. I don't know why I hadn't noticed it before. Maybe it was because she always had covers on her at the hospital, or because I was thinking too much about her being sick and whether or not it was my fault.

Mikey must have noticed it too because he ran to her and started patting her stomach. "Momma, Momma. Where'd the baby go?"

Dad grabbed his hand and held it back. "Stop that, Michael. You'll hurt your mother."

"But where's the baby?" His eyes got wild.

Dad said, "The baby's not with us anymore, son."

Mikey looked back and forth between Mom and Dad and started yelling, "Where's my little brother? Where is he?"

Dad's eyes filled with tears. Mom sat down on the loveseat next to the front door and held out her hand to Mikey. She pulled him close to her and softly stroked the side of his face with her finger. "The baby decided to go to heaven, honey."

Mikey pulled away from her. His face got red and he yelled, "No. He can't go to heaven. He's my brother."

"I know, darling. It's just that--"

Mikey didn't let her finish. He turned around and yelled at me, "You lied, Bethy. You said nobody was going to die. But you lied."

Before I could say anything, he ran upstairs to the bedroom and slammed the door.

I turned to Mom. "Why did the baby die? I thought the doctor said he was okay."

Dad started to say something, but Mom interrupted. "It's okay, Michael. I'll tell her."

She took my hand and held it against her chest. She closed her eyes for a minute, as if it was too hard for her to talk about it. Finally, she said, "The baby came too soon. The doctors tried to save him, but he was too little to make it on his own. He was already gone by the time you gave me your blood."

"But why didn't anybody tell me? I've been thinking all this time he was alive."

"I guess they didn't want to upset you."

"But I am upset. Where is he now? Don't we need to have a funeral for him?"

Dad put his hand on my shoulder. "A prayer was said, Beth, and the baby was . . . taken care of. Now, that's enough. Your mother is tired out and in pain." He got her up from the chair, put her arm over his shoulder, and helped her upstairs.

I couldn't believe how bad things were. How long were we going to have to suffer? First Mom got sick, and now the baby was gone.

I hurried upstairs to find Mikey. He was lying on his bed with his face under his arm. I sat next to him and rubbed his back. "I'm sorry, Mikey. I didn't know the baby would die. Nobody told me."

He wouldn't say anything. He just rolled over so I couldn't see his face. I didn't know what to do. The house was dead silent and there was nobody to talk to for comfort.

I went downstairs to the living room and lay on the couch. I couldn't stop thinking about the baby. I wondered if they'd put him in a coffin before they buried him. I closed my eyes and tried to imagine what it would be like inside that coffin down beneath the earth. It would be dark and cold. It would be lonely. All of a sudden, I couldn't breathe. It felt like there was something heavy on my chest. I sat up, but it didn't help, so I stood up. I still couldn't breathe. I ran outside where there was more air and wandered around the yard trying to breathe normally. Then I lay down on the grass. I still couldn't stop thinking about the baby inside his little coffin.

Finally, I thought of something that helped. My Sunday School teacher had told us that when Jesus returned to earth, during the millennium, parents who lost their babies would get to raise them as if they'd never died. I wondered if Mikey and I would get to be there too. I hoped so. I really wanted to know my little brother. I wanted to see what he looked like.

In the days after Mom got home from the hospital, Dad became very depressed. He couldn't seem to concentrate on anything, not even his scriptures. Sometimes he'd just sit on the couch with his head in his hands and cry.

Mom tried to tell him that loosing the baby wasn't his fault, but he didn't believe her. He kept saying, "If only I'd done what the Lord wanted me to do. If only I'd been worthy of his care."

One day, after Mom was starting to get around a little better, I saw her outside in the chair next to the garden. I went to see what she was doing. She had her eyes closed, and she was talking to herself. I sat down on the grass, leaned my head up against the side of the chair, and listened.

"Tell me what to do, Lord. Michael's confusion is destroying him. I want to support him, but I need to know if his vision was real, or if he was just longing for something important in his life and saw something he longed to see."

I wanted her to open her eyes so she could see the bees buzzing over the marigolds at the edge of the lawn and hear the crows cawing to each other in the apple tree, but she kept praying.

"What if Emma hadn't believed in Joseph's vision? Would he have left her behind? Or would he have turned away from you, Lord? She must have been as confused as I am. She must have wondered why her husband was the one you called on to restore the Church. And then, when you revealed the law of plural marriage, she had to bear all the difficulties of that. Did you bless her, Lord? Did you give her the faith and the strength to endure it? I don't know if I'm that strong."

Two little white butterflies came flittering over the tops of the chrysanthemums. They were so light and playful. I wished we could find some of that lightness in our lives. Even though Mom was feeling better, the weight of Dad's sorrow and guilt had sunk down over our house, smothering any sign of happiness.

I was thinking Mom was going to go on praying forever, when a huge crow swept down from the tree and let out a piercing squawk right over our heads.

We both jumped and Mom opened her eyes. "Oh, Beth. What are you doing here?"

"Umm . . . I was just wondering if you were okay."

She leaned forward in her chair and looked deep into my eyes. "I was thinking about your father's vision. Beth, you were there that day. What did you see? Did your father really talk to someone?" She grabbed hold of my arm, and urgently pulled it towards her.

It hurt and I tried to pull away, but she was holding too tight.

"Tell me, Beth. I need to know."

"I can't remember anymore. It's been too long."

"You've got to try, honey. It's important. Tell me what happened that day at the creek."

"All I know is that I saw a bright light come down through the trees onto Dad's face. He said he was talking to God, and I believed him."

"Did you see anyone?"

"No."

"Did you hear anyone talking?"

"No. The water was too loud."

I tried to pull myself free again. This time she let me go. She leaned back in her chair and looked up towards the sky, as if she thought the answer might be there. I wished I could tell her what she wanted to know. I closed my eyes and tried to remember exactly what happened that day. I imagined myself being on the rocks next to the creek watching Dad out in the water. The water was moving fast and the sound of the rocks tumbling and crashing against each other on the bottom of the creek had terrified me. I thought they were going to smash his feet. I thought he was going to drown.

All of a sudden, I thought of something. "Mom, if he wasn't talking to God, then how come he didn't drown?"

"What do you mean?"

"The water was really powerful, and the floating tree limbs were smashing into him, but when the light came it seemed like nothing could hurt him."

"Did that really happen, Beth? Are you sure?"

"I thought he was going to be washed away. I was scared to death. But then, it seemed like something came and protected him. Maybe it was God. Maybe He really did talk to Dad." I started to cry, and this time I couldn't hold it back. All the worry and fear and the sadness and guilt I'd been feeling all came pouring out at once.

Mom's face softened and tears filled her eyes. She brushed back my hair and said, "I'm sorry, honey. It's been hard, hasn't it?"

I wiped my eyes and nose on my shirt sleeve and tried to swallow the lump of pain in my throat. "Mom, what's going to happen to us?"

She let out a long sigh. "I don't know, honey. I just don't know."

"But what if Dad starts seeing Brother Reuben again? What if he thinks that will make God forgive him?"

"I've been thinking. Maybe he needs to talk to Brother Reuben. Maybe he needs to hear what that man has to say. He's the only one who believes your father."

"But, Mom, why would you want him to do that? Brother Rueben has ruined everything."

"I've got to try something. I've been fighting your father all this time, and all it's doing is tearing us apart. Maybe if I try harder to understand what this all means and let him see that I'm trying, maybe we can survive this."

I looked up and saw that the sky had filled up with gray clouds. I could smell rain, but Mom didn't seem to notice. She said, "You know, Beth. All I ever wanted was to be with your father and you and Mikey, to have our little family go to church on Sunday, and share in the blessings of our Heavenly Father. I had no desire for God to come into our lives directly. It was enough for me to hold Him in my heart and talk to Him through prayer."

She kept talking, but she wasn't talking to me anymore. "I don't know what to do with this God who appears in trees. It's not something I know how to cope with. But I have to learn. I have to find out if there's any truth to it, and if there is, I've got to learn how to live with it."

A long bolt of lightning flashed over the top of the mountains. Before it disappeared the thunder crashed. I grabbed her hand. "Come on, Mom. It's going to rain."

We hurried inside just as huge raindrops began to splatter the sidewalk and darken the wood on the side of the house.

Chapter 15

But the prophet, which shall presume to speak a word in my name, which I have not commanded him to speak, or that shall speak in the name of other gods, even that prophet shall die.

Holy Bible
Deuteronomy 18:20

*A*fter that day in the garden, Mom started disappearing into the study with Dad. I'd put my ear against the door and hear him reading scriptures to her. I guess she was doing what she said she was going to do, trying to find out if what he said about his vision was true. Sometimes she'd come out with her eyes all red from crying, but at least they weren't yelling at each other, and Dad seemed less agitated. I tried not to worry too much.

Dad tried to get Mikey and me involved too. We never knew when he was going to walk in the room and say, "Come, children. Let's pray." We'd have to stop whatever we were doing and get down on our knees. It seemed like the only break we got from praying was when he was at work, or on Sunday when we went to church where other people did the praying.

Then one Sunday, I thought we were heading to church, but Dad turned the other way and took us up to Brother Reuben's house instead. When he pulled into his yard, there were a bunch of cars there. I said, "I'm not going in."

Dad frowned. "Now, come on, Beth. It won't hurt you to say hello."

"I don't want to."

"I'm sure there will be lots of other children here. Maybe you and Mikey can make some new friends."

"I don't want any new friends, Dad."

Mikey wouldn't budge either. He said, "If Bethy isn't going, I'm not either."

Dad said, "Fine. You two can just sit in the car and wait." He headed for the house.

Mom yelled, "Michael."

He turned around. "Well, what do you want me to do? Carry them in kicking and screaming?"

"Let me talk to them for a minute." She opened my door and stooped down to talk to me. "We can do this for your father, can't we, Beth? Maybe it will help him settle himself. Maybe he'll find out he's not interested in what they have to offer."

"Are you sure, Mom?"

"I've thought about it a lot, and I think it might help."

"I don't know. It worries me."

"Please, Beth. I think we should try."

If she thought it was the right thing to do, I had to go along with her. I got out of the car and held my hand out to Mikey. "Come on, Mikey. We've got to do this for Mom."

As we headed across the dusty yard, I heard the goats bleating at the side of the house. Mikey broke away and ran towards their pen. I hurried to catch up with him. When the goats saw him they started bleating even louder. Mikey said, "What's wrong, little goats? Why are you crying?"

He stuck his nose through the space between the boards and patted their heads. They started licking him all over his face. At first, he seemed to like it, but then, all of a sudden, he fell backwards in the dirt. He started crying and spitting and trying to rub the goat kisses off his face.

Dad came and grabbed his arm and pulled him up to his feet. "What do you think you're doing?"

Mikey whimpered as Dad brushed the dirt off his pants. When we got back around front, Brother Reuben was waiting for us on the porch. He looked at Mikey's dirty clothes and laughed. "I see you've been visiting my goats again."

Mikey whispered, "They've got horns. I think they're devils inside."

"Indeed they do have horns." Brother Reuben rubbed Mikey's head and laughed again. "I don't feel any horns on your head. You're too young now, but I'm sure you'll get them. What about you, Beth?" He tried to pat me on the head, but I ducked under his arm and hurried inside.

Even before my eyes got adjusted to the dark, I could hear that the house was full people talking in hushed voices. When I could finally see, I noticed a bunch of women squashed together next to Sister Ella on the old couch and some other women and older girls sitting on green flowered kitchen chairs. The women looked like they could be on a float in the Pioneer Day parade. They all had the same long hair wound up on their head and the same long dresses with long sleeves. The dresses were made out of identical material that looked sort of like a sheet that had been dyed a pale turquoise blue. I wondered what it would be like to look so much the same as everyone else. You'd hardly be able to pick yourself out in a group picture.

There was a nervousness among the women that I didn't quite understand. Then I realized they were afraid of Brother Reuben. Even the men kept their heads lowered when Brother Reuben was talking, as if they were afraid to look him in the eye. I wondered why they wanted to be with him if they were so afraid of him.

I noticed that several of the women were pregnant. And most of them already had babies on their laps and kids crawling around at their feet. One of them, a young girl over in the corner, was so young she still had baby fat in her cheeks. She had big sad eyes and long brown hair, tied back from her face with a blue ribbon. I tried to imagine what it would be like to have a baby at that age, but it seemed too unreal, like it was some kind of mistake. Then I saw Laura and I got the idea that she might be married too. But that was crazy. She was the same age as me, and I wasn't even in junior high school yet. She looked back at me, as if she wondered what I was thinking, but I quickly looked away.

The room got quiet and everybody started staring at me. I realized it was because Brother Reuben had snuck up behind me. He pushed me forward and said, "Brothers and Sisters, this is the lovely Sister

Elizabeth I've been telling you about." He squeezed my shoulders and leaned down so close to my ear his hot breath sent a chill down my spine. "We're happy to have you join us, dear."

Next, he moved over to Mikey. He pushed him toward the group and gave him a quick salute. "And this is Brother Michael Sterling, Junior, a young soldier in our Lord's army."

Mikey squirmed out of his hands and went to hide behind Mom. But that's where Brother Reuben went next.

He pulled Mom forward by the arm and introduced her to everybody. Then he led her over to the couch. "Sister Sharon, these are my girls. You already know Sister Ella, or course, and next to her are Sister Irene, Sister Marie, and Sister Rebecca." He pointed to the young pregnant girl sitting in the corner and said, "And this is Sister Pauline, the newest addition to our little family."

So she *was* one of his wives. I'd thought maybe she belonged to one of the younger men, not Brother Reuben, who already had gray in his beard. The next question that came to my mind was where did they all live? They couldn't possibly live in that one tiny house, so where *did* they live?

Brother Reuben continued to introduce the other women, telling us which ones belonged to which man. But there was one of them that didn't seem to belong to anyone. She was the prettiest one of all, with long silky blond hair and clear blue eyes. I thought maybe she was too young to be married, but then Brother Reuben's newest wife seemed even younger.

Brother Reuben pushed Mom closer to the couch. "Sister Marie, would you please give your seat to our guest?"

Mom quickly pulled away. "Oh no. I'm just fine standing."

He grabbed her arm again. I thought he was going to force her to sit down, but then he stopped himself and let go of her. He went quickly over to Dad, whispered something, and then nodded toward the pretty girl. She smiled at Dad with her shiny blue eyes. Brother Reuben whispered something else, and Dad's cheeks turned red. I didn't know what it was all about, but I wasn't sure I liked it.

I was getting sick of standing there in front of everyone, but the only place to sit was on the floor, and the carpet was really dirty and would have ruined my dress. I went back and leaned against the wall next to the door. Mikey followed me, and after a minute, Mom came to stand there with us too. Her face looked kind of pale, and I thought she might not be feeling very well. I whispered, "Maybe you should have sat down, Mom."

She put her finger to her lips and shook her head.

Brother Reuben talked quietly to Dad a little longer, and then he turned to the people in the room and raised his arms. "Brothers and Sisters, it's time to begin our service."

Everybody quickly got down on their knees, even the women who were holding the babies. I looked at Mom and Dad to see what we were supposed to do. Dad nodded toward the floor. "Sharon. Children. Shall we?" He kneeled down, so we did too.

Brother Reuben began to pray in a loud booming voice. "Oh mighty God, we come before Thee in humility, asking for Thy guidance on the path of righteousness. We are Thy only worthy children, Lord. We have sacrificed our worldly desires and have dedicated our lives to Thy will. Please be with us."

He let out a deep breath and continued praying. "And now Lord, in as much as you have seen fit to send Brother Michael to us, we ask that you reveal Thy plan to him. Open his heart and mind that he may accept your calling. We also ask that you fill the bosom of his wife and children with Thy holy spirit, that they may understand their role in Thy plan. That they may be steadfast in their endeavors to fulfill it."

I thought I heard Mom cough, but when I looked at her, she still had her eyes closed. I turned to watch Brother Reuben pray. In the dim light, I saw the same monstrous look I'd seen that day out on our porch. Something about him scared me. He didn't look like a spiritual man to me. He seemed mean and ugly.

Suddenly, his eyes flew open and he was looking straight at me. He winked and kept praying, while staring at me the whole time. I looked around and saw everyone else's eyes were still closed. It made me nervous and a little bit sick to my stomach. It was almost as if we were the only ones in the room, and I didn't like being alone with him. I looked down at the floor to try to escape his eyes, but when I looked back up he was still staring at me. Why couldn't he leave me alone?

Finally, he smirked at me and finished his prayer. Everybody quickly stood up. I was hoping the meeting was over, but Brother

Reuben swept his arm through the air and pointed to one of his wives. "Please, Sister Lucille, will you lead us in our opening hymn?"

She stood up, raised her arms, and everybody started to sing:

Come, come, ye Saints,
No toil nor labor fear,
But with joy wend your way.
Though hard to you this journey may appear,
Grace shall be as your day . . .

The singing was so loud I thought it was going to burst out the walls. It felt suffocating in the tiny room. I wanted desperately to go outside where I could get some air, but after the song, it was time for the sacrament. It was crazy the way they did it. They served the bread on an ordinary paper plate, and instead of water, they served some kind of red liquid in an regular drinking glass. When they passed it around, Mikey took a big gulp from the glass and then spit most of it out on the floor. Dad gave him a bop on the head, but I was glad he'd done it. I looked over at Brother Reuben to see what he'd do, but he just smiled at me, like he thought it was a good joke.

After the sacrament was over, Brother Reuben pulled Dad to the center of the room, and one-by-one, the men came up to shake his hand. One of the men held his hand for a long time, as if he didn't want to let it go. "This is a marvelous day," he said. "We've been waiting a long time for you."

Waiting for what? I thought. Waiting for him to come build their church, or did they have something else in mind?

The women seemed nervous around Dad, just like they were with Brother Reuben. They kept their heads bowed and kind of curtsied to Dad, then hurried back to their seats. But the pretty girl, the one that made Dad's face turn red, didn't seem shy at all. She smiled, leaned forward, and whispered something to him. Then she bent and kissed the back of his hand. She did it so fast, I almost wasn't sure it really happened. But then, from the look on Dad's face, I was sure it did.

I glanced back at Mom to see what she thought about that, but she was staring at the floor with her hand over her mouth. It made me wonder if she was trying to keep from throwing up.

I leaned toward her and said, "Are you okay, Mom? Should I tell Dad we have to go?"

She shook her head and slumped back against the wall, looking pale and exhausted. I decided I'd better stay close to her.

Everybody went back to their seats, and Brother Reuben gave us all a big smile and said, "Well, Brother Sterling, what a happy day. Our seer and revelator has finally arrived. We are so glad to have you."

Mom let out a little gasp, and Dad looked surprised too. He said, "What are you saying, Brother Reuben? I don't understand."

"Now, now, we are quite certain the Lord has sent you to us for a purpose. You are the one He has commissioned to guide us. Will you speak to us, please?" He stood back, waving toward Dad with a flourish.

Everybody's eyes were on Dad. He cleared his throat a couple of times, but didn't seem to know what to say.

I glanced around and saw the girl who'd kissed his hand watching Mom. She looked as if she wanted to see how Mom would react to the news about Dad being the seer and revelator. When she saw me watching her, she glanced quickly down at her hands and smiled.

Dad was still standing there, stammering. "I . . . I'm sorry, Brother Reuben. I'm not really sure what you expect."

One of the men, with a long beard just like Brother Reuben's, stepped forward and said, "Tell us about your vision, Brother. Tell us what the Lord said."

Then everybody started talking at once. "Yes, do. Tell us, Brother. Tell us what the Lord said."

Brother Reuben held up his hand. "Now, now. This is not a carnival. I'm sure Brother Sterling will reveal the Lord's word to us in time. Perhaps we should just let him get adjusted to our news." He whispered something to Dad.

Dad nodded and then he came back by the wall to stand with us. Mom put her arm through his and pulled him close to her, but he didn't seem to notice. He had a dazed look in his eyes.

Brother Reuben waved his hand towards the couch. "Ella, let's have the children get to know each other in the other room."

She quickly responded by saying, "Laura. Aaron. Did you hear your father? Take the children into the kitchen."

Laura and some of the other girls picked up the little kids off the floor and headed for the kitchen with the other older kids trailing behind. The new babies were the only ones that got to stay with their mothers.

I didn't want to leave Mom alone, but I looked at her and she nodded toward the kitchen. I grabbed Mikey's hand and we followed the others.

There weren't any chairs in the kitchen, so none of us could sit down, but at least it was a little brighter. The sun streamed through the window, sending a broad patch of light halfway across the floor to where the girls had put down the little kids. The older kids leaned back against the counter while Mikey and I stayed by ourselves on the other side of the room, close to the door.

The kids stared at us, like they thought we were a couple of weirdoes. It made Mikey nervous. He pushed me away from the wall and hid behind me with his face against my back. After a few minutes, I couldn't stand it anymore. "What are you all looking at?"

Laura said, "Nothing."

"Well, couldn't you look somewhere else?"

She screwed up her face and said, "It's because your dress is too short."

"Too short for what?"

"Our Heavenly Father. He doesn't want us wearing short dresses."

"What are you talking about?"

She stuck her face towards me. "You should know, you're not supposed to be showing your flesh. It's sinful."

I knew that if you wore temple garments you weren't supposed to let them show, and that meant your dresses had to be at least to the middle of your knees, but all the girls my age wore their dresses shorter than that. It was ridiculous to think you had to wear skirts all the way down to your ankles like these girls did. I felt like putting her back in her place. "If God doesn't want you showing any flesh, why don't you put something over your face, and why don't you wear gloves?"

"He doesn't care about that."

"Is that right?"

"Ask your father. He talks to God, doesn't he?"

The other kids didn't say anything, but I could tell they agreed with Laura. Even the older ones didn't seem to care if Laura did all the talking. I wondered if that was because her father was Brother Reuben, and that gave her some kind of special power over them.

They went back to staring at us, and Laura jumped up on the counter and started swinging her feet, banging her heels up against the cupboards. She smirked and said, "You're father's going to be our seer and revelator, and that means you and your brother will be coming to our church, and you'll get home-schooled, and you'll have to practice all the divine laws, just like we do. That means your father will have to get himself some more wives."

I backed up so fast, I practically smashed Mikey against the wall. I said, "That's ridiculous. He's not going to do that."

She just smiled and said, "We'll see. My father says it's going to happen, and that means it will."

I couldn't bear another minute of looking at her. I pushed Mikey out of the kitchen into the living room. When my eyes got used to the darkness, I saw Dad and Brother Reuben standing in front of everyone. Mom was on the couch, squashed in next to the other women. She had a blanket over her knees. Had they made her cover herself up because her skirt was too short?

Brother Reuben stopped talking when he saw Mikey and me. Everybody seemed to hold their breath, waiting to see what he would do. I didn't care. I went over to Mom and said, "I want to go home."

She looked at Dad, but he shook his head.

Mom said, "You'll have to wait, honey. Go back in the kitchen with the other children."

"No, I don't want to, Mom."

"Please, Beth. Try to think of someone besides yourself."

"I can't stand it. I've got to get out of here."

Mikey said, "Me too."

Brother Reuben came over. "It's okay, Sister Sharon. Let them stay." He put his hands on my shoulders and pushed me down. "Sit there at your mother's feet."

By then, I didn't care if my dress got ruined, as long as I didn't have to go back in the kitchen with Laura. I pulled Mikey down beside me and leaned back against the blanket on Mom's knees.

Brother Reuben started pacing. He seemed agitated about something. He kept looking at Dad, and then at the other men in the room, like he was trying to decide something. Finally, he said, "There are those who see and there are those who interpret. I shall be the interpreter and Brother Sterling, the seer. Together we shall lead you to the Kingdom of Heaven. Let none amongst you turn away from the word of God, lest you be cast into the depths of hell. Brother Sterling, I think it's time for you to speak to us now."

Dad stood up, and I felt Mom's legs shake. I glanced back and saw a frantic look in her eyes. I wanted to take her away from there, but I knew she wouldn't leave without Dad. I tried to get his attention. When he finally looked my way, I jerked my head towards the door and pleaded with my eyes for him to take us home. He whispered something to Brother Reuben.

Brother Reuben nodded. "Certainly, you will need time to consider these things, but don't delay, Brother. It's time to build our church and gather the saints. The second coming of Christ is nigh. We must prepare ourselves lest we be counted among Lucifer's tribe. Lest we perish with the heathens of the underworld. Will you at least lead us in prayer?"

Everyone scrambled to get to their knees again. Dad looked over at Mom as if to ask her if it was okay. When she looked away, he sighed, closed his eyes, and began to pray. "Our Father, which art in Heaven. Guide us to Thy truth. Open our hearts and our minds that we may hear Thy words and follow the path of righteousness . . ."

I hardly heard what he said after that. It was just more words, like the words Brother Reuben had been saying all day. I couldn't concentrate. I was too worried about what it all meant. Mom had said we should join Dad so that he could see that Brother Reuben's people didn't have anything he'd want. But it wasn't like that at all. I could see he was flattered that they wanted him to be their seer and revelator. I wasn't sure what that meant, but it seemed like the beginning of a lot more trouble.

After everyone said amen to Dad's prayer, the room got so quiet I could hear Mom breathing behind me. The men went to the middle of the room and made a tight circle around Dad. They put their hands on each other's shoulders, closed their eyes, bowed their heads, and started praying together, almost as if they were chanting. "God bless our seer. Long may he guide us in Thy ways. Halleluiah, the revelator has come. Halleluiah, we shall no longer walk in darkness. Praise the Lord, for He hath delivered us."

Brother Reuben started singing in his booming voice.

We thank ye oh God for a prophet,
To guide us in these latter days
We thank thee for sending the gospel
To lighten our way with its rays . . .

Everybody else joined in the singing. The kids came in from the kitchen and they sang too. Even Mikey joined in. It was the same song we sang at our church, and he knew it by heart. Everybody kept looking at Dad and smiling, like they were singing the song for him.

Brother Reuben snuck up behind me and whispered, "What do you think now, Sister Elizabeth? Are you proud of your father? Aren't you glad everyone believes in him, that they know he saw God?"

I didn't know what to say. I could see Dad was happy for the first time in months, but I didn't want to be part of Brother Reuben's group. What would the Bishop think? What would everyone else in town think?

I tried to imagine wearing those long weird dresses and the white socks like Laura had on. I'd be a laughing stock. But then, I wouldn't be going to school, so probably no one would ever see me. That was the worse thought of all. I loved school. It was the only place I got to hear about things they didn't teach in Sunday School. And what about Tommy? Would I ever get to see him again?

I didn't know what to do. I felt like I couldn't breathe. I looked around frantically for Mom and finally saw her over in the corner talking to the girl who'd kissed Dad's hand. The girl was holding her arm and jabbering a mile a minute, while Mom frowned and tried to pull away. I wanted to tell Dad we had to leave, but all the men still had him surrounded.

I looked all over the room and saw Mikey in the corner behind the couch all by himself. I hurried over to him. "Come on, Mikey. Let's get out of here." I took his hand and led him to the door.

I felt a lot better outside where there was more air, but then the goats started bleating and Mikey started screaming, "It's the devils. It's the devils" He ran across the dirt yard and headed down the road.

"Wait, Mikey!" I chased him halfway down to the highway before I caught him. "What's wrong with you?"

"The devils are trying to get us, Bethy."

"It's not the devil. They're just goats."

"No they're not. They're devils. I saw their horns."

I finally talked him into going back up the hill, but when the goats saw us they started bleating wildly again. We ran and got in the car and Mikey locked all the doors.

We waited for a long time for Mom and Dad to come out. When they got in the car, they didn't even look at us. All the way home, Mom kept glancing at Dad. She'd open her mouth, like she wanted to say something, but then she'd cover it with her hand and look away. Dad just stared straight ahead, as if he didn't want her to see his sparkling eyes. But I knew what they looked like. I could see them in the rearview mirror.

Finally, I couldn't stand it anymore. I yelled, "What's going on? What's going to happen to us?"

That got Mom talking. She glared at Dad and said, "Yes, Michael. What *is* going to happen? Are you really thinking of being their . . . what did they call it? Their seer? We have a seer and revelator. His name is David O. McKay. He's the prophet of the Church. He tells us what God wants us to know."

"You've read the scriptures, Sharon. You know what they say."

"About polygamy, you mean? Yes, but that's all in the past, or the future . . . in the next life. You know that."

Dad shook his head. "I don't want to talk about this now."

"Oh, is that right? You don't want to talk about it. You want to ruin your family, and you don't want to talk about it!" She slammed her fist on the dashboard.

He turned quickly onto our dirt lane, but he was going too fast. A cloud of dust poured in the back windows and Mikey and I started coughing.

Mom said, "I can't believe you'd think about doing this after all we've been through. I tried to understand. I told myself I'd go up there with you, hoping you'd see it wasn't right for us. I never imagined they'd put you up on a pedestal like that. It must feel really great to be that . . . wanted."

"Yes. Yes, it does, as a matter of fact. I feel a lot more wanted there than I do here."

"How can you say that, Michael? We're your family. We love you as you are, without any miracles or visions. But I guess we're not enough for you now."

"That's ridiculous. You know this is not about you and me. It's about the Lord's work." He looked sideways at her. "Maybe Brother Reuben was right about you."

She glared at him. "What did he say?"

He didn't answer. Instead, he pulled into the carport and slammed on the brakes. He sat there for a minute gripping the steering wheel. "Oh, never mind. This isn't getting us anywhere."

He jumped out of the car and slammed the door. Then Mom got out and slammed her door too. Mikey and I sat there for a long time, staring at each other. I don't think either one of us wanted to go inside to see what would happen next.

Chapter 16

You sisters may say that plural marriage is very hard for you to bear. It is no such thing . . . But it is not the privilege of a woman to dictate the husband, and tell who or how many he shall take, or what he shall do with them when he gets them, but it is the duty of the woman to submit cheerfully.

Brigham Young
Journal of Discourses

*B*y the time Mikey and I got in the house, Dad was in his study and Mom was pounding on the door, screaming, "It's not your decision, Michael. You can't decide this by yourself." She tried to push her way in, but he must have put something behind the door to keep it closed. She started crying, softly at first, and then louder and louder. But he didn't seem to care, he wouldn't open the door.

It terrified me when she went in the kitchen and started opening the cupboards and slamming them shut. I thought she was going to break them off their hinges. Mikey got in the little space between the refrigerator and the wall and hid. When she crashed a dish into the sink, He started to howl and I knew I had to do something.

I ran and pounded on the study door. When Dad didn't answer, I pushed against it with all my weight. He must have moved whatever was blocking the door, because it opened fast, and I went sprawling across the floor. I looked up and saw him kneeling over by the window in a pile of his books and papers. He had his eyes closed and his hands over his ears so he couldn't hear what was going on in the kitchen.

I got up and ran over and yanked his hands away from his ears. "Dad, you've got to talk to Mom. She's going crazy."

"Beth, I can't stand this anymore. You can't ask me to choose between you and the Lord. I have work to do, and I've got to do it."

It sounded like he was giving up on us. I couldn't let that happen. "Tell us what we're supposed to do, Dad."

"We've been around and around on this. I start thinking your mother is with me, then I find out it's not true. Either we do the Lord's work together, or I'll have to do it alone."

I heard another crash from the kitchen. "Don't say that. We can help. I know we can. But you've got to come talk to Mom right now. She's really upset. She's going to destroy the kitchen."

He got up, put his hands on my shoulders, and looked hard into my eyes. He talked to me as if he couldn't hear what was going on in the other room. "We've got to do this, Beth. We have to live the gospel the way it was revealed to Joseph Smith. I'm convinced the leaders of the Church have turned away from the true gospel. In doing so, they've turned away from God. "

I couldn't believe he'd said that. I'd heard him bear his testimony a hundred times, saying how he knew the Church was true and that the prophet, David O. McKay, received direct guidance from God. It set my head spinning to even think about it. "I don't understand. How can everything we've believed all our lives suddenly be wrong?"

"Not everything, Beth. There are just some of God's laws and covenants that we're not obeying. Important covenants that we must follow if we are to progress in the next life. If I am to have my own world."

"Does that mean we have to be polygamists, like Laura Reuben said?" I could hear my voice getting shrill as the implications of his words came down on me. He really did want to be a polygamist.

"I don't know. Maybe so."

"But why is it so important for you to have your own world?"

He looked at me like he couldn't believe I'd said that. "It's why we're alive. It's the reason for everything."

"But polygamy is against the law, Dad. We'll be arrested."

"The Lord will protect us if we do His will. He will guide us, but only if we follow the true teachings of His gospel. It's a test, Beth. If I fail this test, it will be worse than if I hadn't had a vision at all. I've seen the Lord. He gave me his direct guidance. If I deny that, there will be no salvation for any of us and no eternal life together."

There was nothing I could say to that. "Well, then, tell Mom that. Please, Dad. Can't you go talk to her?"

He looked doubtful, but he followed me to the kitchen. I was relieved to see that Mom had calmed down a little. Mikey had his face pressed against her stomach, and she was rubbing him gently on the back. Dad went to her. "Come, Sharon. We can't go on like this. We've got to pray for help."

He took her by the hand and tried to lead her to the living room, but she didn't want to go. He put his arm around her shoulders and whispered something to her. Then she let him guide her out of the kitchen. He pushed back the chairs and kneeled down on the living room floor. "Let's pray. Let's ask the Lord to guide us. Come, Mikey. Come, Beth. Kneel with me."

Mikey and I kneeled down, but not Mom.

"Please, Sharon," he pleaded. "If we don't find an answer to this situation, it's going to destroy us."

He pulled gently on her hand until she finally kneeled beside him. He started to pray. "Heavenly Father, you have given our family a great test, and we are in need of your help. Please help my wife understand the importance of what has happened. Open her heart, that she may know the truth of Thy will. Help her to understand that it is only through my priesthood and through the covenants of our eternal marriage, that she may enter the Celestial Kingdom and receive her exaltation."

He hesitated for a minute and then continued. "Bless me too, Lord, for I am Thy servant. Give me strength that I may withstand the strain of dissuasion that surrounds me. Speak to me. My heart and mind are open, Lord. I am listening. Tell me what you require, that I may instruct my family in Thy holy work. We ask these things in the name of Jesus Christ, amen."

When he finished praying, Mom had tears in her eyes. She seemed sad and worn out, but there was something else on her face. Was it resignation? Had she realized, as I had, that he was going to do what he thought was right, with or without us? There was a look on her face that made me think no matter what he did, she couldn't imagine life without him. He must have seen that look too, because suddenly, he wanted to be alone with her. He told Mikey and me that they were going for a walk.

They went outside, and I took Mikey upstairs to change out of our church clothes. Then we went back downstairs, and I made Mikey a peanut butter sandwich. While he was eating, I went outside to see if I could see which way Mom and Dad had gone. I saw them out in the plum trees fighting.

I hurried around through the carport and across the irrigation ditch to the far side of the plum trees where I could hear what they were saying. Mom was yelling, "You've got it all figured out, haven't you, Michael? You could care less what it does to the rest of us. What about Mikey and Beth? Don't you realize how people will treat them?"

"I'm telling you, it's the Lord's will. He's led me to these people and He intends for us to join them. The children will be fine. They'll adapt. I think you should remember our marriage ceremony, Sharon. You made a promise to honor and obey me."

She didn't respond for a minute, but then she burst into tears and started hitting him. "I can't do it. I just can't."

He grabbed her hands and held them tight against his chest. His mouth was twisted with anger, but his voice sounded strangely calm, "Look, honey. Who knows if it will ever come to that? Who would I marry anyway? I don't know anyone. Why are we worrying about that now? It's just the kind of distraction I don't need."

She stopped crying and yanked her hands away from him. "You don't know anyone you could marry? Don't give me that."

"What do you mean?"

"That girl at Brother Reuben's. I guess you don't know she talked to me. She as much as asked for permission to be your new wife."

"I can't believe that."

"Well, it's true. She kept gushing about how any woman would be lucky to be your wife and how proud I must be to be your first, like Emma was for Joseph Smith. She said she wanted to be my sister and hoped we could be good friends. I couldn't believe what I was hearing."

"What? That anyone else would be interested in me?"

"Oh, I could see they were all very interested in you." She glared at him. "What did Brother Reuben tell you about her?"

"Nothing."

"Don't lie, Michael. I saw him whisper to you. And I saw how those blue eyes shined when she kissed your hand. He's got her all lined up for you, hasn't he? How old is she anyway, fifteen, maybe sixteen at the most?"

"Sharon, I can't tolerate this." For a second he looked mean. I'd never seen his face like that. I was afraid he was going to hit her, but then his voice softened again, "Honey, please. You have to pull yourself together. Don't you realize it would be difficult for me too? It would be a great burden to take care of more than one family. And if I had to leave you alone to spend time with someone else, I know you would suffer and that would be very hard for me. I don't want you to be lonely. I don't want you to be sad, or jealous. I need you to trust me and help me."

"Oh yes, I can imagine how terrible it would be to have a line of women bowing at your feet, waiting for their turn to spend a night with you. And all the Brothers begging you to take their young daughters as your next wife. It would be just awful, wouldn't it?"

He turned away in disgust, but she kept talking. "You think I didn't know this was coming? The first time you brought that man to our house, I knew it. Then, when I got sick and you stopped seeing him, I hoped and prayed it was just a passing thing. Just part of your confusion about that . . . that vision. But you became so hopeless after the baby died. I wanted to help you, Michael. That's why I joined in your studies. That's why I agreed to go with you to their meetings. I never imagined they'd want you to be their . . . whatever it is they want you to be, and that you'd be so eager to do it. What's happening to you, Michael?"

"Losing that baby was God's punishment. Don't you understand? That's the reason I *have* to follow through on this. Do you want God to punish us further?"

He started to walk away from her, then turned back. "When you agreed to go to Brother Reuben's, I thought, *finally* God has answered my prayers. I thought He had filled your heart with knowledge of the truth, but I can see it's only full of hate and suspicion."

He looked suddenly tired. "I'm sorry. I'm not going to argue about this anymore. I think you're right, Sharon. You're not up to it. You have no moral strength. You think only of yourself and your petty jealousy. You can't imagine anything beyond what you've known all your life, and you can't make an accommodation, not even to the Lord God Himself. I can see I'm going to have to go on without you."

She grabbed his arm and spun him around. "You're right, I am jealous. Who wouldn't be? But that's not the main thing. I'm just so afraid of where this is taking us. You're asking me to turn my back on everything I've been taught all my life. Everything I believe."

"I'm not going to listen anymore. You get angry, and then you get soft. You're just trying to work your way in to confuse me. You want to be in control. But it's not your position to be in control. You no longer have any say in this, Sharon. You must support me, or expect that I will do it alone. Do you understand me? I will no longer turn away from God." He yelled those last words and ran out of the plum trees and headed towards the creek.

Mom screamed, "Michael." It was a terrible wailing sound.

The tears streamed down my face as I ran to her and threw my arms around her. "Mom, Mom, don't let him go."

She pushed me away, making terrible gulping sounds. Her face was so red I was afraid she couldn't breathe. I tried to help her, but she pushed me away again and started slapping herself in the face. Then she started hitting herself hard in the chest with her fists. It really scared me, but I couldn't get close enough to make her stop. All I could do was stand there and watch while she hurt herself.

All of a sudden, she stopped. She stared up into the branches of the plum trees with a wild look in her eyes and whispered, "I am strong enough. I can do it. If that's what you want. If that's what you really want. I'll do it. I'll show you I can do it. I'll show you all."

I watched as a fake expression of happiness spread across her face. It was like she had put on a mask, a mask that she could hide her true feelings behind. I went and touched her arm and whispered, "Mom?"

She looked surprised and gave me a strange contorted smile. "Oh, Beth. There you are. Where did you come from?"

It didn't sound like her natural voice. What was she trying to do? I shook her arm and yelled, "Mom!"

"What is it, dear? Is something wrong?"

"You and Dad were fighting."

"Oh, no, you must have misunderstood. Everything is fine. Everything is going to be just fine."

That was crazy. How could everything be fine when she'd just been hitting herself, and they'd been yelling at each other, and now Dad was gone, and she was smiling that strange twisted smile, pretending like nothing had happened? "What if he doesn't come back, Mom?"

"Oh, that's just silly. Why wouldn't he come back? You go find him. Tell him everything is fine."

I didn't want to leave her alone, but she turned me around and pushed me. "Hurry, Beth. Tell him dinner will be ready soon. I'm going to go start dinner right now."

All the way down to the creek, I couldn't get that look on Mom's face out of my mind. Dad had really hurt her this time. He'd scared her so bad she was willing to pretend she was someone else. But what would happen if she tried to keep her emotions stuffed down behind that mask? It didn't seem like a very good thing to do.

When I saw Dad kneeling by the dam, staring up into the trees, I ran to him and jerked his arm. "How can you sit here praying, when Mom's falling apart?"

He opened his eyes and blinked, as if clearing his vision. "What are you doing here, Beth?"

"I told you. Mom's having a really hard time. There's something wrong with her. There's something terribly wrong."

"What do you mean?"

"I don't know for sure. She was really upset. Then, all of a sudden, she was smiling like nothing had happened. But her smile didn't seem real. You never should have fought with her, Dad. What if she gets sick again?"

"God willing, that won't happen."

"But what if it does?"

He didn't answer.

"I heard what you said, Dad. You told Mom you were going on alone if she didn't support you. But what does that mean? Are you going to leave us?"

"No, Beth."

"Then what? Are you going to get another wife, even if Mom doesn't want you to?"

He let out a big sigh. "I've told you, Beth. It's not up to me. It's up to God. I know now that's what He wants us to do."

So it *was* true. Laura said he was going to have to get another wife, and now he was saying it too. But if I told him he couldn't do it, he'd just go away and do it on his own. I knew he would, even if he said he wouldn't. I was going to have to put a mask over my feelings too. I was so upset, I could hardly breathe, but I forced myself to say, "What would it be like?"

"What?"

"To be a polygamist. Where would we live if you had more wives?"

"I don't know. I haven't thought about that. I guess maybe we'd have to build a bigger house where we could all live together."

I looked at him in amazement. "But how could we afford it? Especially when you don't have much work anymore."

He said, "I don't know, Beth. We'll just have to have faith that the Lord will provide for us."

"Wouldn't there be a lot of kids too?"

"Well, yes, I guess there would be . . . in time."

"So the house would have to be really big."

"I really don't know, Beth. I haven't taken it that far."

He seemed irritated with my questions, but I didn't care. There were things I needed to know. "Well, I don't see how we could build a house that big. How many wives would you have anyway?"

"Beth, I don't think we need to worry about these things right now. The Lord will provide the answers. Now, we'd better get back home."

I couldn't imagine why he hadn't thought about what he was getting us into. Maybe he'd never taken it that far because he couldn't really imagine doing it without Mom's blessing, and she'd never given him that. But now, he said he was going to do it, one way or the other. He had his vision and his directions from God, and he had to follow through on that at all cost.

Chapter 17

Whoso findeth a wife findeth a good thing, and obtaineth favour of the Lord.

Holy Bible
Proverbs 18:22

*A*fter Dad talked to me, I spent a lot of time trying to imagine what it would be like to be a polygamist. At first, all I could think of was how everyone was going to ridicule us. I'd seen how that worked with Laura and Aaron. They were total outcasts once everyone found out Brother Reuben was doing it. I wondered if that kind of ridicule was one of the reasons Laura and Aaron had stopped coming to school, along with the fact that Brother Reuben didn't want them corrupted by unrighteous ideas. I ran all kinds of scenarios through my mind, but I didn't really realize what it might mean for my future life until I talked to Tommy.

I'd left a note at his house saying I needed to see him and asking him to meet me down at the creek on Saturday morning. I was there waiting when he came whistling down the trail. He gave me a quick hug and then pushed me back at arms length and said, "What's up?"

"Things are just awful."

"You mean with your Dad?"

"He says he's going to be a polygamist, no matter what any of us say. Either we support him, or he's going to go do it by himself. It's making Mom really crazy."

"Oh, man, that's terrible. What are you gonna do?"

"I don't know. I was hoping you might have some ideas."

He grabbed my hand. "Come on. Let's go find a rock to sit on."

We hopped up through the middle of the creek until we came to a large flat slab of black rock in the shade next to a shimmering pool. We sat down, and Tommy took off his shirt and his shoes and socks. "It's hot as hell."

"Don't talk about hell. I've been hearing too much about hell lately."

He dipped his hands down in the water and splashed it on his head and face. Then he leaned back against another big rock and folded his arms across his chest. "So tell me what's going on."

"Oh, Tommy, it's so weird."

"What's weird?"

"We went up to Brother Reuben's last Sunday. The polygamists were packed in there like sardines, all wearing their weird pioneer clothes. They told my dad that they wanted him to be their . . . seer and revelator."

Tommy raised his eyebrows. "What the hell does that mean?"

"I'm not sure. I guess they want him to talk to God for them. You know, because he had a vision."

"Wow. That's crazy."

"They said they'd been praying and that it was God that sent Dad to guide them."

"So, what did your Dad say?"

"I think it made him feel good to have all those people admire him and for them to believe in his vision. But then he and Mom had a huge fight. I've never seen them fight like that, Tommy. It was awful."

"And now your Dad wants to join them?"

"He believes that's what God wants. He told Mom he's going to do it, no matter what she says. And I think Brother Reuben even has a new wife for him."

Tommy sat up straight and grabbed my arm. "You've got to stop him, Beth. You don't want to be a polygamist, believe me."

"I know, they'll kick Dad out of the Church, and nobody will ever talk to us again."

"It's a lot worse than that. You won't be able to do anything. They'll keep you under lock and key until it's time to marry you off to some old geezer."

"Oh, no! I hadn't even thought about that. But it might be true. I saw all the young pregnant girls up at Brother Reuben's house. Is that what they want me for?"

"You bet. They'll marry you off before you have time to blink. Then you'll learn real quick where babies come from. You won't be able to see me anymore, that's for sure."

"What am I going to do?"

Tommy shook his head. "I don't know. You've got to figure out some way to stop him."

"But he won't listen to me. He won't even listen to Mom."

"I'm telling you, Beth, you don't want to be a polygamist. Your Dad's a real creep for even thinking about it. Doesn't he care what happens to you?"

"I think he cares. It's just that he's totally obsessed with the idea of doing God's will. It's like it's taken over his mind and he can't think of anything else. He believes we're supposed to live exactly like Joseph Smith said. He thinks the Church was wrong when they stopped doing those things."

"Well, I think he's a creep."

"Don't say that. It doesn't help anything."

"Well your mother should just leave him. She should take you away before they get their hands on you."

"Oh, Tommy. She's not going to do that. She loves him."

"She must be crazy." He stretched back on the rock and put his arm over his eyes. I hoped he was trying to think of a solution, but it didn't seem like there was a solution. Dad thought he was doing the right thing. How could I tell him he was wrong?

I'd wanted to talk to Tommy for days, thinking he might be able to help, but he'd only made me more upset. I didn't want to be some old person's wife and have a bunch of babies. I thought about Brother Reuben and how he was always looking at me with his intense eyes and breathing hot air in my ear. Was he thinking I'd be *his* wife?

I tried to focus on the sound of the wind rustling in the top of the cottonwood trees and the sunlight glittering off the flicks of mica in the granite rocks. I watched the skeeter bugs skating across the top of the pool on their spindly legs, leaving long streak marks on the water. I didn't want to be afraid of the water anymore. I didn't want to be afraid of anything. I pulled off my shoes and socks and slipped off the side of the rock into the deep pool. I stood perfectly still, with my arms raised above the icy water, until I got used to it. Then, I took a deep breath and dipped down beneath the surface.

When I came up, Tommy was watching me with a strange expression on his face. I looked down and saw that my T-shirt was sticking to my chest. My nipples were poking up beneath the material. Before I knew what was happening, Tommy was in the water, and he was holding me up against a rock at the edge of the pool kissing me.

I pushed him away and splashed water in his face. He splashed me back, and pretty soon, we were laughing and throwing up handfuls of water at each other like we were a couple of kids.

Finally, we were too tired to play anymore. We climbed up on a rock that was in the full sun to get warm. Tommy stretched out on his side and said, "What are you gonna do, Beth?"

"I guess I'll just have to pray that Dad will decide God doesn't really want him to be a polygamist."

"Pray? It seems like God's the one that's got you in this mess."

"I don't know what else to do, and you don't have any answers."

He shook his head. "Parents are always screwing up their kid's lives. All we can do is leave home as soon as we can."

"Is that what you think I should do?"

"What else can you do? Unless you want to call the police when your Dad tries to get a new wife."

"I could never do that."

"Well . . . I guess you're stuck then." He stared at me with pain in his eyes. I could see he felt really bad about my situation, but there was nothing he could do.

He pulled a strand of my wet hair away from my face and let it drop. "I wish I could help. If I was old enough, I'd take you away."

We looked at each other, not knowing what else to say. I wished he *could* take me away some place, but then what would happen to Mom and what would happen to Mikey? That thought made me remember about Mikey? I'd left him to take care of himself. I told Tommy I had to go home to make sure Mikey was all right.

As we hiked back up to the house, Tommy kept touching my arm and looking at me as if he was seeing me for the last time. I didn't know why. I wasn't a polygamist yet. Maybe he was seeing me different than before. Being a Mormon was one thing, but the possibility of me being a polygamist was something that would separate us forever. It seemed like a play someone wanted me to try out for, and I didn't think I was right for the part. I didn't think any of us were, but Dad had a different opinion, and he was the one that was listening to God.

Chapter 18

If I be wicked, woe unto me; and if I be righteous, yet will I not lift up my head. I am full of confusion; therefore see thou mine affliction.

Holy Bible
Job 10: 15

*M*om kept that fake expression of happiness on her face whenever Dad was around. She'd fix dinner and smile and talk to him about his day when he got home from work. I didn't know how she could pull it off, especially when I saw how she was when he wasn't around. She'd mope around the house all day in her bathrobe and hide out in her bedroom with the door closed. That left me alone with Mikey most of the time. He was moody and crying a lot. I hated to see him like that.

One morning, I went outside to find him. He was in the sandbox playing war with his toy soldiers. He had soldiers everywhere, standing on top of sand mountains, hiding in sand caves, and lying behind sand hills. He had two more in his hands. I watched from behind the apple tree as he marched those two soldiers across the sand towards each other, making shooting noises. Then, he made one of them fall over on its face, and he picked up another one to take its place, and he killed that one too.

I came out from behind the tree and squatted down next to him. "Why are you killing them all, Mikey?"

He gave me a real serious look. "They're bad. They're the enemy."

"How do you know which ones are the enemy?"

"The dead ones are."

"But they all look alike. How do you know which ones to shoot when they all look the same?" For some reason it seemed important for me to know the answer to that question. Who was bad and who was good? Who was right and who was wrong?

Mikey said, "I get to decide." He got a mean look on his face and started shooting until all the soldiers were dead.

I was shocked. I'd never seen him be that mean before. "Why did you do that?"

"I just felt like it."

He sat there for a minute, staring straight ahead with that mean look on his face, and then he started to giggle. He got giggling so hard that it got me giggling. It felt good, and I wanted to keep doing it. I climbed in the sandbox and tickled him so he wouldn't stop. We rolled around and laughed until tears rolled down our cheeks. Finally, I sat up and looked around. I saw that all the soldiers were gone. "Look, Mikey. They're all buried in the sand. We've given the soldiers their funeral."

He started giggling again, but my sides were too sore to laugh anymore. "Come on," I said. "Let's go get an apple from the wine sap tree."

We brushed the sand off each other's clothes and headed for the apple orchard. I got up in the tree and tossed a couple of nice red apples down to Mikey. Then, I climbed down, and we leaned up against the trunk while we ate them.

When I didn't say anything for awhile, Mikey looked over at me and said, "What are you thinking about, Bethy?"

I didn't think he'd understand, but I felt like talking. "All the rules are changing, and it's confusing to me."

"What rules?"

"The Church says we're not supposed to practice polygamy, but now Dad says that's what God wants us to do. He says the Church is wrong. That we've been led astray. And I don't really know why he'd lie."

"What's polygamy?"

"You know. It's when men have more than one wife, and then they end up with a lot of kids too, like Brother Reuben."

Mikey squinted one eye. "Would I get to have a new brother?"

"I don't know."

"I want a brother."

"It's not worth it, believe me. Our lives would be miserable. We wouldn't get to go to school, and I'd have to--"

He tugged on my arm. "I want to be the big brother, Bethy. Can I be the big brother?"

"How do I know?"

"I want to. Please can I?" He started to whine.

"If I knew you were going to act like this, I wouldn't have said anything. How can you be a big brother when you're such a cry baby?" He didn't have a clue how bad it would be, especially for me.

"I'm not a baby. I'm going to tell Momma I want to be the big one." He jumped up and ran towards the house.

I yelled, "Mikey, don't . . ." but he didn't listen. He was going to upset Mom more than she already was. I tried to catch up with him, but he got to the house before me.

When I got inside, Mom was in the kitchen up against the sink. Mikey was in front of her all excited. He was yelling, "I want to be the big brother, Momma. Can I? Can I? I don't want to be the littlest one anymore."

Mom said, "What in the world are you talking about?"

"Bethy says we're going to get lots of kids, but I want to be the big brother. Can I?"

Her eyes narrowed when she looked at me. "Beth?"

"What?"

"What did you say to him?"

"Nothing."

"Now, I know that's not true. Tell me what you said."

"I was explaining about polygamy."

"What about it?"

I could see she was upset. "It's nothing. Mikey's just being dumb."

"I want you to tell me, Beth. Right now!"

I had to say something. "Dad says he's going to do it, and I was just trying to imagine what it would be like."

She put her hand over her mouth and fell back against the sink. I thought she was going to throw up on the spot. When she finally took her hand away, she had a strange look on her face. "It's just grand you're both adjusting so well to your father's plan. I guess it's all been decided amongst the three of you."

"That's not true, Mom. I was --"

"You don't have any idea what you're talking about, Beth, or what it means for us." The way she looked at me gave me an instant stomachache. "I just can't believe you're in on this, Beth." She pushed past me. A few seconds later, I heard the bedroom door slam.

Why didn't she let me explain? I didn't say I wanted us to be polygamists. I was just trying to deal with my own fears, trying to understand what it would mean.

Mom didn't come out of her room for the rest of the afternoon. When she finally came down to fix dinner, I tried to change her mood by smiling and asking her what we were going to have.

She said, "We're having what we're having."

It wasn't like her at all to be so snippy. I sat at the table and watched while she took a chicken out of the refrigerator and started hacking it up.

Without turning around, she said, "Why don't you make yourself useful and set the table instead of sitting there gawking at me?"

"Why are you being so mean? I didn't do anything."

She ignored me.

I found a tablecloth in the drawer, put it on the table, and smoothed out the wrinkles. Then, I got out the plates and the silverware. I put all the silverware on the napkins next to the plates, like I always did, but she came over and said, "That's not right."

"What's wrong with it?"

"The forks are on the wrong side."

"You never cared about that before."

"Just do what I say!"

"Okay, okay. But I don't know why you're all concerned about the forks when everything else is such a huge mess. You'd think we were having company, but we don't ever have company. We don't ever do anything. Everybody probably already thinks we're a bunch of weirdo polygamists."

She turned around real quick and glared at me. "What did you say?"

"Nothing. I didn't say anything." I had to blink to keep the tears away. Why was she blaming me for something I hadn't done?

I heard Dad's truck in the driveway. I was glad he was there. Maybe she'd turn her anger on the person who was really to blame. But it didn't work like that. When he came in the kitchen, Mom turned on her happy face, pretending like everything was just fine. I couldn't believe she could change that fast.

Dad got cleaned up and came down for dinner. After he said the blessing, he smiled at Mom and said "Well, now, isn't this nice?"

Mom seemed nervous and looked away. We all had our eyes on her, but she wouldn't look back. She was staring at her plate.

Dad said, "Well, then, shall we eat?"

Mom hurriedly passed the plate of chicken to Dad.

Mikey gave him a warning look. "Don't take the wishbone, it's mine."

I said, "Chickens don't have wishbones."

"They do too."

"No, really, they don't."

"Do too." Mikey was waving his fork around in the air.

"Michael!" Mom's voice was so sharp it made him drop the fork on the floor. She picked it up and held it out to me with half a smile and said, "Elizabeth, wash your brother's fork, please."

I took the fork over to the sink and ran hot water over it. I didn't know why I had to wash it when he was the one who dropped it. Mom was taking all of her anger out on me regardless of who was to blame. It made me mad. I took the fork back to Mickey and whispered, "Butterfingers."

He tipped back his head and crossed his eyes at me.

Mom smiled, as if everything was all right again. Dad started eating his salad, but he kept looking at us, first at Mom, and then at Mikey and me. It seemed like he wanted to say something, but he didn't get it out before Mikey mumbled something.

Dad said, "What did you say, Michael?"

Mikey repeated what he'd said, only louder. "I want to be the big brother."

"What are you talking about?" Dad looked at Mom and she looked back at her plate.

"Bethy said we might get some more kids. But I don't want any big ones. I hate being the littlest all the time."

Dad turned to me. "Do you know what your brother's talking about?"

Mom was still staring at her plate, as if she was afraid for Dad to see her eyes. I shook my head to warn him not to say anything more, but he plunged right into the trap. "Well, does somebody want to let me in on the secret?"

When nobody would answer, he snapped at Mom. "Sharon, what's this all about?"

She raised her head and looked directly at him. Her face was perfectly calm, but her eyes had turned dark green and were flashing. "They're just wondering about their new life, dear. They're all excited about these new brothers and sisters they're going to have. It's nothing to worry about, though. It's only natural for them to wonder about such things." She stood and picked up her and Mikey's plates and took them to the sink.

Mikey said, "Hey, I'm not done."

Dad said. "Sharon, I don't think we've finished eating yet, do you mind."

"Oh, sorry." She brought the plates back to the table and sat down. She poked her chicken with her fork a few times and tried to eat some lettuce from her salad. Then, she smiled that twisted smile, and said, "I guess I'm not really hungry. If you'll excuse me, I'll just go upstairs so I don't disturb the rest of you with your plans." She got up and left the kitchen before Dad could say anything.

Mikey started eating his chicken real fast. He stuffed it in his mouth with his fingers, all the time looking at Dad to see if he was going to get mad. But he didn't get mad. He just sat there, looking worn out and depressed. After a minute, he let out a big sigh and said, "Beth, could you clean up here?"

When he went upstairs to check on Mom, I looked over at Mikey. He had chicken oil all over his face. "Why did you have to talk, Mikey? You spoiled everything."

"I didn't either."

"You did too. You shouldn't have said anything. Now everybody's upset again."

He screamed, "It's not my fault." He threw his fork at the wall and ran out of the room. Then I heard the back door slam.

All the yelling, and everybody being mad, made me so tired I wanted to go to bed and not wake up until it was all over. But I had to clear the table and do the dishes.

When I finally got all the food put away and the dishes washed and in the drainer, I knew I had to go outside and find Mikey. I'd never seen him run outside like that at night. I should have gone right after him, but I'd thought he'd get scared of the dark and come back in. I was tired of taking care of him, but I knew nobody else was going to. I put my jacket on and went out the back door.

There was a full moon hanging high over the mountains. It was so bright I could see individual blades of grass in the yard, but I couldn't see Mikey anywhere. I went out through the apple trees calling for him, but he didn't answer.

I hurried around the house to the front yard. It was magical out there. The reflection of the moon off the long white sidewalk looked like a floating ribbon, and the leaves on the Russian Olive tree fluttered in the wind like tiny silver butterflies. It was so beautiful, I had to remind myself I was looking for Mikey.

I decided to go out and see if he was in the peach orchard beyond the clothesline, but when I got into the darkness of the trees, I got spooked. I kept thinking something was hiding in the shadows. I stopped where I was and yelled, "Mikey. Stop playing around."

He still didn't answer.

A wind came up out of nowhere. It shook the top of the peach trees and one of them moaned. I told myself it was just the branches rubbing together, but it didn't make any difference. I was still scared. I wanted to run back to the house, but I made myself go all the way through to the other side of the orchard. Just as I was about to turn back, I heard an alarming whooshing sound behind me. I spun around, but I couldn't see what it was. From the sound of it, I thought it might be a bird landing in the top of the tree. If it was a bird, it had to be a really big one. I wanted to run, but I couldn't make my legs move. I stared up into the dense leaves, straining to see what it was. Then I saw two bright yellow eyes. I knew what it was even before I heard its cry, "Whoo! Whoo!"

Mikey came tearing through the trees, screaming, "Run, Bethy, run. It's the owl." He grabbed my hand and pulled me towards the house. We were moving fast, and he kept tripping on dirt clods. I was barely able to keep him from going down. By the time we got out of the trees, my arm was aching. We stopped to catch our breath and Mikey whispered, "The owl's asking us who, Bethy, who has to die. Don't you remember what the book said?"

"I know, Mikey. I know."

"I don't want to be the one to die, Bethy. I'm sorry. I didn't mean to be bad. Don't let the owl get me."

His grip on my hand was so tight it was making it numb. His whole body was trembling. "It's okay, Mikey. I won't let it hurt you. I won't let anything ever hurt you. I promise."

He couldn't stop shaking. I put my arm around him, and we went back up to the house. Just before we went inside, I warned him, "We've got to be quiet. We don't want to get everyone upset again."

Even when we were in the house, Mikey wouldn't let go of my hand. I took him upstairs to the bathroom to brush our teeth, and then we went to our room, and I helped him get his pajamas on. But he wouldn't get in his bed. He just sat on the edge of it, shaking.

I went over to him and pulled back the covers for him. "Mikey, we've got to go to sleep. Everything will be better in the morning."

He wouldn't budge.

I gave him a hug and said, "Do you want to sleep with me?"

He ran over, jumped into my bed, and pulled the covers up over his head. I turned off the lamp and got in with him. He pressed right up against me. I knew I wouldn't get any sleep like that, but every time I tried to move away, he'd start whimpering. He wiggled around and made little moaning noises for awhile, but eventually his breathing got long and slow, and I knew he'd gone to sleep.

I lay there thinking for a long time. I wasn't sure I believed what the Indians said about owls, but maybe it was true. Maybe they really did cry when someone was going to die. If so, who was this new owl crying for? It made me think that Mom was going to get sick again. I hoped with all my heart that wasn't true. I closed my eyes and whispered, "Dear God. Don't let the owl be for us."

Chapter 19

. . . if any man espouse a virgin, and desire to espouse another, and the first give her consent, and if he espouse the second, and they are virgins, and have vowed to no other man, then is he justified; he cannot commit adultery for they are given unto him . . .

Doctrine and Covenants
Section 132:61

*A*s the summer dragged on, Mom's real emotions began to crack through her happy facade. I never knew when she was going to throw something across the room and burst into tears. She must have been hurting so much inside she never even considered what it was doing to Mikey and me.

Dad never admitted he was spending time with Brother Reuben, but we all knew he was. We'd wait for him to come home after work, but more and more frequently, he wouldn't show up until long after we'd eaten and the dishes were done.

Then one night, he came home early and asked for Mom as soon as he walked in the door.

I said, "She's upstairs."

"Well, go tell her I want to talk to her."

"Why don't you tell her?"

"Because I told you to do it. Now go."

I ran upstairs to the bedroom and knocked on the door. When Mom didn't answer, I pushed the door open just a crack and saw her sitting on the edge of the bed. I said, "Dad wants to talk to you."

She didn't even look at me. "He decided to come home, did he?"

"Yes, and he wants to talk to you downstairs."

"Well, tell him I don't want to talk to him."

"Mom!"

"Tell him, Beth. Tell him I have nothing to say to him."

I ran back downstairs, but Dad had already gone in his study and closed the door. When I knocked he said, "Come in, Sharon."

I opened the door. "It's not, Mom. It's me. She says she doesn't want to talk to you."

"Oh, really? Well, tell her to get down here right now."

"I can't. She'll get mad."

"Elizabeth!"

Why couldn't they just talk to each other? It was ridiculous for me to be running up and down the stairs, but I didn't have much choice. Dad was glaring at me with his hands on his hips. I went back up to the bedroom and said, "Mom, he's getting mad."

She went to the window and stood with her back to me.

I went closer. "Please, Mom. I can't keep running back and forth. You have to talk to each other."

I saw her muscles tighten. "He doesn't want to talk to me. He wants to talk at me. He wants to tell me how the world's going to be, and I'm supposed to bow down and kiss his holy feet."

"Why can't you just talk to each other like you used to?"

She spun around and yelled, "Ask your father that."

"He won't talk to me either. Nobody talks to me anymore. And no one asks what I think about what's going on. I'm sick of it."

"Well, I guess we're both in the same boat then, aren't we? You were happy and all excited about you father's plan the other day."

"I wasn't either. I was just trying to make some sense of it. It was Mikey that was excited. And all he wanted was a little brother."

"Oh, really? You didn't support your father?"

"No, Mom, and I don't understand why you're mad at me. It's not my fault everything is so screwed up."

She glared at me for a second, then she started to cry. She sat back down on the edge of the bed with her hands covering her face and sobbed. I sat next to her, but I didn't feel like I could touch her. She didn't want my comfort. I wasn't even sure I knew who she was anymore. I said, "Please, don't cry, Mom. I can't stand it. Can't you just try to talk to him? Please."

"I don't know what good it will do."

"Just try, Mom. Just try. If you think it would help, tell him I'm on your side. I don't want to be a polygamist either. Maybe he'll listen if we both say it."

After a few minutes, she got off the bed and went out into the hall. She stopped in the bathroom and splashed water on her face. Then she dried off and went downstairs to talk to him.

I wanted to listen at the door, but I was afraid they'd catch me. Everybody was getting crazy, and I was afraid of what they'd do. I decided to wait in the kitchen until they came out. Then I could decide by their faces how the conversation had gone.

I was sitting there at the table when I heard Dad yell, "Whether she was or not, is no concern of yours. This jealousy has got to stop. I'm warning you, Sharon."

I couldn't hear what Mom said, but then Dad yelled again, "It's just not true. That is not what this is about. Can't you see how you debase yourself with these accusations? I'll have no more of it."

Someone came out of the study, and then the back door slammed so hard it rattled the windows. I ran outside to see which one of them it was. I looked frantically in all directions and saw something white disappearing into the darkness of the plum trees. It had to be the moon reflecting off of Mom's dress. I raced after her, but by the time I got through the plum trees, she was halfway across the sagebrush field. She was going to the creek. That had to be where she was going.

I hurried after her, trying to keep her in sight, but when I got down to the scrub oak, she was gone. The only thing I could see was the moonlight shimmering down between the thick leaves, and a dark shadow up in the branches that made me feel like there was something up there watching me.

I made my way down through the darkness to the dam. I was startled by how strange and mysterious it looked, not at all like it looked in the day. The moon had turned the cement walls of the dam a ghostly luminous white. The water was completely black and invisible between the white of the rocks, but I could hear it bubbling and gurgling all around me.

I started going upstream, but I couldn't see Mom anywhere. I turned back and scooted down the cement chute into the lower stream. I sidestepped along the narrow cement ridge at the edge of the deep pool of water. Even though I couldn't see it, I knew the water was there, and it made me think of the boy who dove into that pool from the high part of the dam and broke his neck. Was his spirit still down there, whispering with the spirit of Wendy's cousin? The thought sent a cold thread of electricity up my spine, and for minute, I felt like I was going to fall in. I took a deep breath and carefully crept along the rest of the length of the ledge until I was safely past the pool.

I went out into the middle of the creek, hopping from rock to rock, trying to keep my feet dry. I didn't see Mom until I was around the next bend, and then I only saw her for an instant before a cloud covered the moon and turned everything pitch black. I would have to wait for the cloud to pass before I could continue, or I'd risk breaking my leg, but at least I knew I was going in the right direction.

The moon came back out, and I hurried down to where the creek widened out. The water sent up sparkles of light between the rocks that shimmered and melted away and came up again in a new place. I squatted down and put my hands into the water to catch the sparkles, but I could only hold them for a second before the water leaked out and they disappeared. Everything was incredibly quiet and beautiful there. I almost didn't feel afraid anymore.

That feeling of calm disappeared when I heard a forlorn wail. It was like the sound a small animal might make if was caught in a trap, a sound that was so plaintive it hurt my heart. I scrambled downstream, following the sad cry, until I finally found where it was coming from. It was Mom. She was out on a rock in the middle of the creek. I watched, breathlessly, as she pulled her dress up over her head and dropped it to the rock. The moon reflected off her temple garments in a way that made me think of a spirit fluttering in the breeze. She crouched down, and I heard a long sad wail like the trapped animal was about to die. After a few minutes, I saw her stand up and stretch her arms towards the moon, as if she could feel the sensation of its white light shimmering on her skin. She began to touch herself all over, along the back of her neck and down her shoulders. She glided her fingers down to her breasts, along her sides, and across her belly. I held my breath, watching to see what she'd do next. When a cool wind blew down through the trees, I felt goose bumps pop up all over my body. She must have felt that same breeze, because she sank down onto the rock and stretched out on her back, as if she was trying to warm herself on the heat stored in the rock from the day's sun.

While she lay there, I scrambled across the rocks to the edge of the creek where I could go down closer on the trail and hide in the trees. Clouds came again to hide the moon. I couldn't see her anymore, but I could still hear her moaning cries. As my eyes adjusted to pure starlight, I saw something move. Someone besides me was watching her. It was a man. A familiar man. It was Dad. He moved towards her and as he got closer he started taking off his clothes. He threw them down and jumped naked over to the rock where Mom was. She tried to sit up, but he sat on top of her and pushed her down. What was he going to do? Was he still angry with her? Was he going to hurt her?

I tried to push through the trees to get to her, but I got tangled in the branches and fell. I crawled forward, and the closer I got, the more I could hear their strange noises. They were breathing hard, and Mom was making those little moaning cries, and Dad was moaning too. The moans came faster and louder, and all at once, Dad let out a terrible howling wail that split the darkness and echoed down the walls of the canyon.

Mom cried out, "Michael!" and started to sob.

"Don't, honey. Don't cry."

"Why don't you love me anymore, Michael?"

"I do love you. I do."

"Then why? Why do you want to hurt me?"

Dad touched her face and brushed back her hair. He kissed her hands, and her arms, and her cheeks, whispering, "I love you. I love you. I love you. You have to believe that."

"But I don't understand. If you love me why do you want someone else?"

"No. It's not that. You can't think that way. You've read the scriptures, honey. You know what they say. Joseph Smith said, without equivocation, that Celestial Marriage is the foundation of everything. It's a law that God himself lives by, and if we are to become like him, if I am to become a god and keep our family together through eternity, we must follow the same path that he followed. I've studied and prayed and I know these things are true."

"But I'm afraid, Michael. Afraid of Brother Reuben. He's not a good man. There's no way I can bring myself to believe in him."

"Then believe in me, Sharon. Believe in me. Please, honey."

She sat up and faced him. "And what about Brother Reuben?"

"I think you're being unfair to him. He's had a hard time doing what he thinks is right. He's a good man. I've learned a great deal from him. I've come to believe that the Lord brought us together for a purpose. This kind of life we're looking at is too hard to live alone. We'll need support from others. We'll need a community."

"But what about the Church, Michael? What about the community we live in now?"

He shook his head. "I don't know. I expect they'll reject us."

"And you don't care about that?"

"Maybe some of them will join us."

"Oh, Michael! You don't believe that. They'll reject us, and they'll reject the children. How can you ask them to live like that?"

"They'll adapt."

Mom was silent for a long time. The moon passed behind the Cottonwood trees, and the night air grew cooler, as if it was the sun that was being obscured by the branches.

I thought they had finished talking, and that it was time for me to go home. Then I heard Mom whisper, "How can we turn our backs on everything we've been taught all our lives? Why is it so easy for you?"

"No. Not easy. I've been torn apart by this as much as you have. Don't you realize that? I just don't know what else to do. I've had terrible battles with myself. But I'm afraid, honey . . . afraid of what will happen if I turn away from what I know. This is serious. The heavens have opened to me. I have seen God. I can't deny that. It would condemn me to be with the sons of perdition, to burn in hell for all eternity. The scriptures are very clear about that. Is that what you want for me?"

Mom whispered, "No."

"And I'm afraid for you to. How can you enter the Celestial Kingdom without me? Surely, that's what you want for yourself."

"I don't know, Michael. I just don't know."

I sat in the bushes thinking about what he was saying. He really was afraid. There was a seriousness in his voice that I'd never heard before. Would he really burn in hell for all eternity? Or was it just something Brother Reuben had convinced him of? I'd heard about the sons of perdition in church, but Dad would never turn his back on God and say he wasn't real. It had to be Brother Reuben. He was the one making Dad afraid. He was the one saying he'd be punished for all eternity. He was always trying to convince us all that we were sinners, but he was the biggest sinner of all. Why couldn't Dad see it?

The wind started to blow even colder. I was hoping they'd go home, but they were still naked, and I didn't think they'd like it if they knew I'd been watching. I decided I'd better get out of there real quick.

I snuck back through the trees until I got around the bend where they couldn't see me. Then I made my way carefully up through the creek. It was darker now, with the moon falling behind the Cottonwood trees. It frightened me even more to slide along the ledge to the other side of the deep pool by the dam, but I made it safely. I climbed up the cement chute, hurried across the steel bridge, and ran back up to the house as fast as I could. When I got there, I went upstairs and found Mikey lying on top of the blankets with his clothes still on. I was relieved to see he was asleep. He would have been terrified if he had woken up and found himself all alone. I pulled a blanket over him and let him sleep.

I got in bed, but I couldn't sleep. There were too many images and thoughts and sounds rolling through my mind. I kept hearing that terrible howl that Dad made. It wasn't like anything I'd ever heard before. There was such loneliness in it. Such anguish and sorrow. And there was that image of Mom.

I closed my eyes and imagined her standing naked on top of the rock with the moon shining all around her. I pulled my hair up and touched the back of my neck just like she did. Then I touched softly under my ears and down my neck to my shoulders and my chest. Sliding my fingertips across my skin like that felt tickly, almost like someone else was touching me. I used the edges of my fingers to touch along my sides and across my belly, and then, I touched that place between my legs where Tommy said the babies got in. That made the goose bumps pop up just like they did when I was watching Mom, but there was no cold wind blowing this time.

A thought came into my mind. What if that was what Dad was doing when he was lying on top of Mom? What if he was giving her a baby? I realized that had to be what he was doing. I got excited. It would be wonderful if we could have another baby. It would prove to Dad that God wasn't punishing him when we lost the first baby. It would prove that he didn't have to be Brother Reuben's prophet, and he didn't have to be a polygamist, and he wasn't going to burn in hell forever with the sons of perdition.

I felt sure if Dad found out Mom was pregnant, everything would be all right. He'd want to stay home, just like last time she was pregnant. I got so wound up, I wanted to tell Mikey that he might get a little brother after all, but I decided I'd better wait to make sure it was true.

I started thinking about Tommy, and some of the guilt came back over what we'd done together in Matt's hut. I remembered the moaning sound he made, the sound that scared me and made me ask him what was wrong. Was he having the same feeling as Mom and Dad? Is that what it was like when you made babies? I thought of the feeling I had when Tommy touched me there between my legs, how tingly and warm and cold it felt all at the same time. Maybe that's how it felt for Mom and Dad too. Maybe that's what made them moan. But if that was true, why were the moans so sad? Why did it almost sound like they were crying?

I was trying to figure all that out when I heard a noise downstairs. It was Mom and Dad coming back from the creek.

Chapter 20

And thus we see that except the Lord doth chasten his people with many afflictions, yea, except he doth visit them with death and with terror, and with famine and with all manner of pestilence, they will not remember him.

Book of Mormon
Helaman 12:3

*T*he next day, a kind of eerie calm came over the house. Mom moved about as if she was in a dream, and Dad's eyes had an intensity that I could only interpret as love. Perhaps their love-making on the rock had brought back feelings that had been buried for months beneath the pain and chaos. Seeing them like that, and believing there was a baby on the way, I started to believe in the future.

Then two days later, I woke up with a rash. There were little swollen welts and long red stripes over much of my body. When I'd scratch one place, another place would start itching. It was driving me crazy.

I tried lying on my hands to keep from scratching, but the welts burned so bad I couldn't stand it. I jumped out of bed and ran across the hall. "Mom, Mom. There's something wrong."

She sat up, wiping the sleep from her eyes. "What is it? What's wrong?"

I lifted my nightgown. When she saw my rash, she shook Dad's shoulder. "Michael, wake up."

He opened his eyes slowly, rolling over on his side, "What's going on?"

She pointed to the red stripes on my upper legs. "What do you think it is?"

He shook his head. "I don't know. It doesn't look like measles or anything like that."

"No, it looks like an allergic reaction."

Dad turned on the light to get a better look. "I know what it is. It's poison ivy. Look, the blisters are already starting to weep."

Mom looked closer. "I think you're right. Where did you get into poison ivy, Beth?"

I told her I didn't know. It was a lie, but I didn't want her figuring out that I'd been down at the creek watching them. I hadn't even thought about poison ivy. I must have stumbled into it in the dark, when I was hiding under the trees.

Mom must have been suspicious because she gave me a sideways look and said, "Have you been down at the creek, Beth?"

"I don't think so." I scratched beneath my arm and down along my leg.

"You don't think so? What does that mean?"

Dad put his hand on her arm. "Can't you see it's driving her crazy? Let's see what we can do about it."

They took me to the bathroom and Dad turned the water on in the tub. He got a box from the cupboard beneath the sink, poured some white powder into the water, and stirred it around with his hand.

I said, "What's that?"

"Epsom salts. It should draw some of the poison oils out."

Mom put her hand in the water. "Better not make it too hot. It'll make the itch worse."

When the tub was full, Dad went out and Mom stayed with me while I took a bath. She got a washcloth and dunked it in the tub and then pulled my hair up and squeezed the water over my shoulders. The way she touched me brought tears to my eyes. It seemed like a million years since she'd touched me like that, or treated me gently in any way. It made me realize just how hard it had been not only for her, but for me too. We had always had fun together. She used to laugh and make jokes and smile. That was the thing I really missed. Her smile. Where had it gone? And where had her tenderness gone? And her love? All the time she was feeling like Dad didn't love her, I was feeling unloved too. Unloved by both of them. I was sure Mikey felt it too. I could see it in the way he acted. We had all been wounded, and for what? For God's blessings? For some kind of reward in the next life? If that's what God's blessings were like, I could do without them.

I slid down into the silky water and looked up at Mom. I thought she must have been having the same kind of thoughts as I was because there were tears rolling off her chin into the water. She didn't even try to wipe them away. After a minute, she laughed a little and said, "There's a little more salt water for you. Maybe it will help."

When I got out of the tub, she wrapped me in a big white towel, and we went back to their bedroom. I got on the bed between them and sat there, trying my best not to scratch.

Dad winked at Mom and said, "Remember when we got in the poison ivy?"

Mom smiled. "Do I? I itched for weeks."

"But it was worth it, right?"

"You think so?"

"Sure, don't you?"

"You mean, because of what came of it?" She looked at me and squeezed my arm.

"What came of it was good, but the making of it was nice too."

I couldn't believe it. They were talking in code language and teasing each other about making love. I hadn't seen them tease each other in so long, I'd almost forgotten they used to do that. I held perfectly still, trying not to break the spell.

Chapter 21

Beware of false prophets, which come to you in sheep's clothing, but inwardly they are ravening wolves.

Holy Bible
Matthew 7:1

*O*ne Saturday, Mom spent the whole morning in the kitchen with Mikey and me telling stories about her high school days and her old friends. I thought maybe she'd resolved to go on with life, even if she had no idea what life held for her. She laughed and joked, but it didn't hide the deep sadness in her eyes. Still, it was comforting to have that reminder of how she used to be. She even made us oatmeal raison cookies, but before we could eat any, she said we had to earn our reward by raking leaves.

We hurried outside. It was a glorious day, with huge puffy white clouds soaring across a deep blue sky. The last yellow leaves on the poplar trees out along the irrigation ditch were shimmering in the wind. Mom got a couple of rakes from the storage room and gave one to me.

She and I started raking, but every time we got a pile of leaves raked up, Mikey would come running full speed and jump into the middle of it. Finally, Mom put her hands on her hips and said, "Now, how do you expect us to get this job done if you keep scattering the leaves?"

Mikey looked up to see if she was mad, but when he saw the humor in her eyes, he jumped up and went running across the grass and landed in another pile. Mom and I hurried over and started burying him in leaves. It made him giggle, and his giggling got the leaves shaking, and that made us giggle. It felt like a dream to be having that much fun.

I fell into the bed of leaves next to Mikey, and Mom got down on her knees and started burying me too. Then, all of a sudden, she stopped and fell back. She looked scared. I rolled over to see what was wrong and saw Brother Reuben standing there. I jumped up and yelled, "What do you want?"

He moved towards Mom. "Here. Let me help you, Sister."

She scrambled away from him on her hands and knees. I ran over to help her up, but Mikey didn't do anything. I couldn't even see him anymore. It was like he'd burrowed down beneath the pile of leaves and disappeared.

Brother Reuben looked disgusted with Mom when she wouldn't let him touch her, but when he spoke his voice was calm. "Well, Sister Sharon. It's a mighty beautiful day, isn't it?"

Mom folded her arms across her chest and glared at him.

Brother Reuben snickered. "Now why do you look at me like that, woman? You'd think I was the Devil himself come to take you to hell."

She murmured, "Exactly."

"What's that you say?"

Mom shook her head and stepped back. She quickly squatted down, picked up the rake, and held it in front of her like a weapon.

Brother Reuben watched her every move, never taking his piercing eyes off her eyes "I've come to find out why we haven't seen you at our church services, Sister. I thought after you'd met everyone and saw how enthusiastically we welcomed you into our family . . . well, I thought it would open your heart and you'd be eager to join us."

"Oh, really? I thought it was my husband you and the *Sisters* wanted."

"Come, Sister. Jealousy doesn't suit you. The Lord has no patience for a woman who thinks only of herself. Wouldn't it be better if you--"

"How do you know what the Lord thinks of me? Have you spoken to him recently?" Her voice was sarcastic.

Brother Reuben grimaced and tugged on his beard. "It's not me who knows what the Lord wants. It's your husband. But of course, he also knows it's difficult for you. He keeps giving you time to adjust."

He moved towards her. I stepped in quickly between them. He put his hands on my shoulders, and I shook them off while he kept talking. "You are not alone in your jealousy, Sister. Many women have had trouble accepting Celestial Marriage. Why, the prophet, Joseph Smith's, own wife refused to accept the prophecy concerning the doctrine. She actually burned the paper on which it was recorded. Can you believe it?"

"Good for her,"

"Well, you can say that. But we all know she eventually came around. She realized the covenant was her pathway to exaltation in the Celestial Kingdom. Do you think she regrets it now?"

I looked up at Mom. She seemed genuinely surprised by Brother Reuben's question. Maybe it was because it was the first time he asked her something instead of just telling her, or maybe it was because she'd asked herself the same question when she was talking to God out in the garden.

She said, "I'm sure I don't know, but she must have suffered a lot in her lifetime."

"We all suffer, Sister. It's part of life. There are things we desire that we cannot have, even sometimes if we are righteous. Even if we pray every day and open our hearts to the Lord. Even if we know we are deserving." Brother Reuben's thoughts seemed to have drifted somewhere else.

"You act as if it's nothing for a woman to share her husband."

Brother Reuben nodded thoughtfully, as if he understood how she felt. "But there are many who have done it. Plenty who are doing it, even now."

"Maybe it's easier for someone who's been raised that way."

"But you were raised that way, weren't you? Aren't you a good member of the Church? Haven't you heard all your life that the doctrine of Celestial Marriage was only temporarily withdrawn? Weren't you told that it will be practiced in the next life? Even the apostates of your church concede that."

"Apostates?"

"Certainly, they're apostates. They've been led astray by false prophets. The laws of God are immutable. The doctrine of Celestial Marriage should never have been rescinded. Those who have led the

Church astray will be punished, I can assure you of that. They will not reach the Kingdom of God."

His voice was loud, and he shook his finger in her face. "Don't you understand anything? This may be your only opportunity to bring your family into the true gospel. Only you can save yourself and your children. You must join us. And then, if you are righteous and keep your covenants, you will achieve supreme exaltation. You will stand by your husband's side when he becomes a god in his own right. What could be more glorious than that?"

Mom covered her ears and yelled, "Why can't you leave us alone? This is between Michael and me. I want you to leave. Now!"

Brother Reuben's face contorted with anger. "I'll leave, but believe me, Sister, this is not about you and Michael and your earthly . . . association. We're speaking of the Lord's directive. Nothing less. Your husband knows that, as well as I do. He cannot turn away from God. Do you want to lose him?"

Mom gasped. Her eyes got wild, and I thought she was going to hit him with the rake, but she just stood there, her whole body shaking.

Brother Reuben gave her another disgusted look and almost spat out his words. "What's the use? I don't know why I waste my time with you." He waved his arm, as if he was brushing her away. Then he turned and hurried across the grass.

Mom watched him go with her hands clenched tight on the rake and her mouth drawn down into a deep frown. When he disappeared around the corner, she dropped the rake and ran for the house. She went inside and slammed the door. I stayed behind to dig Mikey out of the leaves, but he didn't want to come out. He kept pulling the leaves back over his face.

"Come on, Mikey. I don't want to be out here."

Finally, he crawled out, scowling. "I hate him! I hate him! I'm going to kick him next time he comes."

"I know, Mikey. I feel the same way. But right now we've got to go make sure Mom's all right."

I grabbed his hand and we headed across the grass, but before we could make it to the house, Brother Reuben showed up again.

I pushed Mikey behind me and shouted, "What are you doing back here? My mother told you to leave us alone."

I could see he had no intention of going away. He came over and put his big hands on my shoulders. He leaned down close to my face and said, "I forgot to find out where you stand, young miss? Which path do you choose? Are you with us? Are you going to strive for your reward in heaven, or are you going to follow your mother into the depths of hell?"

I thought of what Tommy said about the polygamists and how they'd want me to marry some old geezer like Brother Reuben. I hit him hard in the stomach and yelled, "Go away! We don't want you here."

He stepped back from the blow, but then laughed and came toward me again. I hit him again, only harder. That stopped his laughing. He grabbed my wrists and held them so tight against his chest it hurt. He kneeled down in front of me, penetrating my eyes with his eyes, not letting me escape from his stare. He was so close, I could smell the staleness of his beard, and I could see his sharp red tongue licking his lips. He whispered, "We need good strong girls like you, Elizabeth. The Lord's work is sometimes hard and strength is an asset . . . as is beauty." He held both my wrists with one hand, and his eyes gleamed as he ran his finger down my cheek. "The Lord loves you, little Sister. He wants you to have his children. He wants you to spread the seed of His loins."

I tried to jerk my hands loose, but his hold was too strong. I tried to kick him, but he pulled me down to my knees and pressed my nose into his shoulder. Then, he leaned back and pulled my hands together in front of my chest and said, "Let's pray, little Sister. Let's pray for your salvation. Let's pray that your mother will find the true path so that you can join us."

I screamed, "Let me go! Mom, Mom, help!"

That's when Mikey appeared. He jumped on Brother Reuben's back and wrapped his arms around his neck. Brother Reuben let go of me and tried to pull him off, but Mikey held on real tight. Brother Reuben's face started to turn red, but I didn't know if it was because he was suffocating, or if he was just bursting with anger.

Once I was free, I scrambled away. When I looked back, Brother Reuben was up on his feet. Mikey still had his arms wrapped around his throat, and he was kicking him in the sides with his heels, as if they were playing that old horsy game. Brother Reuben spun around and finally threw him off, but Mikey was up on his feet in a second, ready to go after him again. I ran over and got a hold of Mikey's arm and pulled him away. He felt all hot and sweaty, and he was panting like a dog.

Brother Reuben was furious. His face was ugly and twisted up with anger. He moved towards us with his arms stretched out wide, as if he was going to gather us up in his horrible embrace.

I screamed, "Run, Mikey! Run!"

Brother Reuben was between us and the house, so we ran behind an apple tree to get away from him. When he came one way, we'd go the other. He kept chasing us until, finally, he gave up. "Oh, to hell with the lot of you. You're children of your devil mother. You can burn in hell, for all I care." He hurried across the lawn and disappeared around the house again.

After I was sure he was gone for good, I turned to Mikey. He was still breathing hard, and his whole body was shaking. "Geez, Mikey, how did you get so brave? I thought you'd disappeared under the leaves, but then you came out and saved me. It was like you were going to strangle him. Were you going to strangle him, Mikey?"

His eyes were wild. "I couldn't stop, Bethy. I couldn't make my arms stop."

I'd never seen him like that. There was a strange darkness in his eyes that frightened me. I said, "I think we better go in the house. I'm cold. I can't stop shaking, and you're shaking too."

Mikey squeezed his hands into fists and then opened them and squeezed them together again. "I'm not cold. I'm hot." He pulled his shirt over his head and threw it on the pile of leaves. Then, he started running in big circles, going first one way and then the other, crisscrossing backwards and forwards across the grass until I got dizzy watching him. He came running towards me with his arms spread out, like he was a giant bird, and crashed full force into my chest.

"Stop it, Mikey! That hurts."

But he wouldn't stop. He kept soaring around the grass and running at me. Finally, he got tired. He fell on the ground and started laughing. It was such a strange laugh, like it had been hiding inside him for a long time, waiting to come out. He kept laughing until, all of a sudden, I realized he was crying. When I asked what was wrong, he started laughing again. I didn't know what to do with him.

Just then, Mom opened the back door and yelled, "What are you doing out there? Come inside."

I shouted, "Quick, Mom, come here. Something's wrong with Mikey."

She hurried over and knelt down beside him. "What is it? What happened?"

Mikey giggled and then started laughing harder and harder like he couldn't stop. She looked at me and then back at Mikey. "What's going on here, Beth?"

"He got all worked up because he had to save me."

"Save you? What do you mean, he had to save you?"

"Brother Reuben came back. He grabbed me, but Mikey jumped on his back and made him stop."

"He grabbed you?"

"Yes. It was horrible. He had a hold of my wrists and he wanted me to pray with him. He told me that God wants me to have his children and spread the seeds of his loins. He said he was glad I was strong because they needed strong girls."

Mom got frantic. She looked around wildly, wailing, "Oh, God. Oh, God. They're just children. How can you let him hurt my children?"

She started pulling on our arms, and patting our faces, and brushing our hair back with her fingers, going back and forth between Mikey and me. I wanted to tell her everything was okay, but I didn't really think it was. I felt dirty. I wanted to go in the house and wash the touch of Brother Reuben off my skin. I wanted to get in bed and cover my head with the blankets, but instead we were sitting on the damp grass, with all the piled leaves scattering across the yard in the wind.

Mikey didn't seem to like all Mom's attention. He glared at her with that new darkness in his eyes. She must have seen it too, because she stopped abruptly and sat back. Then she hugged him again so hard he couldn't move. She moaned, as she rocked him back and forth, but Mikey didn't respond. He kept his arms stiff at his sides and stared straight ahead, as if he was looking at something a long ways away.

Finally, she let him go and got up. She pulled us to our feet and hurried us to the house. "We've got to tell your father. When he hears about this, he'll never see that man again. You tell him what happened, Beth. Make him understand."

"Okay, Mom, I will."

She took us in the house and made us sit on the couch to wait for Dad. She had Mikey on one side of her and me on the other. She must have thought that if we moved, we'd forget to tell Dad what Brother Reuben did.

Mikey started poking at a hole on the edge of the couch arm. Mom didn't stop him; she didn't seem to notice the hole getting bigger and bigger. She kept pulling the curtains back to look out the window. It was getting late, and Dad should have been home. We waited and waited until, finally, she jumped to her feet and yelled, "Where is he?"

I tried to think of something to calm her down. "Maybe he's just working late. Maybe something went wrong, and he had to fix it."

"More likely, he had somewhere to go after work." She got more and more upset, and then she started crying.

I wanted to cry too. I wanted to run away somewhere. Maybe go find Tommy and escape to the creek. I'd find a secret hiding place where no one could find me. I'd let Tommy take care of me and tell me everything was going to be all right. I'd forget I ever had a home. I'd forget about everything. Everybody else could do whatever they were going to do and just leave me out of it.

I didn't hear him drive up, but the door opened and Dad was standing there. Mom jumped up and ran to him. "Where have you been? We've been waiting for you."

He pushed past her, put his jacket away in the hall closet, and came in the living room. He looked at me like I'd done something wrong, and then he noticed Mikey digging the hole in the arm of the couch. He came over and bopped him on top of the head. "Knock it off."

Mikey didn't say anything, but he squeezed his hand into a fist and punched the arm of the chair several times. There was something very different about him, like he'd grown up and gotten mean all in one day. He looked like he wanted to hit Dad, but Dad didn't see it because Mom was yelling at him again. "Don't hit him. This is your fault, not his."

"My fault?"

"Yes, your fault. Do you have any idea what's gone on here today? Tell him, Beth. Tell your father what his dear Brother Reuben did to you today."

He got a funny look on his face. "Yes, Beth. Tell me. I'd like to hear your version. I was truly amazed when Brother Reuben told me what you did."

Mom's eyes narrowed. "What did he tell you?"

"Why don't we hear what Beth has to say first?" He sat down and crossed his legs. Mom sat in the other chair and crossed her legs the same way. They both looked at me, waiting.

Suddenly, I felt dizzy. I didn't know what to say. I'd thought Dad would be furious with Brother Reuben, but I could tell by the way he was acting that he was really furious with me. Brother Reuben must have lied to him and told him everything was my fault.

Dad folded his arms across his chest and continued to wait.

I couldn't speak. I knew he wouldn't believe anything I said. What was the use of even trying?

"Well, Beth?"

I looked to Mom for help, but it seemed like even she was beginning to wonder if I'd told her the truth. I looked at Mikey and whispered, "Tell them, Mikey. Tell them what happened."

He didn't even look up. He had gone back to work on his hole in the couch.

Dad said, "Maybe we better start with Brother Reuben's version. Is that what you want, Beth?"

I shook my head, no.

"Well, then."

I blurted it out. "He had a hold of my arms and wouldn't let go. Mikey had to make him stop."

"He was holding you? Why was he holding you, Beth?"

"I don't know. I guess he didn't want me to get away."

"And why was that?"

"How would I know?" I didn't think I could tell him what I really thought. The way he asked the questions made me feel like crying.

"Do you think it might have been because you were hitting him?"

Mom looked surprised. "You were hitting him, Beth? You didn't tell me that."

"I was hitting him because . . . because he was saying terrible things about you, Mom."

"About me? What was he saying?"

"He said you were going to hell, and that Mikey and I were going there too, and that he didn't care anymore."

Dad jumped up. "I don't care what he said. The fact is, you were hitting him and kicking him. He said you were like a wild animal, and he had to subdue you to defend himself. That's why he was holding you." He looked over at Mikey. "And then you went crazy too, didn't you, Michael? Nearly choked the poor man to death. I couldn't believe it was my children he was talking about."

He turned and glared at Mom. "You say this is my fault? You'd better take a long hard look at yourself. All your anger and jealousy, your moodiness and depression, are having a terrible effect on this family. And to think I was beginning to believe we'd find our way. Every time I see some light, you drag us down into the pit of hell again."

I couldn't believe he'd said the same thing about Mom as Brother Reuben had said. But she wasn't the one dragging us down to hell. Brother Reuben was the one who was doing it. I'd felt something creepy about him the very first time Dad and I went up there and he started winking at me. At the time, I didn't know what it was that made me feel that way, but now, after what he'd done in the backyard, and after talking to Tommy, I was really scared he wanted me to be his wife. The thought of it made me want to throw up.

Chapter 22

We believe that all religious societies have a right to deal with
their members for disorderly conduct . . .

Doctrine and Covenants
Section 134:10

$\mathcal{D}$ad hardly talked to any of us after that. Maybe he thought we would lead him to hell if he listened to anything we said. He'd leave the house before breakfast, and if he came home before we were in bed, he'd go straight to his study. Then, Brother Reuben started showing up again, as if he wanted to challenge Mom to do anything about it. Whenever he was in the house, Mom went upstairs to hide out in the bedroom. I stayed in the bathroom with my ear pressed against the locked door. When I knew they were safely inside Dad's study, I'd sneak out and go to my bedroom, ready to dive under the bed if I heard anyone coming.

When school started again, I was relieved, thinking it would give me a chance to get away from the terrible situation at home. But it was no relief; the kids wouldn't talk to me, except to yell things about my father and Brother Reuben. They must have known it was wrong, because they only did it when there was no one around to make them stop. I didn't even have Tommy to defend me because he'd gone on to Junior High School. All I could do was try to focus on what Mrs. Jones was trying to teach us.

One day in late October, I came into the classroom and everybody started acting weird, pretending not to look at me when I knew they really were. I tried to ignore them and went to my desk. When I opened the top to take my books out, red paint leaked out all over the one new dress I'd gotten for school. I was so shocked and hurt, I burst into tears and ran for the door. Mrs. Jones was just coming in. She took one look at my stained dress and turned to the other kids. "What's going on here?"

Nobody said a word.

She took my hand. "Beth, dear, what happened to your nice dress?"

"Nothing." I ran down the hall to the bathroom and locked myself inside one of the stalls. I sat there with my head in my hands, trying to breathe through the terrible ache in my throat.

I heard the bathroom door open. I could see Mrs. Jones's feet under the stall door, and I held my breath, pretending like I wasn't there. She said, "Beth, honey. Can't you tell me what happened?"

The kindness in her voice broke something open inside me. I started to cry so hard it scared me. I put my hand over my mouth, trying to control it, but there was so much pain built up inside my throat, it made me feel like I was going to suffocate. I opened my mouth and a terrible wailing sound came out.

When I was finally able to calm down a bit, Mrs. Jones said "Honey, won't you come out and talk to me?"

"I . . . can't."

"I know it's hard. But maybe I can help."

"Nobody can help."

"Won't you let me try?"

I pulled some toilet paper off the roll and wiped my nose and my eyes. I took several deep breaths, but I still didn't feel like I could talk. What would I tell her anyway? That my father wanted to be a polygamist?

I knew I had to pull myself together. If she found out about Dad, she might have the same reaction as everyone else. If she did, I wouldn't have anyone at all who'd be nice to me. I stood up and took two more deep breaths and pushed open the stall door. As soon as I saw kind look on Mrs. Jones's face, I started to cry again. She wrapped her arms around me and held me while I cried.

Finally, she took a hanky from her pocket and gave it to me. "I want to help you, Beth, but I need to know what this is all about."

"The kids just don't like me."

"But why? You're a beautiful, friendly girl."

"It's too complicated."

"What is?"

"Everything that's happened."

"I don't understand."

I knew Mrs. Jones couldn't help me. She wasn't even a member of the Church. If she found out about Dad, she might have to call the police if he actually did get another wife. Still, I wanted to trust her. I wanted her to understand. "There're some things I can't talk about, Mrs. Jones. It's the reason the kids don't like me. I'm getting used to that, but I wished they hadn't ruined my dress. Mom's going to be so upset."

"What did they do?"

"They put paint in my desk so it dripped out on me when I took out my books."

"Well, I'll put an end to that. That's the least I can do." She shook her head. "I don't know what this is all about, Beth, but I will not have those children treating you like this." She paused and looked at me. "Do you want to come back to class?"

"I don't know."

She gave me another hug and said, "You try to clean up your dress. Then, if you want to go home for the rest of the day, you can, but you have to promise to tell me if anything like this happens again."

"I will, Mrs. Jones. Thank you."

"I just wish I could help you more, Beth. But I guess you've got your reasons for not telling me what's going on."

"I'm sorry."

"It's all right. But if you ever want to talk, I'm here. Okay?"

"Thank you."

She went back to the classroom, while I tried to clean the paint off my dress. I guess she must have told the other kids what she thought of their behavior, because when I came back in the room, they all looked down at their desks. All except Karen. She waited until Mrs. Jones wasn't looking, then she'd give me looks that sent chills up my spine. That's when I knew she was the one who put the paint in my desk. But why? Why did she hate me so bad?

Then at recess, I found out. She snuck up behind me and whispered, "Your father's going to be excommunicated, just like Brother Reuben. You'll all go to hell."

That just about knocked me over. Was she telling the truth? Would her father really do that? I couldn't believe it. It would destroy Mom. And what about Dad?   What would he do? Make us become polygamists?

When I got home, I washed out my dress with laundry soap and tucked it in with the dirty clothes, hoping Mom wouldn't notice the stains. But a few days later, while she was fixing breakfast, she asked about it. I tried to pretend it was just an accident, but in the end, she made me tell her the truth. At first, she blamed me. She said I must have done something to deserve it

I screamed, "Don't you understand? Everyone hates us. Karen's telling everyone her father's going to excommunicate Dad."

I could see that scared her. I wished like crazy I hadn't said anything. But it was the truth, and I was tired of making up lies.

She looked frantically around the room. ""Oh, dear, I can't believe this is happening. I've got to put a stop to this. I've got to talk to the Bishop." She went to the sink, holding her stomach as if she was going to throw up.

Mikey pounded his fist on the table. "I wanna eat now."

Mom spun around. "What?"

I whispered, "What's wrong with you, Mikey? Can't you see Mom's upset?"

He stood up and knocked his chair over. He grabbed a piece of toast off the plate, smeared jam on it, and stuffed the whole thing in his mouth. He ran out of the kitchen, and then I heard the back door slam.

Mom came over to the table and sat down. "Oh, Beth. If they excommunicate your father, there'll be no place for him to go except with Brother Reuben. It will be the final nail in the coffin. What are we going to do?"

"Maybe Karen was lying, Mom. Maybe she was just trying to be a big shot."

"Do you think she'd make up something like that on her own?"

"Maybe. She's always bragging about being the Bishop's daughter.

She likes to act like she knows everything."

I watched Mom's eyes flick back and forth as she tried to think of a solution. Finally, she said, "You go outside with your brother. I've got to do something."

"What are you going to do?"

"Never mind. Tell Mikey not to worry." She tried to force a smile.

I didn't believe for a minute that there wasn't anything to worry about. If she was right about Dad, we'd soon be spending all our time with the polygamists. Brother Reuben would do whatever he wanted, and there wouldn't be anything any of us could do about it.

Later that afternoon, I came in the house after being outside with Mikey. I found the Bishop in the living room with Mom and Dad. Mikey hurried upstairs, but I wanted to hear what the Bishop would say, so I went and stood behind Mom's chair.

The Bishop smiled. "Hello, Elizabeth. How are you, dear?"

"I'm okay, I guess." It was a lie, but there was no way I could tell him everything that had been going on, especially not with Mom and Dad sitting there.

"Look's like you've been outside having fun. Your cheeks are all rosy."

"I was playing with Mikey in the new snow."

"Oh, that's fun."

I didn't know what to say, so I didn't say anything.

"Well, your parents and I are having a little talk. Maybe you have something you'd like to do in your room until we finish."

I looked at Mom. "Do I have to? I'd rather stay down here."

Dad said, "Beth, go to your room. Now!"

"Okay, okay, I'm going." I ran upstairs. Mikey had his toy soldiers out, and he was making one of his wars on the bedroom floor. It seemed like killing soldiers was the only game he wanted to play anymore. He didn't even look up when I came in.

I went back out and snuck down the stairs far enough that I could see Mom and Dad from the back and the Bishop's crossed legs.

The Bishop said, "I don't understand what you're doing, Michael. You haven't been to church, and I know you've been spending a lot of time with Jacob Reuben."

"Really? Who told you that?"

The Bishop ignored his question. "I thought you needed some time to think things through after we talked in my office, and then, when Sharon lost the baby, well . . . I can see I was wrong in letting it go this long."

"Letting it go? Is that what you were doing? I wondered why we hadn't heard from you." He acted like he was mad at the Bishop for not coming to see us, but it didn't make sense, Dad was the one that stopped going to church.

The Bishop uncrossed his legs and crossed them the other way. "I heard you've been attending Reuben's church meetings."

"Yes, I have. You see, Brother Reuben actually believes in visions and personal revelation. Unlike some people in the Church who preach about such things, but when they actually happen, they call the man a fool."

"No one called you a fool, Michael."

"Not to my face, but it was quite obvious how you felt."

Mom wasn't saying anything, but I could tell she was nervous by the way her leg was jiggling.

The Bishop uncrossed his legs and leaned forward to where I could see the worried look on his face. "Michael, do you know there are people calling for your excommunication?"

So it was true. Karen was right. They really were talking about excommunicating Dad. I wanted to run down and beg the Bishop not to do it, but he'd already told me he didn't want me there.

Dad mumbled his reply, "Perhaps they are the ones who should be excommunicated."

"What? What did you say?"

"Well, you know full well what I'm getting at, Bishop. The Church has stopped teaching the original gospel given to us by Joseph Smith. The Church tells us plural marriage is a Celestial Law. That it's an absolute prerequisite for reaching the Celestial Kingdom. But then, if someone actually practices that law, you excommunicate them. How can that be right? If it's a Celestial Law, then it's God's law. How can it be changed midstream?" Dad stood up and started pacing.

"Now, Michael, be careful what you say. You know the prophet, Wilford Woodruff, had a revelation regarding that issue. If you question the validity of what he said, you'll soon be questioning everything. That would be additional grounds for excommunication. There are some things you just have to accept on faith."

"Exactly. I accept on faith, and through revelation, that God wants me to follow the original doctrine of the gospel. Not the ones made up later by men."

Mom gasped.

The Bishop shook his head. "I don't think you understand the destructiveness of this path you're on. If you're excommunicated, don't you realize that your family will be ostracized? You'll have no place in this community. You have to think about Sharon and the children, Michael."

Dad didn't reply, but he sat back down.

The Bishop turned to Mom. "Sharon? How can you accept this?"

She looked at Dad, but he wouldn't look back. "It's hard, Bishop. I'm very con--"

Dad yelled, "Of course, she's confused. Who wouldn't be? Besides, you know as well as I do, women have always had problems with plural marriage. Nowadays, society tells them they should be monogamous. The Church tells them the same thing, but then it also says we'll practice polygamy in the next world. Don't you think that's a bit confusing? If the Church was consistent with the original teachings, maybe women would know what God requires of them, and a man wouldn't have to feel guilty trying to live by the covenants he's made with God."

The Bishop squeezed his hands together, then put them on his legs and leaned forward. "I must warn you, Michael. Jacob Reuben is not what he seems to be. He is no man of God."

"I would expect you to say that sort of thing, Bishop. After all, you excommunicated him."

"Yes, he was excommunicated, but I'm not referring to the fact that he's gone against the Church by having multiple wives. I'm trying to tell you the man is entirely self-motivated. Don't you realize the sacrifices he'll ask your family to make? Maybe he's already asked you to turn over your worldly possessions."

Dad shook his head in disgust. "Isn't that what we call the Law of Consecration, Bishop? Have you forgotten that too? It's another Celestial principle the Church seems perfectly willing to ignore."

"Yes, I know all about the Law of Consecration, but in Reuben's case it's practiced very differently than in the early days of the Church. What goes into his coffers doesn't necessarily come back out, even to those who desperately need it. Do you understand what I'm saying?"

"You're the one who doesn't understand, Bishop. They want me to be their . . . seer and revelator. The people would listen to me. I'd make sure nothing like that ever happened."

"I see. That's how he managed to convince you. He's telling you you're a visionary. Now why do you suppose a man like Reuben would ask someone from outside his group to be involved like that? If he was really following the true tenets of the gospel, he'd know that such a man must be chosen by God. How can he presume to make the selection himself?"

"The whole group fasted and prayed for a long time. They are unanimous in their belief. A seer is someone who has talked with God. I am such a man, but then you don't believe that, do you?"

The Bishop jumped to his feet. "I'm telling you, Michael, Jacob Reuben is no man of God. He's a predator. Elizabeth is at risk and so is your son. You have to believe me. For heaven's sake, turn away from this madness before you destroy your whole family."

Dad jumped up and Mom did too. She pulled at his arm, trying to reason with him. "Please, Michael. Listen to him."

Dad shook her off and continued with his accusations against the Bishop. "How do you know these things about Brother Reuben? It sounds like a lot of gossip to me. Just exactly what people would say about someone they dislike because they disagree with him."

"It's no concern of yours how I know. Can't you see I'm trying to give you a chance to redeem yourself? You're making it very difficult."

The Bishop was scaring me. What did he think Brother Reuben was going to do? Had he found out what he did to me in the backyard? Did he think Brother Reuben wanted to hurt me and Mikey? Why didn't anyone care?

Dad shook his finger at the Bishop. "I don't believe the things you say, Bishop. I know this man you're talking about. I've spent a great deal of time with him. He's a very spiritual man. It's just that, unlike you, he believes we must live the true gospel."

The Bishop dropped his hands to his sides. "I see. It sounds like you've made up your mind to join him. I guess I'd better proceed with the excommunication hearing." He looked at Mom and said, "I'm sorry."

"No! I haven't made up my mind. Can't you see? I just want to understand what God wants of me. I just want to know the truth." Dad's voice sounded shaky, and I could see he was trembling.

Mom reached for his arm again, but she didn't take it. "Please, honey. You've got to think of the children. What if the Bishop is right about Brother Reuben? What will happen to them?"

Dad dropped back down into the chair and covered his face with his hand.

Mom kneeled in front of him and pleaded. "Please, Michael. You don't want the children to become outcasts, do you? They're already being persecuted at school. It's bad. It's really bad."

He dropped his hand from his face. "What do you mean they're being persecuted? By who? You've never said anything about that."

"I just found out myself."

"But who? Who's doing it?"

She looked at the Bishop, and the Bishop looked away. I couldn't tell if he knew about his daughter putting paint in my desk or not. Had Mom told him that? I hoped not. It would only make Dad angrier with the Bishop.

Mom focused on the floor. "It's the kids at school."

"But why would they do that? What could they know? Did Beth say something?" He looked over at the Bishop. "Or maybe it was you, Bishop. Did you try to get the children involved? Did you think it would put pressure on me?"

The Bishop shook his head. "Don't look to me for what's been done. Look to yourself. I fear something has happened to your judgment. Whatever occurred that day at the creek has affected your mind. I think you need help. If you want me to give you the name of a church counselor, I can do that."

Dad refused to answer.

A deadly silence came over the house. Unable to change the mind of the others, each of them seemed caught in their own mind.

Finally, the Bishop spoke. "I guess I may as well go. I'm not doing any good here."

He stood up and started towards the door, then turned back to Dad. "I think you better give a lot of thought to what you're doing here, Brother Sterling. And I think you'd better do it quickly."

Dad didn't respond, but Mom got up and rushed over to the Bishop's side. "Please, Bishop, give him some time. He said he hadn't made a decision, didn't he?"

"I don't know, Sharon. It seems hopeless. He's turned against the prophet and against the Church. But there's no reason you and the children have to go down that road with him."

"Please, Bishop, let me talk to him. Don't do anything yet. I beg you."

"I'm going to have to do something, sooner or later. I can't let this go on forever."

"I know. But please, just give me a chance to talk to him."

After the Bishop left, Mom hurried back to Dad in the living room. "Oh, Michael, why didn't you tell him you were sorry? You can't let this happen. It'll be terrible if you're excommunicated."

He wouldn't look at her.

"Michael! Don't you care about your children?"

Dad shook his head hard. "What are you saying? Of course, I care."

"Then why didn't you tell the Bishop you'd stop seeing Brother Reuben? Why didn't you say you were sorry for the things you said about the Church leaders?"

"I'm just wondering who got those kids riled up. I don't think they'd do it on their own. Where's Beth? I want to know exactly what happened."

I ran up to the bedroom and sat on my bed trying to think of what I was going to say. If he found out that Karen ruined my dress, I didn't know what he'd do. Maybe he'd never tell the Bishop he was sorry. Maybe he'd decide he didn't care if he was excommunicated.

He came in with Mom right behind him. I looked up innocently and said, "Hi, Dad. Did the Bishop leave yet?"

He came over to the bed and stood towering above me with his hands on his hips. "Elizabeth, I want to know what happened to you at school."

I looked at Mom. I thought she shook her head no, but I wasn't sure what she wanted me to say.

Dad said. "Did you hear me, Beth? I want to know who's been causing you trouble at school."

"It's no big deal. They were just fooling around."

He sat on the edge of the bed and looked hard into my eyes, like he was trying to see what the truth was. "That's not what I heard, Beth. Who's doing it? Anyone in particular?"

Mikey came running over and yelled, "They put paint all over her new dress."

Dad gave me a sharp look. "Is that true?"

I looked at Mom again, but she was staring at the floor. I said, "Yes, but--"

"Who did it?"

"I'm not sure."

Mikey said, "Yes you are. It was Karen. Karen Anderson."

Dad looked from Mikey to me and back to Mikey. "The Bishop's daughter?"

Mikey gave me a smarty-pants look and said, "That's what Bethy told Momma."

Dad looked furious, but he was angry with me, not Karen. "Why are you lying to me?"

Mom came and took his arm. "Oh, Michael, can't you see she's scared? She's more scared of what you're going to do than what the kids did."

"This is unbelievable. You've all been lying to me. My own family. I can't tolerate this." He jerked his arm away from her and hurried out of the room.

"I'm sorry, Mom. I didn't know what to say."

She looked at me sadly. "I know, honey. It's not your fault." She touched my cheek, and then hurried out the door after Dad.

A few minutes later, I went downstairs and found Dad standing in front of the kitchen window, staring out. Mom was behind him with her head against his back. "Honey, please consider what the Bishop said about Brother Reuben. What if it's true? Why would he want you to be their seer?"

"You know why."

"Yes, yes. I know. It's because of your vision. But why couldn't he just tell them he'd had a vision himself?"

He spun around and glared at her. "You mean, make it up? Like . . . like I did?"

"No, that's not what I meant. I meant--"

"I know what you meant, Sharon. You've never believed me. You're just like the Bishop. But I know what happened. There's nothing you or he can say that's ever going to change that. I understand that I might be persecuted. I'm not concerned about that. The Saints have always been persecuted for following the Lord's word."

"But what about the children?"

He pulled away from her and headed for the living room, but then he turned back. "Did you call the Bishop and tell him to come here?"

"What?"

"I said, did you call the Bishop?"

She didn't answer.

"I see." He shook his head. "I never thought you'd go behind my back like that. How can I trust you, if you'd do that?"

"I was worried . . . about the children."

"But not about me?" His mouth was tight. He closed his eyes and let out a deep sigh. "I've got to think. I've got to get away from here and think." He hurried across the living room and stormed out the door.

I yelled, "Stop him, Mom!"

"Let him go, Beth. He has to realize the Bishop is telling him the truth. If he doesn't, then he might as well not come back."

"Don't say that. He's got to come back. You can't let him leave us."

She shook her head, sadly. "I don't know how to keep it from happening."

"But it's getting dark. He doesn't have a coat, and it looks like it's going to snow again."

"I know, Beth. There's nothing I can do. It's up to him."

Chapter 23

And if it so be that the church is built upon my gospel then will the Father show forth his own works in it.

But if it be not built upon my gospel, and is built upon the works of men, or upon the works of the devil, verily I say unto you they have joy in their works for a season, and by and by the end cometh, and they are hewn down and cast into the fire, from whence there is no return.

Book of Mormon
3 Nephi 27:10-11

It seemed like Dad was always being thrown by people telling him what to do. After the Bishop's visit, he stopped seeing Brother Reuben again. I don't know if it was because of what the Bishop had said about Brother Reuben, or if he was worried about being excommunicated. Whichever it was, he still refused to go to church. Mom begged him to go, saying it was the only thing that might keep him from getting excommunicated, but I don't think he could face the people in the Ward. When he didn't go to church, Mom didn't want to go either, so none of us went.

At school, Mrs. Jones protected me in the classroom, but it didn't keep Karen and her friends from yelling and talking behind my back when she wasn't around. At recess and lunch, I stayed by myself. Sometimes I hiked down to the old pioneer cemetery and thought about Tommy, wishing he hadn't gone off to the new school. I missed him terribly. Without him, I didn't have anyone to talk to.

Mikey started having trouble too. The kids pushed him off the merry-go-round, and then called him a crybaby. He got out of school two hours before I did. That meant he had to walk home by himself, so I couldn't protect him. Sometimes when I'd get home, I'd find him in the bedroom with his eyes all red. When I asked him what happened, he wouldn't tell me. I guess he was doing his crying in secret, trying to keep up the toughness he'd found in himself when he fought Brother Reuben.

It was a hard period for all of us. Dad was so tormented with his questions and doubts, he'd often yell at us for no reason. Other times, I could tell he'd been in his study crying, hiding his tears away just like Mikey. I almost wished he'd go back to seeing Brother Reuben so we could have some rest from his terrible battles with himself. He was getting thin again from all his fasting and praying, and it seemed like he never left the house anymore except when he'd have a fight with Mom. Then he'd slam the door and run off to the creek, or somewhere. Mom was upset all the time too. The whole situation was wearing her out, and it showed up in her frustration with Mikey and me. It got harder and harder to be in that house, but there was nowhere else to go where I could feel safe.

Then one day, Dad took off somewhere in his truck. Mom started pacing. I sat at the kitchen table watching her until she finally came to a stop in front of the sink. That's when I asked her something I'd been wondering about. "Doesn't Dad work anymore?"

She turned around and glared at me. "There is no work."

"No work? How can that be?"

"Nobody will hire him."

"But I thought everybody loved his work. They always praised him for being such a great carpenter."

"The word is out, Beth. They're not going to hire someone who's been talking against the Church." She hurried into the living room, as if she wanted to get away from me, but I followed.

"But if they won't hire Dad, how are we going to survive? Won't we starve?"

She wrung her hands. "I don't know. Sometimes I think he doesn't care if he ever works again. I've begged him to talk to the Bishop, but he won't do it." She pushed against her stomach and winced. She'd been doing that a lot lately. It made me worry that she might be getting sick again.

When I followed her back to the kitchen, she spun around and said, "Don't you have something to do besides follow me around asking questions?"

"I just want to know what's going on."

"Well, I don't have the answers." She hurried out of the kitchen and went upstairs.

I wandered around downstairs, and then went up to the bedroom and found Mikey over by his hamster cage. He was holding out a piece of carrot to Petey. Every time the poor hamster tried to bite it, Mikey would pull it away and giggle.

"Don't do that, Mikey. It's mean and there's too much meanness in the world already."

He stuck the carrot in his own mouth and chewed it.

"Why'd you do that? It's got hamster germs all over it."

He stuck out his tongue with chewed up carrot on it and waggled it around. Then he tried to lick me with it.

I pushed him away. "You're sickening."

He giggled again, and then stomped out of the room, making as much noise as he could. He was getting to be a real brat. I knew it was because of all the stress we were under, but it didn't make it any easier to live with.

Later that night, Mom was making mashed potatoes with creamed chip beef. She kept looking up at the clock every few minutes. I was sure she was wondering where Dad was.

Mikey came in. He sniffed the air and said, "Why do we have to have the same yucky stuff every night?"

Mom didn't answer him, but it was true. We'd been having chipped beef a lot lately. After what Mom had said, I realized it was because Dad was out of work, and we didn't have enough money to buy anything else. We'd never had trouble buying enough food. Now, it was just one more thing we had to worry about.

I'd just finished setting the table when Dad came home. He washed his hands at the kitchen sink and sat right down, ready to eat. I was surprised that he looked happy for a change. Mom must have noticed it too. "You look like you have good news, Michael."

"Well, yes. I guess I do."

"What is it? Did you get work?" She wiped her hands on her apron and came over to his side.

"Well, yes, I guess I did."

Mom's face lit up a bit. "Really? Is it a big job?"

"I'd say it's pretty big. Bigger than anything I've ever done before."

I couldn't tell what was going on. Dad seemed happy, but he also seemed hesitant. Was he going to do something to cause trouble? I looked at Mom, but she didn't seem to notice anything wrong. She said, "Oh that's great, Michael. Where is it? Somewhere close by?"

Dad fiddled with his napkin. "Well, that's the thing. I'm going to have to go away for a while."

Mom looked shocked. "Away? What do you mean, away? To where?"

"Uh . . . southern Utah. I think it's somewhere in the desert outside of St. George." He wouldn't look at her.

"Out in the desert? What kind of building project would be there?"

"A church, Sharon. Brother Reuben's group is ready to get started." He met Mom's eyes for a second, and then looked quickly away.

So that was why he wouldn't come right out and say it. He was going to get involved with Brother Reuben again. But there was something confusing about the whole thing. I said, "Why would they build their church down there in the desert when they live here?"

He looked at me like he was trying to be patient. "I guess they want to move to some place where they can live in peace. Some place where people won't torment them, where they can feel safe to practice their beliefs." It seemed like he was talking about himself as much as he was talking about them, and we were the ones doing the tormenting.

Mom clamped her hand over her mouth and turned away, but Mikey grabbed his arm and said, "Can we go with you, Daddy? Can we? Can we?"

Dad smiled a little, "I'm sorry, Michael. There's no place for you down there. Maybe later. We'll see."

Mom went over to the sink and stood there with her back to us. Mikey glanced at her, and then started poking the chip beef pieces down into his mashed potatoes.

After a minute, Mom spun around and faced Dad. Her face was flushed. "You know, Michael, this sounds more like you've decided to join up with them than real work. I can't believe they have any money to pay you."

"They're living the Law of Consecration, Sharon. You heard Brother Reuben say that. They've been pooling their resources. It's what we would be doing if we were following the true tenets of the gospel. I feel very blessed. I've always wanted to see the Law of Consecration in action." His eyes were shining as he thought about his new life away from us.

"You might have talked to me before you made your decision. But then, I guess I have no say in this."

"No, I'm sorry, you don't. I've already told him I'll do it." He said it softly, but we all heard him. It was obvious he didn't care what any of us thought anymore.

Mom turned back to the sink and held onto it with both hands. I could see she was trembling, but she held her voice steady. "How long will you be gone?"

"I don't know for sure. Several months at least."

"I guess that means they've got it mostly finished, if they're ready for carpentry work."

"Well, no. I'm going to help them with everything, beginning with the foundation. They don't really know what they're doing. I'll have to help them get permits and see about getting a well drilled."

Mom spun around. "A well?"

"Yes. I guess the property is some distance from a water source."

"How do you even know there'll be water there?" Her voice was getting shrill.

"They've had it witched. They know there's water."

"Witched? Can't you see what they're doing, Michael? They want you to build the whole thing. It'll take a lot longer than a few months. You know it will. And how can you be sure they'll pay you?"

"Now, don't get all excited. Brother Reuben assured me we'll be taken care of. We'll take this one step at a time." Dad's voice was calm. He seemed relaxed for the first time in months.

"And what are we supposed to do while you're gone? You obviously won't have any other work. Where will we get the money to pay the bills? And what if we need something done around here? Who's going to do it?"

"You'll just have to manage, Sharon. I'll come home from time-to-time, when I can."

"From time-to-time? I just can't believe you decided all this without mentioning a word to me."

Dad pounded his fist on the table so hard the plates jumped. "I'm the patriarch of this family. It's time you started treating me like one. I've been listening to you for months, and where has it gotten us? We're stalled in a world of misery and chaos. I *am* going to do this. You may as well get used to it."

I couldn't tell if Mom wanted to cry or scream. She ran out of the room, knocking the edge of the table with her hip and tipping our glasses over. The milk ran across the tablecloth and dripped down the edges onto the floor.

After a minute, Dad picked up his fork and started to eat his potatoes. Then, he set the fork down again. "In all this anger, I think we've forgotten something. Beth, will you say the blessing?" He folded his arms and closed his eyes.

I said, "Shouldn't we clean up the milk first?"

"Say the blessing, Beth." His voice was firm.

I couldn't think what I was supposed to say. I just sat there until Dad opened one eye and said, "Well? Are you going to bless the food or not?"

I folded my arms and whispered, "Heavenly Father, bless this food and bless this crazy messed-up house. Bring us back together before everything is totally ruined. In the name of Jesus Christ, amen."

I kept my eyes closed until Dad touched my arm. "Eat your dinner, Elizabeth. You too, Michael."

Mikey started eating his potatoes and chip beef in great big spoonfuls. He kept his eyes on Dad. Some of the potatoes escaped out the corner of his mouth and fell back down on his plate. I thought Dad would yell at him to stop it, but he didn't. I guess he didn't want any more trouble.

My stomach was in such turmoil, I couldn't even think about eating. I tried to think of a way to escape. "Maybe I should go see if Mom's okay."

Dad shook his head. "Eat your dinner before it gets any colder."

While I forced the potatoes down past the lump of fear in my throat, I started to wonder if all the polygamists were going down to the desert to help build the church. Would the pretty blond girl with the sparkling blue eyes be waiting there for Dad? Would they get married while none of us were there to stop them?

I pretended I was just curious. "Dad, who's going to be down there? Just you and Brother Reuben, or will everybody be there?"

"I suppose there will be others. We can't build a church by ourselves."

"But are the kids going, and all the wives and everybody?"

"I really don't know. I don't think there's a place for them to stay."

"Then where are you going to stay?"

"At a motel, I suppose."

Dad seemed excited. Was it because he was finally going to get away from us? He'd been threatening to do it for a long time, and now, he had the job of building the church as an excuse. I couldn't stand to think of Mom and Dad being apart. I knew they still loved each other. I'd seen them down at the creek that night. But if they got too far apart, they might forget all that and never get back together again. I started plotting a way to keep us together, telling Dad that we could help him if he'd take us with him.

Mikey got involved too. He grabbed his arm and said, "I can carry your hammer."

But Dad wasn't interested in having our help. He was going away by himself to build the polygamists church, and there was nothing any of us could do to stop him.

Chapter 24

Here, then, is eternal life—to know the only wise and true God; and you have got to learn how to be gods yourselves . . .

Joseph Smith
King Follet Sermon (1844)

*I*t seemed like we were living in a different house after Dad left. It was eerily quiet and everything felt dark and cold and sad. The door to Dad's study remained closed, and after awhile, it was as if that room wasn't part of the house anymore. As if God was locked inside there, and he no longer cared what happened to us.

For the first few days, Mom made a lot of noise, slamming doors and crashing dishes and yelling at Dad, even though he wasn't there to hear it. Then, when he finally called, she acted like she didn't miss him at all. Instead of sitting down and getting comfortable for a long talk, she stood by the phone and wrapped the cord around her finger and said, "Yes, everything's fine, Michael. We're doing just fine. No, we don't need anything from you. . . . I see. So all the men are there. . . I thought you said there was no place for them to stay. . . . Oh, yes, the motel. Must be nice for them to have all that business."

She acted like it was just a friendly conversation with somebody she hardly knew, but I could tell by the gray color of her eyes, and the nervousness of her hands, that she was aching inside.

I tugged on her arm and whispered, "Let me talk to him."

She pretended like she didn't hear me. Then she lied to him and said, "Oh, I'm sorry. They're outside playing right now, but I'll tell them you called."

She hung up the phone. When I asked her why she wouldn't let me talk to him, she said, "He hasn't got time for us."

One day, on my way home from school, I stopped at the mailbox to see if Mom had picked up the mail. She didn't seem to want to do it anymore, so I made it my job. I expected to find the usual bills, but that day I found something disturbing. It was an envelope from the Bishop's office. It was marked, "Personal and Confidential."

I walked down the road turning the envelope over in my hands, worrying about what was inside. Part of me wanted to open it and tell Mom it came that way, but another part of me didn't want to know.

I hurried upstairs when I got home and found Mom sitting on the edge of her bed staring blankly out the window. I got the feeling she'd been sitting there all day.

I said, "I brought the mail, Mom."

She took it and set it on the lamp table.

"Aren't you going to look at it?"

"Why should I? I can't pay the bills."

I went around and leaned against the windowsill so she couldn't avoid looking at me. "There's a letter for Dad, Mom. I think it's from the Bishop."

"Why didn't you tell me?"

"I just did."

She picked up the envelope and turned it over in her hands, just like I had.

"Are you going to open it?"

"It's addressed to your father."

"I know, but maybe you should look at it. Otherwise, how will you tell him what it says when he calls?"

She sighed and slid her finger under the flap to break the glue. She took out the letter. As she read, I watched a frown grow on her face. I was right. It was bad news.

"Is it about Dad's excommunication?"

She covered her eyes with her hand and nodded. "The Bishop has set up a council to talk to him."

"When?"

"Right away."

"What are we going to do?"

She thought about it for a minute. "I'd better write the Bishop and tell him your father's out of town working. I'll say I'll let him know about the letter when he returns. That way, maybe they won't do anything until he gets back."

"That's a good idea, Mom. You won't be lying because he really is out of town working."

"That's right. Now go put this letter in his study where it won't get lost."

I ran downstairs and put the envelope in the middle drawer of his desk. Then, I moved some papers over the top of it, thinking it might be better if it did get lost. One thing was for sure, it wasn't something Dad was going to have worry about. That was for me and Mom to do.

It had been almost a month since Dad left, and he still hadn't been home to see us. There was always some reason why he couldn't make it. When he said he was going to make it home for Thanksgiving for sure, Mom said, "Don't count on it."

She was right. On Thanksgiving Day, he called. I was the one who answered the phone. He said there was a big rainstorm coming in. He had to get the church protected so the wood wouldn't warp.

I said, "But why can't somebody else do it?"

"They've all gone home for Thanksgiving."

"That's so unfair, Dad. Why do they get to have Thanksgiving and we don't? Mom even cooked a turkey for you. Don't you realize how bad that makes her feel?"

"I know, honey. I'm really, really sorry. I miss you all so much. I just. . ." His voice cracked, and I realized he was telling the truth. But if he missed us so bad, why didn't he do something about it?

"You've got to come home sometime. Mom needs you. We all do."

"I know. I know. I absolutely promise I'll be there for Christmas. Can you wait that long?" His voice sounded really sad. It made me wonder if things weren't as great down there as he'd thought they were going to be.

I said, "I guess I can wait, but I don't know about Mom. You better talk to her."

I told Mom it was Dad on the phone. She took a long time to answer, then she just said things like, yes, no, and I don't care. She listened for a minute more and said, "It's always the same story,

Michael. I don't want to hear it anymore." She slammed down the phone and went back in the kitchen.

I didn't think it helped for her to get mad at him. If she made him feel like he wasn't welcome here, he might never come home.

I followed her into the kitchen and lied to Mikey, saying, "Dad said to tell you Happy Thanksgiving."

Mikey didn't seem to care about that. As soon as I sat down, he said, "The wishbone's mine."

"Oh yeah. How come?"

"I need it. I've been saving up my wish for a long time."

"Well, you have to break the wishbone with somebody else. How do you know you'll get the biggest part?"

"I'm going to break it with myself. That way I'll be sure."

"That's cheating, Mikey. Your wish probably won't come true if you cheat."

"It will too. Momma, tell Beth to stop lying."

Mom yelled, "Will you two please shut up!" She clamped her hands over her ears and started to cry.

It hurt to have her yell at me, but I still tried to make her feel better by telling her that Dad absolutely promised to be home for Christmas.

She said, "You're a fool if you believe that."

It got hard to know what to do with Mom. I didn't like it when she cried, but it was even worse when she got mad because it felt like she was blaming me for everything that went wrong. To make matters worse, whenever Mom got mad, Mikey got mean.

One day, Mikey and I were in the bedroom, when we heard Mom yell, "Michael J. Sterling, how many times have I told you not to leave your soldiers in the tub?"

Mikey squeezed his eyes shut and put his hands over his ears as Mom came storming into the room. She pulled him up off the floor and dragged him by the arm to the bathroom. The next thing I heard was a loud thump. I ran to see what it was and found Mom standing with her hands on her hips looking at a round hole in the wall behind the door.

"What happened?"

"Your brother decided to make life worse than it already is. He's put the doorknob through the wall."

Mikey was over by the bathtub. His face was bright red, and he had a look that warned me not to get too close to him. He had a handful of toy soldiers, and he was bouncing them off the backside of the bathtub. Mom rubbed her temples and left the room.

I looked at the hole and saw that it went all the way through the drywall. I pushed the door towards the wall, and sure enough, the handle fit exactly inside the hole. I looked at Mikey in disgust. "Why'd you do that? Do you want to ruin everything?"

He just kept throwing his soldiers.

I wondered what Dad was going to say when he saw that hole. The window in the back door already had a cardboard patch over it from when Mikey threw a snowball with a rock inside it. If Dad didn't come home soon, the whole house was going to be wrecked.

About a week before Christmas, Mikey was outside building a snow fort in the new snow, and Mom was upstairs in her bedroom. I'd been wondering if we were going to have any kind of Christmas, so I decided to look in Dad's study to see if Mom had hidden any presents in there.

Once I was inside the study with the door closed, I looked in the closet and through all the drawers in the desk, but I couldn't find any presents. I'd already checked all of Mom's usual hiding places, and I was beginning to think that there weren't any presents. I didn't care about myself, but I knew it would make Mikey feel real bad.

I sat down in Dad's chair and was tilting it back and forth to make it squeak, when a beam of sunlight slipped between the curtains and lit up Dad's Book of Mormon on the desk. I got the idea that the light was telling me to look inside that book. I picked it up and it fell open to a page that was all marked up with red underlines and exclamation points and little notes written in the margins. I turned to the next page and saw it was the same as the first one. I looked through the whole book. Some of the pages had more underlines and notes than others, but all of them were marked. I read some of the scriptures, trying to figure out what Dad was making notes about, but he'd underlined so many places, it was like he was questioning and reacting to everything. There was something about it that worried me.

I put the Book of Mormon down and picked up his copy of the Doctrine and Covenants. I had to hold it very carefully because some of the old yellow pages were starting to fall out. There were notes and underlines, just like in the Book of Mormon. Some of the pages had arrows pointing from one scripture to the next, or there were numbers, one, two, and three, inside of circles next to the scriptures. I read the scriptures that had the arrows between them, but I couldn't see what the connection was.

I noticed a small blue notebook on the desk that said, Record of Michael J. Sterling, 1963. Inside, it was full of Dad's writing. The first page said, James 1:5 - 'If any man lacks wisdom, let him ask of God.'

Below the scripture, he'd written a question:

> *Does this mean we can speak to God directly? I spoke to God. Did he speak to me? Was it God or an agent of God?*

I looked at the top of the page and saw a date which showed he'd written the notes about the same time he had his vision. That meant he really didn't know if it was God that talked to him. It was just like Mom had said, he'd made that part up later. Was it because of Brother Reuben? Was he the one who convinced Dad it was God that talked to him, or had he convinced himself?

I read the next scripture: D & C 93:1 - 'Verily, thus saith the Lord: It shall come to pass that every soul who forsaketh his sins and cometh unto me, and calleth on my name, and obeyeth my voice, and keepeth my commandments, shall see my face and know that I am.'

That was followed by a list of Dad's questions:

> *- How can we keep our covenants with the Lord when the government and the Church itself will not allow it? If we cannot rely on the Church, can we receive salvation on our own? Can I still become a god?*

> *- Who is God?*

> *- If a man is righteous and keeps the covenants he has made with God, he will become a god in his own right. Brigham Young has said Adam is not only our father, but the God of this world. If he is our physical father and our God, then who is Jesus and what is his relationship to Adam?*

- We are God's spirit children. Jesus is our eldest spiritual brother, but he also had a physical body. He is God's only begotten son, so he is also our physical brother. Adam is the father of our physical bodies. If Adam is the God of this world, then who is God the Eternal Father? And who is Jesus? The son of Adam, our God, or the son of God our Eternal Father? What will God's relationship be with the inhabitants of my world when I become a god? If I do become a god? If I can become a god?

All of his questions were about who God was, and about being a god himself. I'd heard him talk about it before, but I didn't know how bad it was. Is that what he was trying to figure out by reading and marking the scriptures? Was that the obsession that was driving him crazy and leading him to destroy us all?

I turned quickly to the next page in the notebook. It had a drawing with a title that said, The Eternal Celestial Family. There was a circle at the top, labeled Man/God (myself). I decided that circle was supposed to represent Dad, because there was a line connecting it to another circle just below it with Mom's name inside. There were two other circles next to Mom's labeled Wife 2 and Wife 3. Were those supposed to be the other wives that Dad might have some day? Did he already know who they were?

Underneath each of the wife circles, there were a bunch of circles labeled, Progeny. Under Mom's name, there was a circle for me and one for Mikey, plus a couple more. Maybe one of them was for the little brother we lost, and the others were in case Mom had more babies. I looked at the progeny circles under the unknown wives and realized that Dad had planned the whole thing out. He was going to have babies with them. Did Mom know about this? Had she seen the notebook? Did she think he was down there in the desert getting his new wives?

My stomach ached, and I was getting that tight feeling in my chest, but I couldn't stop looking. I turned the page of the notebook and saw more of Dad's questions and some of his answers:

- How does a man become a god?

-Through the Priesthood - It is written, a man can receive the highest priesthood directly from God and those who so receive it are of the Church of the First Born and shall have their calling and election made sure and when this is done they shall be exalted to the highest kingdom.

- But a man must live the Law of Consecration - the United Order - without it a man cannot enter the Celestial world.

- And he must live by the divine covenant of plural marriage, having at least three wives. He cannot otherwise become a god. It is essential to the function of the patriarchal family -- a man, his wives, and his children, and all who come through his line, will be together in the Celestial Kingdom. And he and his wives shall conceive the spirit children to inhabit his world when he becomes a god. But what of his mortal children, what is their role in the Celestial Kingdom?

It looked like Dad had figured out what he had to do to become a god. He had to do all the things that Brother Reuben talked about. I couldn't figure out if he had found the answers in the scriptures, or if they were answers Brother Reuben had given him during those long hours they spent in Dad's study. As I turned the pages, the writing got harder and harder to read. The letters looked like scribbles, like he was writing so fast he couldn't finish one word before he started the next.

I closed the notebook and held it against my chest, feeling the pounding of my heart against the cover. I was thinking of all Dad's questions about becoming a god, and I was remembering how many times he and Brother Reuben and talked about that. Brother Reuben was always saying that certain things had to be done if Dad wanted to be a god, and that there were things Mom had to do if she was going to sit by his side in his kingdom. Was it really true that an ordinary man could be a god? It was such a huge question it made my head spin.

I tried to imagine Dad being a god, sitting up in heaven with all his spirit children around him, and them all getting ready to get their mortal bodies and go to a world that he had created for them to live on. I tried to imagine me and Mikey and Mom being there, but I couldn't figure out what my role would be. The more I thought about it, the more it seemed like one of Mikey's fairy tales. But maybe I shouldn't have been thinking about it like that when Dad was treating it so seriously. Maybe he knew something that I just couldn't understand. Maybe it was something he'd learned about in the men's priesthood meeting, something that couldn't be discussed with a girl. There had to be something to it, or why would Dad have spent so much time thinking about it, and why would he be willing to risk everything by going against the Church and going with Brother Reuben and making us all so miserable?

I noticed that the beam of sunlight had moved and was now shining on the floor in front of the window. It suddenly felt very important for me to talk to God to try to find out if what Dad was doing was right or wrong. Maybe a girl could talk to God, if she had faith. I hurried over and knelt down in the light. For a minute, I couldn't think of anything to say, but then I closed my eyes and prayed with all my heart. "Dear God . . . or whoever you are in the light, can I ask you a question?"

I waited for a minute, but when I didn't hear or feel anything, I continued, "Is Dad right about what you want him to do? Are we really supposed to be polygamists? Will he come home soon, or are we supposed to go live with him and the polygamists in the desert? I need to know what you want. I need to know what is true. Please, God, answer me."

I stayed there for a long, long time with my eyes closed, waiting. But no answer came. I thought about Mom and wondered how it could be all right with God for her to be that sad and lonely. I thought about Dad in the desert with the polygamists. He was lonely too, but he was still willing to break us apart over his obsession with being a god. How could that be right? I wanted so bad for us to be back together again and for us to laugh and enjoy life like we used to. Then I got a feeling under my heart like Dad said happened when the Holy Ghost talked to you. But it wasn't warm and glowing like he said it would be. It was cold and aching. I wanted it to go away. I pressed on my heart and opened my eyes. The beam of sunlight had disappeared, and I was kneeling alone in the dark.

Chapter 25

But if any provide not for his own, and specially for those of his own house, he hath denied the faith, and is worse than an infidel.

Holy Bible
1 Timothy 5:8

I don't know why we believed Dad was coming home for Christmas. Maybe it was because he'd said he was bringing a Christmas tree and he told Mom to get out the decorations. Or maybe it was because he said he'd be home on Christmas Eve day, like he had it all planned out and knew just when he'd be leaving. I hadn't seen Mom that excited in a long time. She seemed almost giddy. She immediately wanted to start cleaning up the house and getting ready for him. We moved the furniture around, vacuumed the living room, and then we washed and waxed the kitchen floor. When we finished, we were both sweating.

We plopped down on the couch and I said, "What about presents, Mom? Aren't we going to get Dad something?"

She shook her head. "We don't have that kind of money, Beth. You know that."

"But we have to give him something. Maybe we could make him a present."

She smiled. "Oh, that's a good idea, Beth. We could all make presents for each other this year."

"It'll be fun. But we don't have much time. Christmas is only a few weeks away."

"Well, then. We better get started. Let's see if we can find anything we can use."

We ran around the house looking for leftover cloth, ribbons, buttons, paper, and anything else we could work with. Then we got out the crayons, the colored pencils, the stapler, the tape, and the shoebox that held all the odds and ends. We sat at the kitchen table and looked at all the stuff, but neither one of us could think of what to make. Then I got an idea. "Mom, do we have any old Sunday newspapers?"

"I don't know. Probably."

"If we do, we can make Mikey a camera."

"A camera?"

"Yes. We can get a little box and cut holes on both ends to look through. Then we can . . . never mind, I'll show you. Do we have a little box?"

Mom thought for a minute. Then she went and opened the cupboard over the stove and took down a box of kitchen matches."

"Oh, that's perfect."

She emptied the matches into a bottle and brought the box over to the table.

"Can you find the newspapers while I cut the holes? I especially need the funny papers."

She hurried away to get the newspapers while I cut little holes on both ends of the box with a knife.

When she came back, I got the scissors and started cutting out pictures of characters from the comics. "See. We can put these inside the camera. Then, when Mikey takes a picture of somebody, he can take out one of these cartoon characters, as if that's what they look like. Don't you think it's funny?"

Mom laughed. "It's very funny, and a clever idea." She got another pair of scissors and started helping me.

I said, "Here's Dagwood. That's a good one for Dad. And we can put in Linus with his blanket, in case Mikey takes a picture of himself. I guess I'll have to be Sally or Lucy, even though they're too young. It's strange that there isn't anybody my age in the comic strips."

"Maybe you better put in Charlie Brown too. Mikey might not like being Linus."

"That's right. He might think Linus is too much of a baby." I gave her a sideways look. "Now, who do you want to be, Blondie? Or would you rather be Mary Perkins or Olive Oyl?"

She laughed again. "I don't know. I guess it depends on what mood I'm in."

"We'll put them all in and you can decide later. I think I'll put Prince Valiant and Rex Morgan, MD in the box for Dad." I grinned at her. "Then you can be the glamorous, June Gale, if you want."

"Put them all in. It'll make it more fun."

When all the cartoon characters were inside the box, Mom had the great idea of putting an elastic band around the whole thing. That way the pictures wouldn't fall out, and Mikey could flip the elastic against the box to make the clicking sound when he wanted to take a picture. We wrapped the camera in some leftover wrapping paper Mom had, and she put it inside a brown paper grocery bag and took it upstairs to hide.

While she was gone, Mikey came running in the house all excited. "I finished it, Bethy. I built a high wall all around my fort. Now the enemy can't get in."

"That's good, Mikey, but if you built the wall all the way around, how are you going to get in?"

"Oh, no. I didn't think about that. I've got to go make a door."

"You should wait until tomorrow. That way, nobody can get in tonight while it's dark."

Mikey thought about it for a second and decided that was a good idea. He went to take off his coat and boots. By the time he got back to the kitchen, Mom had come downstairs. We told Mikey our idea about making Christmas presents, and we all sat down to decide what to do next.

After a few minutes of us looking at each other, I said, "I know. Maybe we could make Dad some coupons that he can use to get things done."

Mikey said, "Like what things?"

"You know. One coupon could say, 'good for taking out the garbage,' and another one could say, 'good for a back rub.' We could think of all kinds of things, and then we could make the cards and decorate them."

Mom said, "I think he'd like that." She looked through a box of old Christmas cards we'd received from other people. "These might work." She cut the cards in half and handed Mikey and me the part with the pictures of Christmas trees and Santa Clause and the baby Jesus.

"That's great, Mom. They're already decorated. We can write our coupon message on the back where it's blank."

Mikey grabbed one of the cards and said. "I'm going to make a coupon that's good for a piggy back ride."

Mom and I both laughed. She said, "Are you going to ride him, or is he going to ride you?"

Mikey just looked at her like she was dumb.

After we finished making the coupons, Mom cleared some of the stuff off the table and said, "Okay, what else?"

Mikey and I shrugged.

"You could make your father a collage."

Mikey screwed up his face and said, "What's that?"

"You know, it's a picture made out of other pictures. For example, you could find pictures in old magazines and paste them together in a way that tells a story. I think I have some poster board somewhere."

I said, "What kind of story would we tell?"

"I don't know. How about something that will remind your father of us."

Mom found us the poster board and went upstairs to work on something else while Mikey, and I ran around the house gathering whatever old magazines we could find. They were mostly Ladies Home Journals, Life magazines, and Mom's old plant and flower catalogs.

Mikey started cutting out all the animal pictures he could find. I looked at them and shook my head. "We're supposed to make a story that reminds Dad of us. We don't have any dogs or cats or cows."

He frowned. "Then what am I supposed to do?"

"I've got an idea. See if you can find a big tree in the garden catalog, and I'll look through the Christmas cards for a picture of Jesus."

"Why do we need a tree?"

"Find one and I'll show you."

He found a big weeping willow tree, and I pasted it in the top left corner of the poster board and put the picture of Jesus I'd found in a church magazine up in the top branches.

"What's Jesus doing in the trees?"

"It's Dad's vision."

He gave me a look like he wasn't so sure he liked where the story was going, but when I told him to find me a little angel, he went back to work looking through the magazines and cards. We spent the next several hours finishing the whole story of everything that had happened.

It started to get dark. Mom came downstairs to fix dinner. When she saw our collage, she sat down at the table and spent a long time looking at all the pictures. She ran her finger over the face of the sad woman down in the corner. "Is this supposed to be me?"

I didn't think she liked it. I'd told Mikey he should have found a happier picture, but he said that Mom wasn't happy most the time so it wouldn't be real. He must have realized it was a mistake, because he put his hand over his mouth and waited to see what she would do.

Mom's eyes filled with tears as she ran her finger over the top of the other pictures. "You've made your father quite handsome, haven't you? I haven't noticed that for a while, but you're right. He is handsome." She stared at the picture representing Dad for a long time, but I got the feeling she wasn't really seeing it.

She moved her finger over to our picture of Brother Reuben and her eyes narrowed. She shook her head. "It's all here, isn't it? Even the baby with its little wings flying up to heaven." A tear ran down her cheek and dripped onto the collage. "We've been through a lot, haven't we? I'm sorry it's been so hard." She put her arms around us and hugged us while she cried.

Over the next few days, we were constantly making presents. We made cookies, taffy, bookmarks, and picture frames. We drove up to the mountains and got pine branches and decorated them with red bows, and we made Christmas tree ornaments out of pinecones that we painted white, and then glittered. I decided it was a lot more fun than going to the department store to shop for presents. But we did go down to the grocery store one day, and Mom picked out a small ham for Christmas dinner. She said she'd make mashed potatoes and homemade rolls to go with it, and she bought nuts for a pecan pie, even though they were way too expensive.

I was getting excited for Dad to come home. I just knew if he saw how nice everything was, he'd want to stay with us, even if the stupid polygamist church never got finished.

On Christmas Eve day, we were all on edge, wondering what time Dad would be home. Mom tried to keep us occupied with last minute cleaning. Then we took our baths, and Mom curled her hair, and then mine.

We were all feeling fidgety, and after a few minutes, Mom said, "Maybe we ought to play a game of Perquackey or something."

I said, "Oh, that would be fun."

Mikey said, "It's not fair. I don't know hardly any words."

"We'll help you, won't we, Mom?"

"You'll try to steal my words."

"That's ridiculous. You can't steal someone else's words."

"Yes you will. I know you will."

He stuck out his tongue at me, but Mom grabbed our hands and pulled us to the living room. "Sit," she said. Then she went to the game closet and got out the game of Perquackey.

We sat there shaking out the dice on the table and making up words until two-thirty in the afternoon, but Dad didn't come. Mom frowned and said, "Maybe I better put the ham in the oven."

At five o'clock, when the ham was all dried and shriveled up and the mashed potatoes were getting cold, Mom said, "We might as well go ahead and eat."

Halfway through the meal, the telephone rang. Mom answered and just kept repeating, "I see. I see."

I pulled on her arm. "Is he coming?"

She pushed me away and said, "What's wrong with it?" She closed her eyes and rubbed her forehead "Well, why didn't you let us know sooner, Michael? We've been waiting all day."

I kept looking at Mom trying to read what he was saying in her eyes, but she kept moving away from me. She looked so let down, I just knew Dad wasn't coming home.

When she hung up the phone, she turned and looked at Mikey and me. She didn't say anything for a minute while she tried to control her tears. Finally, she sat down on the loveseat and pulled us towards her. "I'm sorry. He's not coming."

"But why, Mom? He promised. Even you thought he was coming this time." I tried to blink back my tears, but I couldn't stop them. It was so disappointing, after everything we'd done to get ready. I couldn't understand how he could do that to us.

Mikey punched the arm of the loveseat, "I knew he wasn't coming. He's just a big stupid liar."

Mom took Mikey's hand and touched it against her cheek. "He couldn't help it, honey. He really did try this time. He started out early this morning, but then his truck stalled. He said he had to walk for hours to get back to where he's staying. Then he and Brother Reuben had to drive all the way back out and tow the truck in."

I said, "What's wrong with the stupid truck?"

"I don't know. He said it acted like the carburetor was gummed up. Like something got in the gas."

"But what could it be? How could that happen just when he was supposed to come home?"

"I wonder. It sounds fishy, doesn't it? And I don't know how he's ever going to get home if he doesn't have his truck."

"And what about all the presents we made? How are we going to give them to him?" I could hear myself whining, but I didn't care.

Mom rubbed her forehead again, as if she had a headache coming on. "I don't know."

Mikey kicked the wall. "I bet he never wanted to come home in the first place. I hate him."

That was more than Mom could take. She burst into tears and ran upstairs. Mikey ran outside and slammed the door.

Once again, everything was ruined. All the joy we'd had making presents and getting the house ready for Dad was completely gone. He wasn't going to see the collage Mikey and I made, and he wasn't going to get his coupons, or see the decorations. And there wasn't going to be any Christmas tree. It was all just a big stupid waste of time.

That night, I didn't say my prayers. I couldn't make myself talk to someone who didn't care what happened to us, someone who would let Dad's truck break down just when he was finally coming home.

Chapter 26

And you are to be equal, or in other words, you are to have equal claims on the properties . . .

Doctrine and Covenants
Section 82:17

*D*ad not coming home for Christmas put a cloud of despair over the house. We all got snappy and irritable with each other, especially Mom. She was so stressed by the fact that we didn't have any money, she'd yell at us if we asked for anything. I prayed Dad would come home, but Mom said, with the truck not working, it would be up to Brother Reuben to bring him. Evidently, that wasn't something Brother Reuben wanted to do. The situation just got worse and worse.

One day in February, the phone rang. I knew it was Dad; he was the only person who called anymore. I raced to answer it, but Mom got there first. After listening for a minute, she frowned and said, "That's all very nice, but when are you going to send some money?"

She plopped down on the loveseat and started jiggling her leg. "What do you mean, they haven't paid you? You said you'd send something last week . . . I know, but the bank account is empty. What am I supposed to do, borrow against the house to pay the bills?"

She listened to Dad for a minute more, then her face got red and she started yelling. "You did what?"

She jumped up and headed down the hall, pulling the phone cord after her. "If you got a second mortgage, then where's the money?" She jerked the cord so hard the phone jumped off the table. "That's insane, Michael. How could you do such a thing?"

I crawled over and put the phone back on the table, but I could see it wasn't going to stay there for long. Mom was madder than I'd ever seen her in my whole life. But she looked scared too.

She came back and sat down hard on the loveseat, taking a few deep breaths before she could talk again. "Michael, I know you believe in the Law of Consecration, but what are we going to live on?" She rubbed her forehead so hard it left red streaks across it. "If Brother Reuben isn't even willing to pay for your work on the church, why would he ever give us anything back? It's our money, Michael. It's all we had left. How could you give it to him?"

Her leg was jiggling again, and I was getting worried about what was going on. "Oh, right. You had to prove your loyalty. What about your loyalty to us? Did you ever think of that?"

She got up and leaned her head against the wall. "I don't know what to say. We haven't seen you in months, you've sent us nothing to live on, and now you're telling me everything we've worked for is gone."

She started banging her head against the wall. I jumped up to stop her, but she pushed me away.

"They'll take the house, Michael. How can we pay the second mortgage when we can't even pay the first? And what are we going to do when they turn off the phone and the electricity and the gas? You won't be able to call."

The phone was still at her ear, but I could tell she wasn't listening anymore. She blinked hard, trying to keep back the tears. Then she suddenly slammed down the phone without even saying goodbye.

"Oh, no, Mom. What did he do? "

"He's given away everything. He doesn't care about us, Beth." She looked frantic, but then her face changed to a look of disgust and she started mocking his voice. "We have to put our faith in God, Sharon. If we do what God says, He'll protect us and provide for us."

"What are we going to do?"

She reached toward me, but before I could respond, she turned and ran upstairs.

The next day at school, I could hardly concentrate on what Mrs. Jones was saying. I was too worried about Mom and the fact that Dad had given away all our money. When school was finally over, I ran all the way home and hurried into the house. "Mom, I'm home. Where are you?"

She didn't answer, and I couldn't find her anywhere, but I found Mikey sitting on the floor in the bedroom tearing holes in his homework assignment. "Where's Mom?"

"I don't know."

"Well, wasn't she here when you got home from school?"

"No."

"You mean you haven't seen her?"

"So what if I did? She wouldn't talk to me."

"Well, she isn't downstairs, and she isn't in her bedroom. What if she's gone away, Mikey? You should have kept a watch on her."

Before he could say anything, I heard a terrible sound coming from the bathroom. I ran down the hall and pushed open the door. Mom was on her knees in front of the toilet. She glanced over at me. "Oh, Bethy. I'm so sick."

That's all she could say before she had to throw up again. She started coughing and gagging and her whole body was trembling. I went to brush the hair out of her eyes, and I felt how cold and clammy her skin was. "Maybe you should get in bed, Mom."

She moaned and said, "I don't know if I can."

"You've got to. You can't stay here."

I got a clean nightgown and helped her put it on over her temple garments. Then I helped her in to bed and covered her up. I said, "Should I get you something to eat? Your stomach must be completely empty."

"I don't think I can keep it down, honey."

"How about some licorice tea? Could you drink that?"

"I don't know." She rolled over on her side and started to moan again.

"I'll make some and you can try it." I ran downstairs and put water on the stove to boil. Then I pulled over a chair to look on the top shelf where the licorice was supposed to be, but I couldn't find any.

I looked in the refrigerator for something else to give her, but there wasn't anything that would work. I desperately needed to talk to Dad to ask him what to do, but I didn't know how to call him. If only there was someone else I could call, but Mom had warned me not to let anyone know where Dad was and what he was doing for fear they'd excommunicate him. I slammed the fridge door, wondering what I was supposed to do.

I was getting really scared. We needed help, but there was no place to get it. Dad had said God would provide for us, but that didn't seem to be happening. Things were just getting worse and worse. Then I realized we'd never asked God for help. Since Dad left, we hadn't been doing much praying at all. Maybe that was the problem. Maybe we should ask God what to do.

I ran upstairs to find Mikey. He was lying on his bed with his arm over his eyes. I pulled at his arm and said, "Mikey, we've got to do something. Mom's sick, and the only thing I can think of is to pray for her." He put his head under the pillow and wouldn't come out.

"Come on, Mikey. We've got to do something." I dragged him off the bed, but when I got on my knees to pray, he just sat there staring at the floor with an ornery look on his face. I tried to fold his arms, but he let them go limp and fall back down in his lap. "At least close your eyes, Mikey. You can do that much."

He finally squeezed his eyes shut, and I started to pray, "Dear Heavenly Father. We desperately need your help. Please bless our mother and make her well and bring our father home. Life has been really hard for us. We need your blessings now more than ever. Please hear our prayer and provide for us, like Dad said you would. In the name of Jesus Christ, amen."

Mikey whispered amen too. We turned around and sat on the floor next to the bed looking at each other. I tried to sense if anything had changed, but everything felt the same.

Finally, we got up and went to Mom's room. She was still lying on her side moaning a little, but I thought she was asleep. I whispered to Mikey, "At least she's sleeping. Maybe that's a good sign."

When I got up the next morning, I went in Mom's bedroom first thing. She didn't look any better. In fact, I thought she looked worse. Her face was pale and sticky. When I touched her arm, she moaned and pulled her legs up closer to her chest. She opened her eyes just a slit, then closed them again.

She was getting thin, looking almost like Dad did when he was fasting all the time. She had dark circles under her eyes and her cheekbones pressed up beneath her skin. I realized I couldn't leave her alone. Mikey would have to go to school by himself.

I went back to the bedroom and woke Mikey up. He rubbed his eyes and grumbled. I got him a shirt and some pants from the closet and laid them on his bed. "You get dressed for school, while I make breakfast."

I hurried downstairs to look for something for him to eat, but I couldn't find anything. How could I make breakfast if there wasn't anything to make it with? I went through all the cupboards again, then I remembered the food in the closet under the stairs. Dad had said it was only for emergencies, but this seemed like an emergency to me.

When I looked in the closet, I found out that Mom had already been using the emergency food. There was hardly anything left except a few cans of string beans, some canned tomatoes, and a quart of bottled peaches that one of the women in the Ward had given Mom back when people were still talking to us. There were some other things, like cooking oil and sugar and powdered milk, mostly stuff you couldn't really eat. But I could use the powdered milk for Mikey's oatmeal, if I could just find some oatmeal.

I pulled out a gunnysack that was on the floor and wheat kernels came pouring out the bottom. It looked like a mouse had decided to have some of the wheat, but luckily he hadn't eaten it all. Maybe I could do something with that later.

I still hadn't found any oatmeal. I ran to the kitchen and got a chair so I could look on the upper shelves of the closet. In the very back, on the far side, I finally found one round box of Quaker Oats. It made me so happy, I almost cried.

By the time I'd finished making the oatmeal, Mikey still hadn't come down. I ran upstairs and found him back in bed asleep. But at least he was dressed. I dragged him off the bed and pulled him out of the room and all the way downstairs to the kitchen.

I put some oatmeal in a bowl, poured milk over it, sprinkled on a little brown sugar, and gave it to Mikey. He took a big spoonful, and immediately spit it back out in the bowl.

"What's wrong now?"

"The milk's sour."

"It can't be. I just made it."

"It tastes bad."

"It's the only milk we have, Mikey. It's just different because it's powdered. Try to taste the sugar."

"I don't like it." He sent the bowl sliding across the table and sat there with his arms folded across his chest.

I felt like slapping him, but I knew it wouldn't do any good. "Well, then what are you going to eat? You can't go to school hungry."

"Why can't I have toast and eggs?"

"Because there aren't any. Don't you understand? Mom hasn't been to the store in weeks. The refrigerator's empty."

He got up, ran over to the fridge, and pulled open the door so hard it hit the wall. I went and stood behind him and we both looked. There was half a jar of strawberry jam, a little bit of peanut butter, some ketchup and mustard, a few dill pickles, and some Miracle Whip. The only thing in the vegetable drawer was a piece of dried lettuce and two shriveled-up carrots. That was all we had.

Mikey grabbed the jar of strawberry jam. He took it back to the table and started eating it straight from the jar with his spoon.

"Wait a minute, Mikey. Don't eat all the jam yet." I'd remembered that Mom always kept extra bread in the freezer. Maybe there was some of that left.

I opened the freezer, but it was so full of snow and ice, it was hard to see what was in there. I got the spatula and scrapped off as much of the snow as I could. Then I got a sharp knife and chipped off some of the ice. Sure enough, I found a frost covered loaf of Jack Spratt Bread way in the back of the freezer. I didn't know how long it had been in there, but I didn't care. It would have to do.

When I set the frozen bread on the counter, Mikey ran over. "Oh, boy, we can have toast. Make me some toast, Bethy."

I took it out of the package and tried to pull the bread apart with my hands, but it was almost like it had never been sliced. I got the sharp knife and forced it down between the pieces. Finally, the heel popped off. After a minute, I got another piece free. I stuck them in the toaster while Mikey stood there with his jar of jam, waiting.

By the time we finished making the toast, it was already eight-thirty. Mikey was going to be late for school. I yelled, "Come on, get your jacket on. You've got to go now."

"But you're still wearing your nightgown."

"I'm not going."

"Why not?"

"I've got to look after Mom."

"Then I'm gonna look after her too."

"No, Mikey. You have to go to school."

I tried to lead him out of the kitchen, but he got down on the floor and wrapped his arms and legs around the table legs.

"Please, Mikey. Why can't you just do what you're told?"

He didn't say anything, but he wouldn't budge either.

"Okay, then, don't go. But I've got things to do, so don't expect me to play with you all day."

He crossed his eyes and stuck out his tongue. "Who wants to play with you anyways?"

I left him in the kitchen and went to check on Mom. I was shocked when I saw how her lips were all coated with white stuff. She needed to have something to drink. I whispered, "Mom, Are you awake?"

She opened her eyes a little. "Oh, Beth. Shouldn't you be at school by now?" Her voice was so weak I could barely hear her.

I sat down next to her. "I couldn't go. I'm too worried about you."

"I'm sorry. I don't know what's the matter with me. I'm so tired."

"You're probably just hungry, after throwing up. I tried to find you something last night, but there wasn't anything. Then you fell asleep, and I didn't know if I should wake you up or not."

"I should have something."

"I know, but nearly all the food's gone, even the stuff in the closet under the stairs."

"I'm sorry, honey. I've hardly had any money for groceries."

"But what are we going to do when everything's gone?"

She groaned and rolled over on her side, pulling her legs up to her chest. Seeing her all rolled up like that just about broke my heart. "Maybe we should call somebody, Mom."

"There's nobody to call."

"Maybe we could call, Mrs. Jones. She's always nice to me, and she's not a Mormon so she wouldn't try to get Dad excommunicated. I'm sure she'd help."

She moaned again. "No, don't do that."

"I'm sure she wouldn't mind."

"I don't want outsiders involved."

"But, Mom, we've got to do something."

She gave me a desperate look. "Please, honey. Just do what I say."

"Okay." I stroked her hand softly trying to comfort her. "It'll be okay. I know Dad will come and bring some money. Maybe he's on his way right now."

She opened her eyes and said, "There is no money. Don't you understand? It's gone. He's given it all to Brother Reuben." It shocked me how strong her voice was.

I was feeling completely hopeless when I remembered the peaches I'd seen with the emergency food. I told her I'd be right back and raced downstairs. It was hard to pry the lid off the bottle, but it finally came up. I got a big spoon and plopped one of the fat yellow peaches into a bowl along with some of the juice. Then I ran back upstairs to Mom. I rubbed her arm and she opened her eyes. "I found something for you to eat. I think you'll like it."

I helped her sit up and gave her the bowl. At first, she just tasted the juice, but that seemed to taste good and she tried a few tiny pieces of peach. I was happy to see her eat. "It's good, isn't it?"

She smiled a little. "It's the best peach I've ever had in my life." She licked her lips, ate a little more, and smiled again. When she'd finished eating everything in the bowl, she said, "Ahh, that was good. But it made me thirsty. Could you make me some hot water, honey? Maybe it will stay down better than cold."

When I got back down to the kitchen, I couldn't believe what I saw. Mikey had eaten the whole bottle of peaches. I was furious. "You little brat. Why did you do that?"

He looked at me like he was afraid I was going to hit him. "I was hungry, Bethy."

"But now what's Mom going to do? It's the only thing she can eat."

He whined. "I didn't know."

"Well, why didn't you ask? You're so stupid, Mikey. You're stupid and you're mean and you're selfish."

"I'm not either." His bottom lip started to quiver.

"Well, why can't you think about somebody besides yourself? You only care if you're hungry, even when Mom's sick and starving."

"It's not my fault." His eyebrows wrinkled, and I knew he was about to cry.

"Look, Mikey. Why don't you just go to your room? I don't have time to argue. I have to make Mom some hot water."

I put the water on the stove and looked back towards the table. I felt bad I'd said those things to Mikey, when he was hurting as much as me and Mom. His face was red, and he was squeezing his eyes open and shut, trying to keep his tears from falling.

I was about to tell him I was sorry when his face got mean. He picked up his spoon and threw it as hard as he could at the refrigerator door. It clanged and almost hit him in the face when it bounced back. I tried to grab him, but he pushed me away and ran out of the kitchen. I yelled, "You better mind your Ps and Qs, Michael Sterling."

When the water started to boil, I took a cup of it up to Mom. She had already gone back to sleep so I put it on the nightstand next to the bed. I set a piece of paper on top of the cup to keep it hot a little longer. I stood there watching her for quite awhile, wondering if she was dreaming, and if that was what made the expression on her face keep changing.

I went around the bed to the dresser and looked at the picture of her and Dad on the day they got married. They looked so happy then. Mom's wedding dress spilled out on the floor all around her feet. Her hair was pulled up, which made her neck look long and pretty. She'd told me that Dad gave her the pearls she was wearing. I wondered where the pearls were now and why she didn't wear them anymore.

Dad was a handsome man with his dark hair, and his dark suit, and his white shirt, and dark tie. He looked mischievous, like he had a secret. I looked at the picture for a long time, thinking about how good life used to be and wondering if we'd ever be happy again. I turned around and looked at Mom lying on her side with her face turned away from me. It made me feel so alone. I went over and carefully got on the bed and lay next to her. I just wanted to listen to her breathe and be close to her. She let out a little moan, and I held my breath so she wouldn't hear me and wake up. I wanted to hug her and tell her everything was going to be all right, but I didn't really believe that. Besides, she was sleeping and that was the best thing for her.

Chapter 27

. . . let there be a famine in the land, to stir them up in remembrance of the Lord their God, and perhaps they will repent and turn unto thee.

Book of Mormon
Helaman 11:4

*T*he days went by and Mom didn't get any better. Every day, I stayed home from school to take care of her. Mikey wouldn't go either. I expected the school to call to find out where we were, but they never did. I decided they didn't care if we went to school, just like the people in the Ward didn't seem to care if we went to church. It was as if we'd dropped off the edge of the world, and it didn't matter to anyone.

One morning, when I went in to see how Mom was doing, she opened her eyes and whispered, "Honey, I've made a terrible mess of myself. Can you help me change the sheets?" She looked miserable and something smelled really bad.

When I started to help her, she said, "First, you better get me a clean nightgown."

I got the nightgown and helped her sit up while we took off the dirty one. She tried to take off her temple garments, too, but she was having trouble undoing the little buttons.

"Let me help, Mom. My hands are smaller."

I undid the buttons, and when she pulled off the garments, the awful smell got worse. She must have messed in her garments because they were all brown between the legs. I hurried and rolled them up so she wouldn't have to look at them and be embarrassed.

She started to put on the clean nightgown, but I said, "Don't you want to take a bath first?"

"I don't feel very well, but I guess I should try."

I got the water going, then went back for Mom and helped her to the bathroom.

She sighed as she sank down into the warm water. "It feels nice, Beth. Thank you."

She closed her eyes and let out another long sigh. Her poor body was so thin, her breasts were sagging, and I could see her ribs. I wanted to stay with her to make sure she didn't fall asleep and slip down beneath the water, but I had to go clean up the bedroom.

I took everything to the laundry room and started the washer. As I was putting her garments in the water, I noticed there was quite a lot of blood mixed in with the brown stain. Oh no. Had she been bleeding down there, like when she lost the baby? But she couldn't be pregnant again, she was too thin. So what did it mean? Why was she bleeding?

I hurried and remade the bed and got back to the bathroom just in time. Mom was asleep and had slipped part way down into the water. I pulled gently on her arm. "Come on, Mom. Your bed's ready."

She opened her eyes slowly, as if she was waking up from a dream. "Oh, I guess I dozed off. The water was so soothing."

I was helping her back to bed when the phone rang. It got me all flustered, and I didn't know if I should go answer it or stay with her.

She said, "You better go see who it is."

I raced downstairs and grabbed the phone. For a minute, I didn't think there was anyone there, but then I heard Dad's voice. "Is that you, Beth?"

"Yes, Dad. It's me. It's Beth."

"What's going on, honey? You sound all excited."

"I'm not excited, I'm scared."

"Scared? Why what's wrong?"

"It's Mom. She's bleeding again."

"Bleeding? What do you mean?"

"I don't know for sure. She had diarrhea, and when I went to wash her garments there was blood there too. What does it mean, Dad? Does she need to go to the hospital again?"

"Was there a lot of blood?"

"Quite a bit."

"Well, Moms bleed sometime. It doesn't mean anything's wrong necessarily. It's just . . . part of how God makes women so they can have babies."

"I know about that, Dad, but this seems . . . different."

"Well, she hasn't mentioned any problem to me."

"But, Dad. She's really sick"

"What do you mean?"

"She's throwing up all the time."

"Throwing up? Why that could mean . . . Does she throw up in the morning?"

"She throws up all the time. It doesn't matter what time of day it is. Where have you been anyway? Why haven't you called?"

"I'm sorry, honey. It's hard to get to a phone, and I didn't think I should be making too many long distance phone calls given the situation."

"We have to be able to talk to you. If you don't call, how can I tell you that Mom's sick, and how can I tell you that there's hardly any food left."

"No food? Why wouldn't there be any food? Why didn't your mother tell me?"

"She did. She said we didn't have any money for anything after you gave it all to Brother Reuben. How are we supposed to buy food if there isn't any money?"

"Why didn't you use the three year's supply? It's there for emergencies. I thought you'd be using that."

"I told you it wasn't enough for three years when you put it there. It's practically gone. We can't just eat wheat and beans and powdered milk. That's the only kind of thing that's left."

"Where did it all go?"

"We ate it! It's all we had!" He was acting so casual about the whole thing, I couldn't stand it. He was probably down there with plenty to eat, while we were starving.

"I'm sorry, honey. I didn't know."

"You've got to come home, Dad. Why won't you come home? Don't you care about us anymore?" I started crying and I couldn't talk anymore. There was a sharp pain in my back between my wing bones that went all the way to the top of my head, and my chest felt like it was going to break open from the pressure that was building inside me. Then, all of a sudden, I couldn't breathe. I started gasping.

I could hear Dad shouting over the phone, "What's going on? Beth? Beth? Are you there?"

I tried to talk, but it was hard to get the words out. "I . . . can't . . . breathe."

"Why, what's wrong?"

"I . . . don't know."

"Now, I want you to listen to me, Beth. Do you hear me?"

"Yes." I gasped for another breath.

"I want you to concentrate . . . Beth? Are you listening?"

"Uhf." Was all I could say.

"I want you to breathe slowly. Let the air flow into your belly, not your throat, or your chest. Do you understand? Don't try to get a lot of air all at once, just breathe gently."

I tried to do what he said, but I started coughing and wheezing.

"Honey, listen to me. I want you to close your eyes and concentrate on your belly. I'll count to five and you let the air just come in slowly. Don't try to force it. Put your hand over your belly button so you can feel it pushing out with air. Now breathe in . . . one . . . two . . . three . . . four . . . five . . . six . . ."

I lay back on the loveseat and put my free hand over my belly. I closed my eyes and listened to Dad's voice. I tried to breathe in and out softly, like he said. At first, my throat felt closed off, and I had to gasp for air, but then it got a little easier.

Dad kept counting, "One . . . two . . . three . . . four . . ." Then he added other words. "You're doing fine, honey. That sounds good. Just keep breathing slowly. I'm coming home. I'll be there just as soon as I can. Everything's going to be fine. Just fine."

I wanted him to keep talking, to keep telling me he was coming home. His voice was comforting, and the more I listened, the more relaxed I got until finally my breathing was almost back to normal. I felt like I could just fall asleep listening to his voice.

Dad must have realized what was happening because he said, "Beth, are you all right now?"

I opened my eyes and sat up feeling a little woozy. "I think so."

"That's good. Now, do you think your mother can make it down to the phone?"

"She's too weak, Dad. I can hardly get her to the bathroom."

"Then we better not bother her. You tell her I'm coming home just as soon as Brother Reuben can bring me."

I felt my chest getting tight again. "But you've been saying that forever. When will he be able to do it?"

"I'll tell him it's urgent. I'll come soon."

"You've got to, Dad. Things are awfully bad. We need you."

"I need you too, honey." His voice cracked, and after a minute, he whispered, "I love you."

"Do you really? Mom said you didn't have time for us anymore."

"Of course I love you. I love you all . . . more than you'll ever know. Tell your mother that, will you? Tell her I'm coming home."

"I will, Dad. I'll tell her. But make sure you do."

I hung up the phone and went back upstairs. When I opened the door to the bedroom, Mom was leaning back against the headboard, waiting. "What did he say?"

"He's coming home."

"Oh, really? He said that?"

"He said he's going to tell Brother Reuben it's urgent."

She looked away. "I've heard that before."

"It's really true this time. I know it is. He said that he loves us and that he's going to come home. He didn't tell you himself because I told him you were too weak to make it downstairs."

"I see." She looked at me as if she didn't believe me.

"I told him you were sick and that you were bleeding."

"You said that?"

"Yes."

"What did he say?"

"He said something about God making you that way so you could have babies. Then he asked if you were throwing up in the morning."

"That sounds about right. That's all he's interested in."

"I told him I didn't think it was that kind of bleeding. He knows something's wrong. He's coming home, Mom. I'm sure of it this time."

She slid down and pulled the covers up to her chin. Then she rolled over on her side so she didn't have to look at me. Something I'd said had upset her. Didn't she want Dad to come home? I thought she'd be excited. But maybe she was just too sick and tired to be excited.

"Maybe if you eat something, you'll feel better, Mom. Should I see if I can find something?"

She shook her head and pulled the covers up over her nose. She still wouldn't look at me. "Dad really loves you, Mom. He misses you. He told me to tell you that."

She started to cry, covering up the sound of it with the blankets. I didn't know if she wanted me to stay with her or leave her alone. When she pulled the blankets over her head, I knew she didn't want me there. I went out and closed the door. I was disappointed about how she acted when I told her Dad was coming home. Maybe he *was* lying again, but why couldn't we be optimistic for at least a second? It couldn't hurt. If we believed him, maybe it would really happen.

The rest of the day, I couldn't stop listening for Dad. One time I was sure I'd heard a car in the driveway. I ran to the living room and pulled back the curtains, but all I saw was a flock of black crows scattering up into the sky from the bare branches of one of the apple trees. I wanted desperately for him to come home, and not knowing if he would really do it made it one of the longest days of my life.

Mikey didn't make it any easier. He'd been playing outside and came in the house yelling, "I'm hungry. I'm hungry."

I'd already told him there wasn't any food, but he started chanting, "I want ice cream. I want a cherry pie. Make me a hamburger, Bethy, or else I'm going to die of starvation."

I wondered if he knew he'd made a poem, but he didn't look like he knew it; he was just saying how hungry he was. "I already told you we don't have anything."

"But can't you at least make me a peanut butter and jam sandwich."

"We ate the last loaf of bread."

"I want one anyway. Please." He cocked his head to one side and gave me a charming smile, as if he thought that would help.

"It doesn't matter if you want one, because there's no way to make it. So please stop asking."

He sat down at the kitchen table and started pounding it with his fists, screaming, "I want one. I want one."

"Okay. Okay. Calm down. You'll wake Mom up."

He kept pounding his fists, so I got the nearly empty bottle of peanut butter from the refrigerator and went and got the last big can of honey from the closet under the stairs. Mikey sat and watched as I tried to pry the lid off the can with a knife. Every so often, he'd pound the table to make me move faster. When I finally got the lid off the honey, I got a plate from the cupboard and put a big spoonful of peanut butter in the middle of it. Then I covered the top of the peanut butter with honey and handed it to him with a spoon. "There."

He looked at me like he thought I was crazy. "That's not a sandwich."

"I know, but the only thing that's missing is the bread."

He started eating the no-bread sandwich. He put some of the peanut butter and honey in his mouth, chewed it a little bit, then stuck out his tongue with all the gooey mess on it. Then he started giggling. That got him coughing and sputtering, so I had to get him a drink of water to keep him from choking to death. "It serves you right for being so disgusting." I pretended like I was mad, but I was actually glad he was doing his old gooey tongue joke.

When Mikey got through eating and had gone upstairs, I tried to think of something I could fix Mom. It seemed impossible, but then, out of the blue, I remembered the root cellar. Maybe there would be something there. Maybe I could make her a baked potato. I don't know why I hadn't thought of it before, but then there were a lot of other things to think about.

I found a paper sack and put on my coat. When I got outside, I remembered another thing I'd forgotten. Brother Larsen's chicken coop. Maybe there were some eggs over there that nobody had found. I decided to go find out. I knew it would be stealing if I took them, but they'd probably just go to waste anyway. Besides Mom had to have something. Scrambled eggs might be the perfect thing.

On my way over to Larsen's place, I got nervous about getting caught, but then I remembered it was Sunday. Everybody would be at church. Still, I could see that my shoes were leaving deep tracks in the snow. If they discovered that there were some eggs missing, they'd know exactly where to look for the thief, but I had to do it anyway. As I walked across the barren field between our apple orchard and theirs, the cold gray sky seemed to press down towards the ground taking the oxygen out of the air. It made it hard to breathe. I shivered and pulled my coat tighter around me.

I came to the old walnut tree, on the borderline between our property and Larsen's, and saw a bunch of crows up in the top of the branches. Why were they hanging around all the time? They reminded me of the day Tommy and I came across the crow funeral. I didn't think these crows were having a funeral because they weren't making any noise. They just followed me from tree to tree, as if they wanted to see what I was going to do. I was glad they wouldn't be able to tell anyone that I was stealing eggs.

When I got to the chicken coop, I looked around to make sure nobody was watching, then I pushed back the gate and went in. The rooster and all the chickens came flapping toward me. I was afraid they were going to peck me, so I backed up holding the paper sack in front of my legs. I waved my hands to try to shoo them away, but it didn't help. I decided I had to be brave and ignore them. I walked all around the cage looking for eggs. I found a couple that were broken, and it looked like the chickens, or maybe the rooster, had been eating the brown shells. I looked some more and finally found one unbroken egg behind a board leaning up against the fence and another one under some straw in the corner. I hoped they hadn't been out there so long they'd frozen, or gone rotten.

The chickens continued to follow me around, pecking at the ground everywhere I went. They acted like they were starving. I tried to think if we had something I could feed them. Maybe if I fed them, it wouldn't be so bad that I took their eggs. But what did we have that they'd like? Then I remembered the big bag of wheat in the hall closet. It wasn't anything I knew how to cook, so I might as well feed it to the chickens.

I hurried out of the coop and closed the gate. I put one of the eggs in one corner of the sack, and the other one in the other corner, then rolled the whole thing up and held it in the middle so they wouldn't come together and break while I carried them. I ran all the way back to the house and put the eggs in the refrigerator.

As I dragged the bag of wheat out of the closet, the grains leaked out of the hole the mice had chewed in the corner. I just let it keep coming, then I got the broom and the dustpan to sweep it up. I dumped the grains into the paper sack. I was sure the chickens wouldn't mind a little dirt mixed in with their wheat.

Mikey had come downstairs and was watching me. "What are you doing with the wheat, Bethy? Are you going to make us some bread?"

"No, I don't know how to make bread. I'm going to feed the chickens."

"What chickens? We don't have any chickens."

"Brother Larsen's."

"Why do you have to feed them?"

"Because they're hungry, and I want to pay back the Larsen's for taking their eggs."

"Eggs? Oh, boy. Do we get to have scrambled eggs?"

"No, Mikey. The eggs are for Mom. Don't you even think about eating them."

He started to get that ornery look on his face, so I said, "Maybe you can help me find some more eggs. If we do, then you can have one too. But get your coat on, it's cold out there."

He grabbed his coat and followed me outside. We ran all the way back to the chicken coop. I had Mikey throw handfuls of wheat at the chickens, while I looked around for more eggs. I searched everywhere, but I couldn't find anything except more broken shells. Maybe the chickens were eating their own eggs, or maybe some of the Larsen boys had been in there having an egg fight, like I'd seen them do. When Mikey had thrown all the wheat, I promised the chickens I'd bring them more later, if I could.

We walked back toward the house until we got to the root cellar. I told Mikey I had to see if there were any potatoes. The snow on top of the board that covered the entrance was really deep, and I nearly froze my bare hands brushing it off. Then I had to pry around the edges of the board because it was frozen shut. When it finally came loose, a gust of cold air whooshed up into my face. It smelled like old stale dirt that was starting to rot.

Mikey pinched his nose and said, "Yuck. It stinks."

"I know. It's been closed up too long."

I was nervous about going down there into the cold and dark. I knew there would be spiders and maybe even rats. I should have brought a flashlight, but there was a little bit of light going down into the pit from the entrance, so I decided it would be okay. I climbed slowly down the ladder into the little room below. When I got to the bottom, I had to stay in one place and wait while my eyes adjusted to the dark. It reminded me of how scared I'd gotten thinking about our little dead brother inside his coffin, and it scared me all over again.

I kept looking up at the light to make myself feel better, but every time I did that, it only made it darker when I looked back inside the cellar. I thought about what Brother Reuben said to Mom that day, about falling into the pit of hell, and how Mikey and I were going to go there with her. Was the pit of hell like this? All dark and cold and musty? Or was it burning with fire like the Bible said?

Maybe I shouldn't have stolen the eggs. Maybe I'd be punished. I knew it wasn't right, but what were you supposed to do if someone you loved was starving? I knew I'd convinced myself it was all right because I wanted to help Mom. But maybe in the eyes of God stealing was bad no matter what reason you had for doing it. Maybe I really was going to go to hell like Brother Reuben said.

I looked up and saw Mikey's head floating above me in the light. I wanted to be back up there with him. The sickening smell of the rotting dirt was filling up my lungs. It was suffocating. I started to gasp for air. I was about to get out of there when I remembered Dad saying, "Breathe slowly, Beth. Breathe deep down in your belly. One . . . two . . . three . . . four . . ."

I pulled some of my shirt out of the top of my coat, covered my nose and mouth with it, and tried breathing gently down into my belly. When I could breathe a little better, I felt my way over to the long box against the wall where the potatoes and carrots were supposed to be buried.

I didn't think Dad had put any vegetables down there during the fall. He'd been too busy reading scriptures and meeting with Brother Reuben, but maybe there'd be some good ones from the year before. I swept back the straw and pushed my hands down into the cold dirt.

I knew spiders loved to live in places like that, and it was too dark for me to see them if they came out. It smelled even worse there than over by the ladder, like there was mold growing in the dirt. I held my breath and reached deeper.

I found lots of round lumps, but when I squeezed them, they broke up, so I knew they weren't potatoes. I kept squeezing the dirt until I got over to the edge of the box. Then I felt something hard. It was more like the shape of a carrot than a potato. I put it in the sack and felt around for more. I leaned over and something tickled my face. I jumped back and tried to brush it away, but when I moved my head, there was more of it. It had to be cobwebs. I was feeling frantic, but I had to see if there were any more carrots. I forced myself to keep squeezing the dirt until I found two more carrots and four potatoes, but after that there wasn't anything else.

I folded over the top of the sack and scrambled up the ladder as fast as I could. When I came out into the open, I took a huge gasp of fresh air.

Mikey started giggling. "You look like a Halloween monster, Bethy."

"I do?"

"You've got dirt all over your face and dirty black spider webs in your hair."

"Quick, Mikey. Make sure there aren't any spiders." I bent over and shook my head.

He stood back and leaned towards me. "Hold still or I can't see."

I put my head down farther and held it still, but he wouldn't get very close, so I didn't know if there were any spiders there or not. When I lifted my head, I was shocked at what I saw. Mom was sitting on the steps over by the back door. She only had her nightgown on. She was trying to wave at me, but it seemed like she could barely lift her arm. I yelled, "Hurry, Mikey. Bring the sack."

I raced across the yard, yelling, "Mom, what are you doing out here? Why aren't you in bed? You're going to freeze."

"Oh, Beth. Where were you? I thought something was wrong. I called and called, but nobody came. I thought something terrible had happened. Why did you leave, Beth? Why didn't you tell me where you were going?" Her face was all wet, but I couldn't tell if she'd been crying, or if it was sweat on her face. I felt really bad for leaving her, but how could I know she would wake up?

"We were just looking in the root cellar to see if there was anything for you to eat."

Mikey pulled one of the carrots out of the sack so she could see.

"You should have told me, Beth. I was worried sick."

"I'm sorry. I thought you were asleep."

"Even if I was asleep, you should have told me where you were going. Don't ever do that again!"

"I said I was sorry. I was thinking you were going to starve if you didn't get something to eat. You've got to get inside, Mom. It's too cold out here."

She leaned back against the door and closed her eyes. She seemed too exhausted to move. Finally, she opened her eyes. "I'm sorry. I feel so worthless. I should be taking care of you, not the other way around."

"But you're sick, Mom. How can you?"

"I've got to pull myself together." She held onto the door frame and tried to pull herself up, but she couldn't do it. Mikey and I got on each side of her and helped.

Once we were inside, we let Mom rest on the loveseat for a few minutes. Then we helped her upstairs and put her back to bed. When she was settled, I said, "I'm going to make you a scrambled egg and a baked potato. By the time Dad gets home, you'll be feeling a lot better."

She just moaned and pulled the covers up around her neck. I ran downstairs to start cooking.

Chapter 28

The man has brought upon himself his misery; therefore I will stay my hand, and will not give unto him of my food, nor impart unto him of my substance that he may not suffer, for his punishments are just--

Book of Mormon
Mosiah 4:17

*T*hat night in bed, I kept whispering to myself, "He's coming home. Dad's coming home. He's coming home, and we'll all be okay." I tried to believe what I was saying, but there were questions that wouldn't go away. Even if he did come home, would he stay with us? Or would he try to take us back to the desert with him? If that's what he wanted, would Mom go? I couldn't imagine that she would. If she didn't, would he go back by himself? Or would he tell Brother Reuben he'd have to finish his church by himself? I worried about the money, too. Mom didn't believe Brother Reuben would give us anything back, so how were we going to buy food and pay the bills, even if Dad did come home? My biggest question was about Mom. Would she get better if Dad came home?

The next morning, I heard a tentative knock on the front door. I thought it had to be Dad, but why would he knock at his own house? When I opened the door, Tommy was standing there. I couldn't believe it. "Oh, Tommy, where have you been?" I hurried outside, pulling the door closed so Mom wouldn't hear us and wake up.

"I got kicked off the bus. When I was walking home, I saw your teacher, Mrs. Jones. She asked me why you hadn't been in school."

"I wondered why she never called to find out."

"She said she'd heard you went down south with your father, so I came over to see if it was true. But I didn't really think you'd go away without telling me."

"Dad went down to the desert to build Brother Reuben's stupid church. He left us here, and now Mom's sick and all the money's gone. We don't even have anything to eat."

"What? Why didn't you tell me?"

"How could I? You don't have a telephone, and I couldn't leave the house because there's nobody else to take care of Mom. That's why I couldn't go to school."

"Why didn't you call somebody in the Church?"

"Mom wouldn't let me."

"That's crazy. Why not?"

"She's afraid they'll excommunicate Dad if they find out where he is and what he's doing."

"Would they?"

"The Bishop said he would. I think Mom's trying to pretend we're not here so they won't do it. Oh, Tommy, I don't know what's wrong with her. She just keeps throwing up, and sometimes she has diarrhea, and she's been bleeding. She can't even get out of bed. I keep trying things, but I don't know how to fix her. I'm scared, Tommy. I'm really scared." I started to cry.

He put his arm around me. "Come on, let's sit down."

We sat on the edge of the porch. I couldn't talk because of crying, and I guess Tommy didn't know what to say to comfort me. We just sat there looking out at the front yard. I was amazed to see how much of the snow had melted, even though it was only March. I hadn't even noticed that the weather was changing.

A robin flew down and hopped towards us pecking around in the grass. Tommy touched my arm. When I looked at him, he crossed his eyes and tilted his head from side-to-side so that he looked just like the bird. Then he got up and waddled around the grass, lifting up one leg and then the other real quick, as if he had spindly bird legs. It was just a silly little act, but it made me laugh so hard I started crying again. Tommy came back and sat next to me. He put his hand on my leg to comfort me.

"Oh, Tommy. I've missed you so much."

"I've missed you too, Beth. We used to have some good times together, didn't we?"

"I don't know what's happened to me. It almost feels like a sin to laugh."

Tommy shook his head and looked away like he was disgusted with the whole situation. "When's your bad old dad supposed to come home?"

"I don't know for sure. I told him about Mom this morning. He said he'd come right away, but Mom doesn't believe him."

"Well, if your mom doesn't believe him, we'd better do something ourselves."

"But what?"

"I don't know. Let me go see if I can figure something out."

"But you just got here."

"Don't worry. I'll be back." He got up to go, but then looked back with a concerned look on his face. "Will you be okay?"

"I don't know. I really need you, Tommy. More than I've ever needed anyone."

He squeezed my arm, and then he took off across the lawn. He turned around once to wave just before he disappeared into the apple orchard. I didn't know what he could do for us, but I was glad that there was finally somebody who wanted to help. We'd been on our own for so long it seemed like the whole world had forgotten us.

I didn't want to go back in the house, so I sat on the porch and looked around the yard to see what I'd been missing. Although the snow was almost gone, the apple trees were still just bare limbs sticking up against the gray sky. They seemed so forlorn without their leaves. The walls of Mikey's fort had almost all melted away. When did that happen? I guess I hadn't been noticing anything, except for how sick Mom was, and how hungry Mikey was, and how empty the house was without Dad.

When I finally went back in, I found Mikey standing in front of the refrigerator, like always, looking for something to eat. I said, "You're going to have to wait until Dad comes. Maybe he'll bring some food."

"I'm hungry now." He slammed the refrigerator door.

"Then eat some honey. I'm going upstairs to check on Mom."

He opened the refrigerator and slammed it shut again.

As I left the kitchen, I said, "It doesn't matter how many times you slam the refrigerator door. There still won't be any food in it."

A few hours later, I was staring at the clock, wondering why the hands didn't seem to be moving, when I heard someone at the front door again. This time I knew it just *had* to be Dad, but when I swung open the door, it was Tommy again. He was carrying a big paper sack, and this time, Mrs. Jones was with him. I was so relieved to see her, I wrapped my arms around her and said, "Mrs. Jones, I'm so glad you're here."

"I'm sorry I didn't come sooner, Beth. Some of the children said your family had gone down south. But when Tommy told me about your mother, I knew I had to come right away. Why didn't you let me know how sick she was, honey?"

"She wouldn't let me. I thought maybe you'd call, but you never did."

"I did call, but nobody answered. I thought it must be true that you'd gone with your father."

"I must have been in the bathroom with Mom. She's always in there throwing up."

Tommy grunted. "Can I put this bag down somewhere? It's heavy."

I looked in the sack. "What did you bring?"

"It's food. I didn't want you to starve while you were waiting for your dad, so I got some stuff from my house."

I led him and Mrs. Jones into the kitchen where Tommy set the bag down on the table. "This is all we had right now, but I'll bring more after my mother goes to the store. Here's some bread." He pulled out a long loaf of Wonder Bread. It wasn't the kind of bread we usually ate, but that kind of thing didn't matter when you were starving.

Next, he pulled out a package of Saltine crackers and a bottle of Seven Up, saying, "My mother thought these might help settle your mom's stomach."

Mrs. Jones touched my shoulder. "How long has your mother been sick, dear?"

"It seems like forever."

"Maybe I should talk to her. Would she mind?"

"I don't know. She was asleep last time I checked, but maybe she's awake now."

"You better ask her if it's okay if I come up."

I ran upstairs. Mom was still asleep, but I rubbed her arm until she opened her eyes. "Mom, Mrs. Jones is here. She wants to talk to you."

She opened her eyes a little more. "What did you say? Who's here?"

"It's Mrs. Jones. She's downstairs. She wants to talk to you."

"Why is she here? I thought I asked you not to call her."

"I didn't. Tommy brought her. He came over this morning to find out why we weren't in school, and I had to tell him. Then he told Mrs. Jones. He only wanted to help, Mom. He brought us some food too. It's in the kitchen."

"Well, I guess I'd better talk to her, but I don't know if I can make it downstairs. She'll have to come up here." She struggled to sit up in bed. "Oh, dear. I must look a sight. Get me a comb."

I ran and got her comb and mirror from the dresser. She tried to pull the comb through her hair, but it was full of knots. She tried a few more times and gave up. "Get my bathrobe, Beth."

I ran to the closet and brought back her pretty blue terry-cloth robe. I helped her put it on and tie the belt. Then I went down to get Mrs. Jones.

Tommy said he'd wait in the kitchen.

I led Mrs. Jones upstairs. When she saw Mom, she put her hand over her mouth and gasped. "Oh, my."

Mom said, "I'm sorry. I know I'm a mess."

"Oh, no. Don't worry about that, dear. It's just that you're so thin. You must have been sick for a long time."

"I haven't had much of an appetite, and now I've got this nausea. I can't seem to keep anything down."

Mrs. Jones looked upset. "You know, Mrs. Sterling, I don't want to intrude, but I think you should see someone. Do you have a family doctor?"

"Yes, Doctor Wilson. But he's all the way down in Midvale. I don't think I can drive there right now."

"You most certainly cannot drive. Don't you have a friend who can take you?"

Mom looked down at her lap. "I'm afraid I'm a little short on friends right now."

"I see. Well, I'll take you then."

Mom looked alarmed. "Oh, no. That's not necessary."

"But it's plain to see you need help."

"That's very kind of you, but . . . my husband is on his way home. He should be here any time. Isn't that right, Beth?"

I could see Mom was desperately looking for an excuse, so I said, "It's true, Mrs. Jones. I talked to him a few days ago. He said he'd come just as soon as he could."

The conversation was making Mom tired. She slumped back against the headboard, trying hard to keep her eyes open.

"I don't know, Mrs. Sterling. I don't think I can leave you like this in good conscience. And what about the children? It's a lot of responsibility for them. They must be worried to death about you."

"I appreciate your concern, Mrs. Jones, I really do, but I think I'd like to wait to see if my husband returns. He'll probably come this weekend. Maybe, if that doesn't happen . . ." Mom grabbed her stomach for a second, and then tried to pretend like she hadn't done it. She forced herself to smile a little.

Mrs. Jones sat down on the edge of the bed and touched Mom's arm. She spoke softly, "Why won't you let me help you?"

Mom shook her head. "I'm sorry . . . you're so kind . . . I just don't know how I'd . . . I'm sorry." She turned away and started to cry.

Mrs. Jones looked at me, but I didn't know what to say. Mom obviously didn't want to go to the doctor with her. I said, "She probably doesn't feel good enough to go anywhere in the car. Maybe she's afraid it will make her throw up. Or maybe she's afraid Dad will come home, and he won't know where we are. Is that it, Mom? Is that why you don't want to go?"

"Yes, that's it, Beth. He wouldn't know where to find us."

Mrs. Jones must have decided not to try to convince her anymore. "Can I at least pick you up some things from the grocery store? Tommy brought a few things from his house, but that won't last long. How about if Beth and I make a list?"

Mom nodded and touched Mrs. Jones' hand. "Thank you. I'm sorry to be so much trouble."

"Don't worry about that for a second. I'll stop by tomorrow after school and bring you some things. Will that be all right?"

"I guess so." Mom relaxed a little.

"And then, if your husband isn't home by Monday, we'll get you in to see your doctor, okay?"

"Yes, okay. Thank you."

"All right then. Beth, come down and help me make a grocery list." She squeezed Mom's hand. "You take care of yourself, dear. I'm going to give Beth my home phone number, just in case you need anything tonight."

Mom squeezed her hand back. "I don't know how to thank you."

"I'm just glad I found out what was going on here. We've got to get you fixed up. That's all that matters." She stood up. "Ready, Beth?"

We went downstairs. Tommy, Mrs. Jones, and I sat down at the kitchen table and made a shopping list. I told her Mom might like some chicken noodle soup, and maybe some more peaches, and Jell-O would be good too. "And don't forget peanut butter and jam for Mikey, and maybe some tuna fish and bananas, and some more bread and eggs."

I realized my list was getting big, but it was just because we'd been hungry for so long. I wanted to have something Mom could eat and something Mikey would like too, but I didn't know for sure how much all those things would cost. I turned to Mrs. Jones. "I'm just giving you some suggestions, but maybe it's too much. I'm sure that whatever you get will be fine."

She gave my arm a squeeze. "Don't worry about that. You've got enough to worry about."

When we finished making the list, Mrs. Jones wrote down her phone number and left. Tommy and I walked out to the backyard. I said, "I wish Mom would have let Mrs. Jones take her to the doctor."

"Maybe she can't afford it. That's why we never go. My father thinks it's a waste of money."

"Maybe that's the reason. But if something isn't done soon, I don't know what's going to happen to her. "

"Hell, if your Dad doesn't come, me and Mrs. Jones will take her to the doctor ourselves."

"But how could you pay for it?"

"I don't know, but we're not going to let her just lie there and die."

"Oh, no. Why did you say that? Do you really think she's going to die?"

"No, I was just saying we can't let things get worse. We've got to do something."

"But what if she does die, Tommy? What if she can't ever keep anything down? Won't she eventually starve?"

"That's not going to happen. I promise." He gave me a quick hug and took off across the back lawn. I wanted to believe what he said, but I wished he hadn't said that about her dying. I couldn't stop thinking about it the rest of the day. What would we do without Mom?

Chapter 29

And whosoever among you are sick, and have not faith to be healed, but believe, shall be nourished with all tenderness, with herbs and mild food, and that not by the hand of an enemy.

Doctrine and Covenants
Section 42:43

*T*hat afternoon, Mikey and I took a picnic up to Mom's bedroom. We sat in a circle on the bed. She had soda crackers and Seven Up, while Mikey and I ate peanut butter and jam sandwiches on Wonder Bread. After being hungry for so long, it seemed like a feast made for a king. Suddenly, Mickey's eyes got real big. I turned around to see what he was staring at and saw Dad. We hadn't even heard him come in.

I was shocked by the way Dad looked. His hair had gotten long and he was growing a beard like Brother Reuben's. Mom looked up and let out a little gasp. She clapped her hand over her mouth.

I said, "Geez, Dad, why didn't you say something. You scared us."

"I wanted to get a good look at you all before I broke in." He hurried over and sat on the edge of the bed next to Mom. I could tell he was shocked by how she looked. "Why didn't you tell me how bad things were, honey?"

Mom shook her head and looked away.

I said, "I told you she was sick."

Mom still didn't say anything, but she reached out, touched his beard, and then quickly pulled her hand away.

Dad laughed a little. "Oh, I'd almost forgotten about that. I guess I look a little different, huh?" He tugged on the end of his beard, and then he gently touched Mom's cheek. "I came as soon as I could, but you don't seem very happy to see me."

"I can't quite believe you're here. It's been so long, Michael." She really *didn't* look very happy, and neither did Mikey. He had crawled off the bed and was peering over the edge of the mattress at Dad. I tried to get him to come closer, but he wouldn't do it.

"You know I'd have come home if I'd known what was happening here."

"Beth told you I was sick."

"I know. I came as soon as I could after she told me. But why didn't you tell me before?"

I didn't like the way Mom was acting. She was going to make Dad think we didn't want him there. I couldn't let that happen. "We're all glad to see you, Dad. It's just that Mom's been sick for so long it's hard for her to be happy about anything."

"I can see that. It hurts me to see you like this, Sharon. What is it? What's wrong?"

Mom started to cry, and Dad wrapped his arms around her. "Tell me what's going on, honey. Can't you?"

"Something's wrong, Michael. It hurts really bad."

"What hurts?"

"I don't know. I've got this aching pain in the left side of my abdomen, and I'm sick all the time. I can't stop throwing up. I need help. Please, help me." Her tears seemed to be making it hard for her to breathe, and she was gasping for air.

Tears ran down Dad's face too. "I'm sorry, honey. I didn't know."

Pretty soon all of us were crying, except Mikey. He was staring at his hands and biting his lower lip so hard I was afraid he was going to make it bleed.

Dad gently wiped away Mom's tears. "You need a blessing, Sharon. It's obvious we need the Lord's help with this. I'll go now and call someone to join me."

Mom grabbed his arm. "Michael, I--"

"It's okay. Everything's going to be fine." He hurried out of the room before anyone could stop him.

Mom got a wild look on her face and struggled to get out of bed.

"What's wrong, Mom? Are you going to throw up?"

She pushed me aside and put her feet on the floor. She stood and tried to make it to the door, but she must have gotten dizzy because she stopped and held herself up against the bedpost.

"Where are you trying to go, Mom? Can't I help you?"

She gasped, "Don't let him do it, Beth. Tell him . . ." She tried to make it to the door again, but she was too weak. She held herself up against the wall for a minute, and then slowly sank to the floor.

I got down next to her. "Please, Mom. Get back in bed. I'll tell him whatever you want. What do you want me to say?"

She started to sob. Everything was such a mess. I thought things would be better when Dad got home, but Mom was even more unhappy than before.

Dad came back in the room. "I called Brother Reuben. He'll be right here." When he saw us on the floor, he said, "What in the world are you doing down there?"

Mom tried to get up, but she only made it to her knees. "How could you do that, Michael? I don't want that man to bless me. I don't want him in this house."

Dad helped her up and carried her back to the bed. He covered her up with the blankets and sat down next to her. "Now don't be like that. We need him. We need the full power of the priesthood. I can't bless you by myself."

"But, Michael, I don't need a blessing. I need a doctor. Please." She was sobbing again.

Dad put his hands on her shoulders. "You've got to have faith, my love. The Lord will heal you if you believe in him. We don't need doctors and medicine or . . . that sort of thing. We need faith. Now, try to calm yourself. It can't be good for you to get so worked up."

He took her hands in his, stroked them gently. Then he held them to his lips and kissed them over and over. Mom seemed to relax a little. She closed her eyes and made a little whimpering sound. Dad smiled. "There, that's more like it."

After a few minutes, he whispered to me, "Elizabeth, take your brother downstairs and wait for Brother Reuben. You can show him upstairs when he comes."

Mikey was still hiding behind the mattress. I grabbed him by the hand and pulled him out of the room.

When we got downstairs, Mikey said, "If he blesses her, she'll get more sick."

"What do you mean? Why would Dad want to make her sicker?"

"Not, Dad. Brother Reuben. He's the Devil. The Devil hates people. He only wants to hurt them."

"I know, Mikey, but what are we going to do? If we turn against Dad, he'll just go away again."

"I don't care."

"You do too."

"No, I don't."

"What are you going to eat if Dad isn't here to take care of things and make the money to buy food?"

"Nobody wants him to work anyways."

We heard a knock at the door, and Mikey ran for the stairs. He was scared of Brother Reuben, and so was I, but I had to let him in. When I opened the door, Brother Reuben gave me a creepy smile and said, "Oh, there you are, little Sister. I've been wondering when I'd see you again."

He reached for my arm, but I knocked him away. "Dad said to come to the bedroom."

I ran up the stairs ahead of him so he couldn't get too close. When we got to the bedroom and Dad saw Brother Reuben, he jumped up and hurried across the room. "Thank you, Brother. Bless you for coming so quickly."

He shook Dad's hand, but he was scrutinizing Mom. "We move quickly when the Lord's blessing is needed."

Dad asked if he'd brought the consecrated oil, and Brother Reuben pulled a small blue bottle out of his pocket. "It's already been blessed."

"Thank you, Brother."

Mom had pushed herself up so that she was sitting against the headboard with the covers pulled up tight around her neck. She looked so small and fragile compared to Dad and Brother Reuben. It seemed like they could break her in two if they weren't careful.

Brother Reuben went closer to the bed and leaned over Mom. "I'm sorry to hear you've been ill, Sister Sharon."

Mom glared at him.

He cleared his throat and straightened up. "Well, should we get on with it?"

Dad sat down on the edge of the bed next to Mom. "Do you think you can sit in a chair if I get one? I think it would be easier to give you the blessing that way."

She shook her head and pushed him away. Dad went downstairs and brought up a chair anyway. He set it a little ways from the bed, and then went back for Mom. She pulled the covers up even higher. "I'd like my bathrobe."

"Elizabeth, get your mother's robe."

I got it out of the closet. As I handed it to her, she frowned at Brother Reuben. "Do you mind?"

He turned his back, and I helped her put the robe on. After Dad got her over to the chair, she started pulling her fingers through her hair. "It's such a mess. I can't seem to get a comb through it."

"That matters not to the Lord, Sharon. We are here to bless you, not judge you." Dad looked around the room. "Where's your brother, Elizabeth?"

"I don't know."

"Well, go find him, please. I think we should all be here. We need everyone's help."

I ran to our bedroom, but Mikey wasn't there. I looked in the bathroom, then I went downstairs and looked in every room. I even looked in Dad's study, although I knew he'd never go in there. I went outside and ran around the whole house, but he wasn't there either. Where in the world could he be?

I hurried back in the house and stood in the middle of the living room trying to think of some place I'd missed. The only place I hadn't checked was the laundry room. I ran back upstairs and threw open the door. I couldn't see Mikey anywhere, but I thought I heard a muffled noise in the dirty clothes cupboard, so I pulled open the door. At first, I wasn't sure he was in there. Mom hadn't done the laundry for so long there was a ton of clothes. I pushed some of them aside, and there he was. He had his hands over his face, like he thought I couldn't see him if he couldn't see me. I pulled on his arm. "Mikey, Dad wants you to be there for Mom's blessing. He says he needs your help."

"I'm not going."

"Please, Mikey. Everyone's waiting."

"No."

"Mom's sitting in the chair, Mikey. She can't sit there forever. It will only make her sicker if she has to wait. You don't want that to happen, do you?"

"No."

"Okay, then. Come on."

I moved back, and Mikey crawled out. I pushed the dirty clothes back in the cupboard, grabbed Mikey's hand, and hurried him into the bedroom.

I could tell Dad was upset that we took so long coming, but he just said, "Why don't you two sit up there on the bed."

The men stood on either side of Mom, and Brother Reuben handed Dad the little bottle of oil. He opened it, carefully poured some on his fingers, and then set the bottle on the nightstand. Mom had her eyes closed, but she wrinkled up her forehead when Dad started to rub the oil there. The wrinkles deepened when they both put their hands on top of her head and Dad started to pray. "In the name of Jesus Christ, and by authority of the Holy Melchizedek Priesthood, I lay my hands upon your head and anoint you with this consecrated oil which has been dedicated for the blessing of the sick. Sister Sharon Sterling, we ask that you open your heart and allow the Lord's blessing to enter. Let your faith grow. Let your bosom swell with the presence of the Holy Spirit, that the Lord may bless you and make you whole."

Dad finished praying and opened one eye. He nodded to Brother Reuben who cleared his throat and began his part of the prayer. "Sister Sharon Sterling, in the name of Jesus Christ, and by the authority of the holy Melchizedek Priesthood, we seal and confirm upon you this anointing. I say unto you, if you desire the Lord's blessing, you must renew your promise to honor and obey your husband. Humble thyself before the Lord, Sister, and begin this very day to follow each and every one of His covenants, then surely thy sorrows shall be washed away. But if you heed not my words, surely you shall feel the Lord's wrath upon you, and you shall be punished, even unto the end of your days. I say these things in the name of Jesus Christ, amen."

I watched as Mom shrunk beneath Brother Reuben's words. When the prayer was over, Dad pulled him to the other side of the room and whispered, "Why did you say those things, Brother? This is no time to proselytize. She needs comfort not threats of retribution."

Brother Reuben didn't even try to lower his voice. "Don't blame me. It was the Holy Spirit speaking through me. The Lord is mightily disturbed by her attempts to interfere with your work." He walked over to Mom and shook his finger in her face. "Follow the Holy Spirit's admonitions, and you will be healed, Sister. Do not, and you shall continue to be punished."

She tried to hit Brother Reuben, but her hand only struck air, and she nearly fell out of the chair. Dad ran over and helped her back to bed. "I'm sorry, honey. I didn't know he was going to say those things." He turned around and glared at Brother Reuben. "I think you'd better go now."

Brother Reuben turned on Dad. "Don't be pulled in by her, Brother. We know from experience that she will do whatever she can to dissuade you from your work. Remember you are weak when it comes to your wife. This illness is surely a ploy."

Dad took Brother Reuben's arm and jerked him out of the room. A few minutes later, I heard him drive away.

When Dad came back up, Mom was sobbing. He put his arms around her and tried to comfort her, but she couldn't stop.

I whispered to Mikey, "Come on, we should let them be alone."

Once we were outside in the hall, Mikey turned to me with his hands on his hips. "I told you he was the Devil."

He was right. The whole blessing was a disaster. I couldn't believe what Brother Reuben had said. Sometimes it felt like he really was the Devil. If he was, then what would his blessing do to Mom? Would it make her sicker like Mikey said?

Mikey pulled on my sleeve. "Look."

"What?"

"I've got the cons-crated oil." He took the lid off the little blue bottle and sniffed it. Then he poured a little bit on the end of his finger and tasted it. "Yuck. It tastes just like regular oil."

I put some on my finger and tasted it too. Mikey was right again. It was just plain olive oil. How could olive oil make Mom better?

Chapter 30

But, behold, faith cometh not by signs, but signs follow those that believe.

Doctrine and Covenants
Section 63:9

*T*he next morning, while Mom was still asleep, Dad ran up to the mailbox to get the mail. When he came back, he had already opened the envelopes. He had a troubled look on his face.

I said, "What's wrong, Dad?"

"It's nothing."

"Are you worried about the bills?"

"There's nothing to worry about. The Lord will provide for us."

"How? Is He going to send us some money in the mail?" I knew it was a smart aleck remark, but I didn't really believe God could take care of things that way anymore. Maybe he could help Dad get a job, but that would mean the people in the Ward would have to change their mind about him.

"The Lord works in His own way. Sometimes He tests us before He opens a path through which our problems can be solved. We have to trust Him. We have to believe that He knows what is best for us."

"But what if Mom doesn't get better? What if she just keeps getting sicker? How long are we supposed to wait?"

"Until we know God wants us to do something different."

"But how will we know that?"

"He'll give us a sign if we keep our hearts open to the Holy Spirit." He went into his study with the bills and left me standing there..

I hoped Dad was right about God. I didn't understand why He would give Mom a test and then make her wait after she'd already been sick for so long. Why couldn't He just make her better? Why did she have to suffer so much?

I'd just gone to the kitchen to do the dishes when I heard someone at the front door. I didn't want to open it. I was scared it might be Brother Reuben. The knock came again.

Dad came out of his study. "Open the door, Elizabeth?"

"I don't want to."

"For heaven sakes, why not?" He nudged me out of the way and opened the door himself.

It was Mrs. Jones, with two large brown paper bags in her arms.

Dad said, "Yes, can I help you?"

"It's my teacher, Dad. It's Mrs. Jones."

Mrs. Jones looked past him to me. "Hello, Beth, dear. I've brought the groceries I promised."

Dad looked at me, and then back at Mrs. Jones. "The groceries?"

"Yes. I was here yesterday and found out there was no food in this house."

"Well, I'll take care of that now. Thank you for your concern."

Mrs. Jones came in and set the bags on the loveseat by the front door. "You might as well take it now. I've no use for it."

It looked like Dad was going to argue with her, but she turned to me and said, "How's your mother, Beth?"

"She's--"

Dad pulled me to the side and said, "She's just fine."

Mrs. Jones didn't seem convinced. "Well, I've been worrying about her all night. Has she been to see a doctor?"

"I'm sorry you had to worry. But I'm home now. I'll take care of my wife."

I gave Dad a sideways look and said, "We gave her a blessing. We're waiting to see if it's going to work."

Mrs. Jones raised an eyebrow. "Really, Mr. Sterling? Do you think that's wise? It seemed like something was seriously wrong with her."

"Mrs. Jones, I appreciate your concern, but I'll take care of my family." Dad pulled the door open a little and held out his arm towards it, inviting her to leave.

But Mrs. Jones didn't want to leave. She stepped closer to the stairs. "And what about the children? Will they be back at school on Monday?"

Dad looked flustered. "Well, I think they should be. I mean . . . haven't they been there? I don't see any reason why they can't go. I'll send them tomorrow, I mean Monday." He held out his arm again to show her the way out.

Mrs. Jones still wouldn't go. "I think you should really consider taking your wife to a doctor. How will you feel if she doesn't get better? If something is seriously wrong, you'll be responsible for not getting her help. Can you live with that?"

The blood rose to Dad's face. "Please, don't continue this. It's not your business to intrude in this way. I'll take care of my wife and children." He turned, walked down the hall, and went into his study. He closed the door, leaving Mrs. Jones and me standing by the door.

Mrs. Jones shook her head. "I'm sorry to be so forceful, Beth. I'm just very concerned about your mother."

I could feel a knot growing in my stomach. I knew Mrs. Jones was right about how sick Mom was. If she was willing to stand up to Dad that way she must have thought Mom was in real danger. Did she think she was going to die?

She took my arm and pulled me outside. "Beth, is she as sick as she was yesterday?"

"She almost seems worse."

"Then she's got to be checked out. This illness has lasted so long it must be something serious. You've got to convince your father to take her to the doctor."

"I'll try, but I don't know if he'll do it. He's sure that God's going to make her better."

"If your father doesn't do it, we'll have to get someone else involved to make sure it happens. Do you hear me, Beth? Your mother has to get some help. You come to school on Monday and tell me what's going on. If he isn't going to take her to the doctor, you tell me. You understand?"

"Okay." I could hardly keep from crying. I wished she would stay and make Dad do it. I wanted to believe in him, but hearing what Mrs. Jones said made me feel like it wasn't going to work.

She put her arm around my shoulder and hugged me. "I'm sorry, dear. I know it's not right to put this kind of pressure on you, but something has to be done."

"I'm so confused, Mrs. Jones. I've been taught all my life that blessings can heal people. I even remember one time when Mikey's earaches were healed after my dad blessed him. But I'm not sure it's going to work this time. Maybe it's my fault. Maybe it's because I don't have enough faith."

"Oh, Beth. I don't know what to say. If your mother wasn't so sick, it might be okay to wait and see. It just worries me how weak and thin she is. I've got to tell you, I'm very concerned."

"But what can I do about it?"

"Like I said, you have to try and convince your father to at least let a doctor look at her. And if that doesn't happen, you let me know and I'll see what I can do." She hugged me again. "I better go now."

After Mrs. Jones drove away, I stood on the porch thinking about what she'd said. I'd been so glad when Dad said he was coming home. I thought he would take care of Mom and that everything would be alright. Now, Mrs. Jones said he wasn't doing the right thing. Who was I supposed to believe? Dad wanted God to heal Mom, but Mrs. Jones thought we should take her to the doctor. I was confused, and I was scared for Mom. Somebody had to figure out what was right for her. Then I remembered what Dad said about God giving us a sign when we were supposed to do something different. What if Mrs. Jones was the sign? What if God was using Mrs. Jones to tell us that we should take Mom to the doctor? If that's what God wanted, then that's what we should do, wasn't it? I hurried in the house to tell Dad.

He was still in his study with the door closed. I went in and stood in front of him until he looked up. "Dad, we have to take Mom to the doctor."

He shook his head. "We'll wait for the Lord."

"You said He'd send a sign when we were supposed to do something different. I think Mrs. Jones is that sign."

"Don't be ridiculous, Beth. Why would God send a gentile to do his speaking?"

"A gentile?"

"Yes, someone outside His Church."

"How would *you* know if she's a gentile?"

"Why she isn't wearing temple garments. But she's married, isn't she?"

I didn't know what to say. Maybe Dad was right. Maybe God wouldn't use someone outside the Church to deliver His message. But what if Mrs. Jones was right anyway? We couldn't take that chance. "I think we should take Mom anyway."

"Now, I want you to stop this, Beth. We can't let that woman throw us off course. The Devil will send temptations, but we've got to hold fast to our faith."

I couldn't believe he was saying that about Mrs. Jones. "She hasn't got anything to do with the devil! She's my teacher. She's my friend. She helped me when the kids at school were mean."

Dad looked surprised. "I'm sorry. I was just saying she knows nothing about the ways of God."

"I don't know if she knows about God or not, but she knows about Mom. She's worried about her, and I'm worried too. We've got to take her to the doctor, right now. If you don't do it, I'm going to tell Mrs. Jones and she'll make you do it." I made my voice as strong as I could to make sure he would listen to me.

Dad stood up quickly. "Sounds like you think you're the head of this household now."

"I'm sorry, Dad, but I think we have to do something for Mom."

He came around the desk and kneeled in front of me. He held unto my shoulders and looked deep into my eyes. "Come, Elizabeth. Kneel with me. Let's ask for the Lord's guidance."

I pushed his hands away. "No! I'm tired of praying. I'm sick of relying on God." I ran to the door, and then turned back and shouted. "If anything happens to her, it's going to be your fault. I'll tell everybody that you refused to take her to the doctor." I went out and slammed the door.

My throat tightened up, and I hurried to the living room and lay down on the couch. I closed my eyes and put my hands over my belly, trying to breathe gently, like Dad had taught me, but I was too upset. I tried to empty my mind, but instead it filled up with fear.

Suddenly, I remembered Mom bleeding on the couch the last time she went to the hospital. I jumped up and lifted up the cushion to see if the blood was still there. It didn't look like blood anymore. It was just a big brown stain that was going to be there forever. Something about looking at the stain gave me an overwhelming feeling that something was terribly wrong.

I raced upstairs to Mom. She had pushed back the covers and she was up on her hands and knees. She was whimpering and trying to crawl away from where she'd been lying. The sheets were all dirty, and there was even more blood than the last time. When she saw me she cried out, "Oh, Beth. Help me. Please help me."

I ran downstairs and threw open the door to Dad's study. "Come quick. Mom's in trouble."

"What is it? What's happened?"

"She's bleeding again. It's bad. It's really bad. You've got to do something."

We ran upstairs. When Dad saw the sheets he said, "Oh, dear God. Oh, honey."

Mom cried out. "It hurts. It hurts so much. I'm afraid, Michael. Please help me. Please."

He pushed me toward the bed. "Stay with your mother. I've got to make a call."

Mom reached out to him as he ran from the room. Her eyes were wild. I knew she was afraid of what he was going to do. "Stop him, Beth. Don't let him bring that man back."

I ran downstairs as fast as I could. "Dad, Dad. Please don't call Brother Reuben. It'll make Mom worse."

"What? I'm not calling *him*. I'm trying to find Doctor Wilson's number."

He held the phone to his ear with his shoulder while he flipped through the pages of the telephone directory. "You're right. We can't wait any longer. We've got to take her to the doctor."

I grabbed the phone directory from him. I turned to the W's and told him the number. He quickly dialed it, but it didn't seem like anyone was going to answer. He kept saying, "Come on. Come on. Where are you? It's only three. You've got to be there."

I crossed my fingers, and prayed that someone would answer the phone. Finally, Dad said, "I've got to talk to Doctor Wilson . . . No, it can't wait."

After a minute, Dad said, "Thank God you're there, doctor. It's Michael Sterling. It's my wife . . . I don't know, exactly . . . She's been sick for awhile, can't eat much or keep it down, but now there's blood. I think she's bleeding internally . . . I don't know, there's quite a lot. And diarrhea."

Dad hit himself in the forehead with his fist. "I'm sorry, doctor. I've been out of town. When I got home, I didn't think it was that bad. I don't know why I didn't see it. I guess I thought . . ."

He hit himself even harder. "What? Can't you just see her in your office? Oh dear God, please don't let it be that . . . Okay, I will. I'll take her right now." He hung up the phone and stood there for a minute with his hand over his eyes, moaning.

"What, Dad? What did he say? Is it bad?"

"We've got to take her to the hospital. Get some blankets and a pillow and make her a bed in the back seat of the car. Hurry, Beth, hurry." He ran up the stairs two at a time with me right behind him.

I got the pillow off my bed and grabbed two blankets out of the linen closet. I ran back downstairs, out to the car, and made the bed. Then I raced back upstairs.

Mom was sitting on the edge of the bed pleading with Dad, "Please, Michael. Don't make me go like this. At least clean me up a little. It'll make me feel better. Please, honey."

Dad shouted at me, "Run some water in the bathtub. Hurry. Turn it up full blast."

I ran to do what he said. After a minute, he came in the bathroom carrying Mom. He took off her dirty nightgown, then he lifted her gently down into the water while it was still running. He said, "Get me a clean washcloth, Beth."

I grabbed one from the cupboard. It didn't take Dad much time to clean her up, and while he was dressing her, I ran to get Mikey.

I finally found him outside in the backyard throwing sticks at the crows. "Come on, Mikey, we're taking Mom to the hospital."

I dragged him into the house, just as Dad was carrying Mom downstairs. We got her into the car, and I sat on the hump in the back seat holding her hand while Dad drove. I was trembling with fear, but I felt relieved for the first time in months. Finally, somebody was going to take care of Mom.

Chapter 31

And again, if there shall be properties in the hands of the church . . . every man who has need may be amply supplied and receive according to his wants.

Doctrine and Covenants
Section 42:33

*D*ad jumped out of the car when we got to the hospital. He scooped Mom out of the back seat and carried her into the emergency room in his arms. Doctor Wilson had already arrived and was waiting inside. He took one look at Mom and said, "It's a good thing you brought her in, Michael. It's not a minute too soon."

Dad told Mikey and me to go sit in the waiting room while he went to move the car. I found Mikey a book about trains that I didn't think he'd seen the last time we were there, but when I put it on his lap he started jiggling his knees, like he was trying to make it fall on the floor. He had a mean look in his eyes, and I was worried about what he was going to do. After a minute, the train on the cover must have caught his attention because he stopped jiggling and looked inside. He turned the pages quickly, only stopping to look at the pictures. Before long, he was making train sounds, real softly, so only I could hear him.

It was quite awhile before Dad came back. And when he did, he looked worried. I jumped up and said, "What's wrong? Has something happened to Mom?"

"No, no. They're taking good care of her. It's just that Doctor Wilson wants to admit her to the hospital."

"Can't they just do something for her and let her go home?"

"It's not that simple, Beth. Now, I've got to go talk to the admitting office." He headed down the hall and disappeared through a door with a sign above it that said, "Admitting and Billing."

I sat down and tried to concentrate on Mikey's book, but it was almost impossible. I kept thinking about Mom. If they were going to keep her, she must be really bad. But what was wrong? What could make her bleed inside like that?

A few minutes later, I looked up and noticed Dad talking on the phone over by a little table in the hall. I told Mikey I'd be right back and went over to see if he was saying something about Mom. He was talking in a low voice, as if he didn't want anyone to hear. "This doesn't sound like the Law of Consecration as I know it. I gave you that money in good faith, Brother. You're responsible for our welfare. I've nothing left but the few dollars you gave me for food and utilities."

He had to be talking to Brother Reuben.

"Well, I can't wait. Sharon is very ill. The doctor says she needs surgery. The hospital is asking me if I can pay for it. That's right, the hospital."

He jumped up. "How can you say that, Brother? You know I believe in the power of the priesthood, but she's bleeding inside. The doctor said I never should have waited this long."

Dad leaned his head against the wall in despair. "She's my wife. I love her. If she doesn't make it through this, what will I tell the children? That God wanted it that way?"

I couldn't believe what he was saying. Did he really think Mom was going to die? It was impossible. How could we live without Mom?

I was beginning to feel that terrible tightness in my chest, when I heard Dad yell, "She is not a wicked woman! She's sick and lonely and scared." His voice cracked and tears ran down his cheeks. "You're a cruel man. You're a bully and a liar and a cheat. You're no man of God. I can't believe I ever thought you were." He slammed down the phone and sat down hard. He put his face in his hands and started crying, making a terrible gulping sound. There was so much pain in that sound, I realized things had been really hard for him, just like they'd been hard for us. He must have missed Mom terribly while he was away, and now, he was going to have to live with what his actions had done to her.

I put my arms around his trembling shoulders and said, "Don't cry, Dad. Please don't cry. Somebody will help us. They just have to."

He looked at me pitifully. "We have no money to pay the doctor or the hospital. I don't know what to do." He started to cry so loud the people in the waiting room looked over to see what was wrong.

Mikey ran over and stood there with his hands on his hips, staring at Dad. "What's wrong with him?"

I didn't even try to explain.

I kept hugging Dad, and rubbing his back, until he finally stopped crying. His body had gone limp. When he looked at me again, his eyes were empty. I didn't know if he could even see me. He looked down at the floor, shaking his head and muttering, "What have I done? I've ruined everything. I've given it all away. And for what?"

I tried to think of something that would give him hope, something that he'd believe. "Maybe you should pray, Dad. Maybe God will tell you what to do? Maybe if he knows that you're never going back to Brother Reuben, He'll listen."

He shook his head in misery. "God has forsaken me."

"But He wouldn't do that. You always said He'd take care of us."

The tears streamed down his face, and I grabbed his hands and shook them, trying to bring him out of his despair. "Come on, Dad. Maybe if God won't help us, Doctor Wilson will. Or maybe Mrs. Jones knows what we can do. We'll figure out something. Now that you're back with us, everything will be okay. I know it will."

Finally, he lifted his head and wiped the tears off his face with the back of his hand. He shook his head real hard, like he was trying to make his brain work. Then he got mad. "I'm not going to let him get away with this. He has to provide for us. It's God's law. He can't change that."

He stood up, put his arms around Mikey and me, and led us back to the waiting room. "I have to talk to Doctor Wilson. You stay here."

We sat back down to wait again. The waiting was getting intolerable. I wanted to do something to help, but I had to rely on Dad. And now, Dad had to rely on Brother Reuben, even though it looked like he wasn't willing to do anything. I got so agitated, I finally picked up a book and forced myself to see it. I realized it was the one with the owl that I'd read about before. I flipped through the pages until I saw him. His intense yellow eyes seemed to penetrate to my soul. It frightened me and made me believe that maybe owls really did give a warning when people were about to die. But I didn't want to believe that. I searched the words for something else and found a part where it said owls were good luck for some people. Good luck. That's what we needed. I closed my eyes and prayed to the owl. Please owl. Bring us good luck. We really, really need it.

Dad came back into the room, moving fast. I tried to catch him as he headed down the hall toward the Admitting and Billing room, but he said, "Sit down, Beth. This isn't resolved yet."

I worried about what was happening with Mom while Dad was running around. And what was happening with Dad behind the closed doors. And now Mikey was squirming in his seat.

"Do you need to go to the bathroom?"

"No."

"Then why are you squirming?"

"Because my butt hurts."

"I know, mine does too. Maybe we should go to the bathroom, just so we can walk around?"

"Yeah. Maybe we can find something to eat. I'm starving."

"I doubt it, Mikey. This is a hospital, not a restaurant, and besides we don't have any money."

"Well, what do the sick people eat?"

"I don't know."

"They've got to eat something."

"Come on. The bathroom is down the hall this way."

When I came out of the girl's bathroom, I couldn't see Mikey anywhere, but there was a nurse pushing a gurney down the hall. Dad was beside it, so I knew it had to be Mom. I hurried towards them. "Where are you taking her?"

Dad said, "She's going to her room."

The nurse stopped and said, "There's a waiting room on the third floor, Mr. Sterling. Your daughter can come and wait up there if you like."

Dad looked around. "Where's Michael?"

"I don't know, Dad. He went in the bathroom, and he hasn't come out yet."

Dad was flustered. He looked at the nurse and said, "I'm sorry."

"It's okay, Mr. Sterling. We can wait here for a minute, if you want to get him."

He hurried into the boy's bathroom, but when he came out Mikey wasn't with him. "Oh, dear. Where has he gotten too? You should have kept a closer eye on him, Beth."

"It's not like I could go in there with him."

"I'm sorry. I know that. I just can't imagine where he's gone."

"He said he was hungry. Maybe he went to find something to eat."

Dad looked exasperated. "We don't need this right now."

The nurse said, "Look, Mr. Sterling. How about if I take your wife up to her room? When you find your son, you can all come upstairs to visit with her for a few minutes. She'll be settled in by then. She'll be in room three sixteen."

I squeezed Mom's hand, and then the nurse took her to the elevator. Dad and I walked down the hall to see if we could find Mikey. I asked him why they'd decided to let Mom stay. He said it was only for one night, and then he'd have to find a way to pay. I asked him how we were going to do that and he said, "I don't know."

We got to the end of the hall and turned into another hall, and then another one. We caught a whiff of something cooking, and we kept following our noses until we came to the room where the smells were coming from. Sure enough, Mikey was there. He was sitting at a table, right next to the man at the cash register, eating a piece of chocolate cake.

Dad hurried over to him and put his hand on his shoulder. "We've been looking all over for you."

Mikey ignored us and kept eating his cake. I thought Dad would take the cake away from him, and Mikey must have thought the same thing because he started eating it in huge bites.

The man at the cash register shrugged at Dad and said, "Sorry. He said he was starving."

Dad gave him a grim smile. "Well, I guess he is. Thank you for taking care of him. What do I owe you?"

"That's okay. It's on me."

"That's not necessary."

"Well, I'm the one who gave it to him."

"Never mind that. I'd like to pay for it."

"Okay. It's twenty-five cents."

Dad found a quarter in his pocket and gave it to the man. He let Mikey finish his cake and handed him a napkin to wipe off his face. Then we went up to see Mom.

She was in a room with three other ladies. She had the bed by the window where a wide beam of sun was shining in across the bed. I was glad for the sun because Mom had been cold for such a long time.

Her eyes were closed, but when Dad touched her arm she opened them a little and said, "I see you found Mikey. Where was he?"

"Just where you might expect. In the cafeteria . . . eating chocolate cake."

Mom looked at Mikey and tried to smile. "I'm sorry, honey. It's been a long day, hasn't it?" She held his hand for a minute, and then seemed to drift off to sleep.

Dad leaned down and whispered, "You rest now. I'll take the children home and come back first thing in the morning."

Her eyes fluttered open. "Take care of them, Michael. If anything happens to me . . . take care of my children."

Dad brushed the hair back from her face. "Nothing's going to happen to you, I promise." He kissed her forehead and whispered, "I missed you, honey. I love you."

Mom moaned, and a tear rolled down her cheek. Then Dad started crying. They gazed at each other in silence. Even after all the hurt they'd caused each other, there was still a lot of love in their eyes.

I went over and held Mikey's hand. He looked at Mom and Dad, and then he looked at me and blinked. He didn't cry, but his eyes were shiny and wet. That brought tears to my eyes too. Maybe we did have a chance to recover and get our life back to how it used to be. If Mom could get better, it just might be possible.

Chapter 32

And he became Satan, yea, even the Devil, the father of all lies, to deceive and to blind men, and to lead them captive at his will, even as many as would not hearken unto my voice.

Pearl of Great Price
Moses 4:4

I looked over at Dad as we pulled out of the hospital parking lot. He seemed very distracted, and I knew he must be trying to figure out how to pay for Mom's treatment. I still couldn't get used to his beard. I didn't like it. It made him look old, and it reminded me too much of Brother Reuben. I told him I thought he should shave it off now that he was home.

"What?"

He seemed irritated, so I didn't say it again

The drive home was hard. Dad kept forgetting what he was doing. He sat at the traffic lights long after they'd turned green, and then drove too fast in between. Then, once we got away from the busy city streets and up on the long deserted road to our town, he started muttering to himself and driving even faster. He kept hitting the steering wheel and then hitting himself in the head with his fist. He had to be thinking about Brother Reuben.

I caught a glimpse of pink light reflecting in the rear-view mirror, and I looked back at the sun. It was just about to go down over the Great Salt Lake, and it was bathing the landscape in a sweet golden light that filled me with hope. It felt almost like a blessing from God. But that feeling didn't last long. When we came to the road to our house, Dad didn't turn. I knew where he was going; he was going to see Brother Reuben, and that could be nothing but trouble.

He roared up the hill to Brother Reuben's house and slammed on the brakes in the front yard. Then he jumped out of the car and said, "Stay here."

I slid over into the driver's seat and watched him go towards the house. Before he got there, Brother Reuben came out and ran down the porch stairs. He hurried part way across the yard and then stopped. They were two dark silhouettes against the brilliant red-orange sky burning like fire above them. That sky, or something else, must have scared the little goats at the side of the house because they started bleating wildly and butting their heads against the wood of their cage, as if they wanted to break out. Mikey grabbed my arm and screamed, "Don't let the devils get me."

A wind came up and rattled the branches of the dead tree in Brother Reuben's yard, sending a flock of crows squawking and scattering up like big black splotches of ink against the burning sky.

Brother Reuben stayed at a distance and yelled above the sound of the birds. "Why have you come here? I've nothing to say to you."

"You know why I'm here. You've got something that belongs to me."

"Belongs to you? Now, you know that's not true, Brother. What's given unto the Lord remains with the Lord."

Dad moved closer to Brother Reuben. "You're not the Lord, more likely you're Satan. You know full well what was given to you under the Law of Consecration must be returned when there is a need."

Brother Reuben scoffed. "Oh, yes. Your sick wife. She's being punished, Brother. I can't intervene in the Lord's wrath."

"You're right about that. She is being punished. But it's not by God. It's you who are punishing her. And it will be on your head if you don't make provisions for her."

He shrugged. "I've many brothers and sisters to provide for. They all have needs. Your wife is not even one of us. She must join the fold, Brother. Then, and only then, will she be forgiven and healed. Only then will she be provided for."

"By what power do you judge her? You're no man of God. I'll go to your people. I'll tell them what you've done."

Now Brother Reuben was the one that moved closer, until his nose was right in Dad's face. "They won't listen to you. I've told them how you've turned against us, how you've blasphemed against the Lord."

Dad pushed Brother Reuben on the chest so hard he stumbled backwards. "You lied to them, after all I've done for you? Why would they believe what you say? I've spent time with them. They know who and what I am."

"I'm afraid you don't understand. We needed your help to build the church, that's all. There wasn't a carpenter or a builder among us. But you've done most of the work now. I think we can manage just fine without you."

Dad's arms stiffened at his sides. "You're saying everything you told me was a lie? And that you were all in on it? I don't believe you. Those men down there treated me with respect. You were the only one who didn't. I've become friends with them. I'd know if they lied."

"Well, you can believe what you like. But the truth is God sent you to us. We prayed and you were the answer to our prayers. We thought you would join us permanently, become one of the Brethren, but that's not necessary now. You've done the Lord's work. With your wife the way she is, you've become more trouble than you're worth."

Dad made a loud roaring sound. He leaped at Brother Reuben and knocked him down. He sat on his chest, and with his knees on Brother Reuben's arms, he raised his fist in the air as if he was going to hit him. Before he could do it, Sister Reuben came screaming out of the house. She ran across the yard, grabbed Dad by the hair, and tried to pull him off Brother Reuben, but she wasn't strong enough. She searched around until she found a big thick stick, and she started beating Dad on the back with it. He held up one arm to protect himself, but he wouldn't let go of Brother Reuben.

Sister Reuben was hitting Dad so hard I was afraid she was going to kill him. I screamed, "Come on, Mikey. We've got to help Dad."

We jumped out of the car and ran over and grabbed Sister Reuben's skirt from behind. We pulled it as hard as we could until she twirled around and tried to hit us with the stick. Her legs got wrapped up in her skirt so she couldn't get to us. Mikey ran forward and butted her in the stomach with his head, and she fell down on her knees and wailed, "God, save us, save us from the heathens."

Dad was still struggling with Brother Reuben. I ran to him and said, "Hurry, Dad. Let's go before she gets back up."

He looked at me, then he looked down at Brother Reuben. "Oh, my dear God. What am I doing? I've never hit another person in my life." He rolled to the side off of Brother Reuben, but before he could get to his feet, Brother Reuben grabbed him and pulled him back down into the dirt. He sat on Dad's chest and hit him, first on one side of his face, and then on the other. His eyes were blazing and his mouth twisted with hate as he hit Dad again and again.

I jerked the stick away from Sister Reuben and hit Brother Reuben on the back, while Mikey kicked him in the side. But we couldn't stop Brother Reuben.

I looked up and saw that the sky had turned a dark violet blue out over the Great Salt Lake, but up there on the side of the mountain, there was still a little light. The goats were bleating louder and louder and Sister Reuben was wailing. The crows came back all excited and circled above Brother Reuben's head, squawking and diving. Brother Reuben didn't even notice. He kept on hitting Dad until the blood was running down his face and his eyes were full of terror. He groaned and said, "Run, Beth. Run, Mikey. Get help."

We couldn't run. Where would we run to? The other houses were too far away. What if Brother Reuben just kept hitting him? I had to make him stop, but what could I do? It seemed like Brother Reuben was getting bigger and stronger all the time.

Suddenly, Mikey grabbed the stick away from me. He ran and stood on the side of Brother Reuben. Just as he was raising his fist to hit Dad one more time, Mikey positioned the stick like it was a bat and Brother Reuben's face was the ball. He swung the stick so hard it was like he was trying to hit a home run. It made a loud crack when it hit and Brother Reuben fell over, grabbing his face and rolling onto his back. He howled as the blood ran out between his fingers.

I helped Dad up, and we all ran for the car. As we drove away, I looked back and saw the dark shadow of Brother Reuben still lying in the dust with Sister Reuben crying over him.

We didn't talk on the way home; we were all too upset over what had happened. Dad drove slowly. It felt almost like we were floating in a dream. When we got home, we sat in the car unable to move for several minutes, and then we got out and somehow made it to the house. Dad pushed open the door and we went inside, but he didn't turn on the lights. He just stood there, tilting his head one way and then the other, listening. I listened too. Then I realized the thing we were listening for was Mom. But she wasn't there. It was such a strange feeling of absence. Mom had always been there. How could our world exist without her? What were we going to do if she never came home? I already missed her, and she hadn't even been gone a whole day. How could I bear it if I had to miss her forever? It hurt too much to let my mind think about it.

I hurried over, turned on the light, and looked back at Dad. His face was covered with dirt and blood and pain. Somehow, I knew the pain wasn't from the beating. It was from his aching sorrow about Mom. I grabbed his hand and pulled him upstairs to the bathroom. He sat on the toilet seat while I got a washcloth and soaked it in warm water and gently wiped the blood and dirt off his face. It was hard to get it all off, especially the blood that was stuck in his beard. I said, "Maybe you better rinse it with water, Dad. I don't think it's going to come out otherwise."

He went to the sink and splashed water on his face again and again, moaning with each splash. When he was finished, and all the dried blood and dirt were finally gone, I could see how terribly bruised and cut up his face was. One of his eyes was already starting to swell up. I got out a box of Band-Aids. He sat down again, and I helped him put them on the cuts. His poor face looked so sad with all the red puffiness and the Band-Aids. It brought tears to my eyes. "Oh, Dad. I'm so sorry you got hurt."

He closed his eyes and sat there for a long time until I said, "Maybe we'd feel better if we ate something."

I took his hand. He let me lead him downstairs to the kitchen, but when we got there, he said, "You go ahead, Beth. Fix something for yourself and Mikey. I'm not hungry."

"I'm not hungry either, but Mom would tell us we have to eat if we're going to have strength when we need it."

"I'm sorry. I can't."

I heard him pacing between the living room and his study the whole time I was making sandwiches. Then, while Mikey and I were eating, he went upstairs. After a minute, I heard the faint sound of the hair clippers. I looked at Mikey and he looked at me, remembering when Mom had used the clippers to cut off all her hair. I felt a catch in my throat, but I tried to convince myself he was just cutting off his beard, like I'd asked him to.

When he came downstairs, it wasn't just his beard that was gone; he'd shaved his head too. It shone under the fluorescent lights of the kitchen, just like Mom's did when she shaved off her hair. Dad looked even more bizarre with his bruises and the Band-Aids and his swollen eye. The top half of his face was sun-tanned from the desert, while the bottom half was baby-skin white. I couldn't stop staring at him and neither could Mikey.

Pretty soon, Dad was back in the living room pacing again. Mikey leaned toward me and whispered, "He looks like a scary Frankenstein monster."

"Don't tell him that. You'll only make him feel worse."

Dad paced the house all night while I listened from my bed under the light of a pale shimmering moon. It was so bright, I could see it even with my eyes closed. The light had a heavenly quality to it. It got me thinking about God again and wondering why he didn't help us. Was he really up there in his heaven? Where was heaven, anyway? I'd been taught about God, as far back as I could remember, and I'd always believed in Him. But now, it occurred to me, the only reason I believed in God was because of the stories people had told me, not from anything I'd seen for myself. Dad had totally believed in Brother Reuben. He believed what Brother Reuben said so much he was willing to destroy us all, but now, suddenly, he didn't believe in Brother Reuben at all. How could that be? I understood it was because Brother Reuben had turned out to be a liar. But why hadn't Dad seen it before? I did. I knew there was something wrong the first time I met Brother Reuben. And Mom did too. So why was Dad so blind?

Chapter 33

Wherefore, I command you again to repent, lest I humble you with my almighty power . . .

Doctrine and Covenants
Section 19:2

I went downstairs the next morning and found Dad just hanging up the phone. He stood there staring at the floor. His face was turning blue from the bruises, and his right eye was bright red and almost swollen shut.

"Oh, Dad, your poor face. Does it hurt a lot?"

He pressed his palm against his eye, as if he thought he could push away the swelling. Then he glanced at me. "I talked to the Bishop."

"What did he say? Can he help Mom?"

"He can, but I don't know if he will. He wasn't willing to talk about it over the phone. He's coming over."

That's when I remembered the letter the Bishop sent while Dad was down in the desert. Had he ever opened it? What if the Bishop was just coming over to tell Dad they were going to excommunicate him? I said, "Uh . . . did the Bishop seem mad? I mean, do you think--"

"What?" His eyes fluttered, as if he was having trouble staying awake.

It obviously wasn't a good time to talk about excommunication. "Never mind."

"Yes . . . well, let's see, he'll be here in a few minutes. What should I do? Got to clear my head somehow." He rubbed his forehead, and then the top of his head. He seemed surprised that his hair was gone.

"Maybe a shower would make you feel better."

"That's right. A shower. That's a good idea, honey."

Dad was still in the shower when I heard the Bishop's car in the driveway. I wasn't so sure I wanted to let him in until Dad came down. What if I said something wrong and it made him not want to help us?

I waited for a minute when the knock came, but then, not wanting him to leave, I opened the door. The Bishop stood there in his dark blue suit and his red tie, just the way I remembered him, but somehow he didn't seem as tall as before. He smiled grimly and said, "Hello, Elizabeth. It's been a long time. How are you, dear?"

"I'm fine, Bishop . . . I mean, I'm not really fine. Nothing's very fine around here." I stood back so he could come in. "Dad's in the shower. Do you want to sit down and wait for him?"

I led him to the living room, and we sat down together on the couch. We looked at each other for a minute, and then the Bishop said, "Maybe we can talk while we're waiting."

"What should we talk about?"

"Things have been rough, haven't they?"

I nodded, blinking hard to keep the tears back.

"Beth. Why didn't you call me when your mother got so ill?"

"She wouldn't let me. She said nobody wanted to talk to us."

"Why would she think such a thing?"

"Because nobody ever did talk to us, and nobody ever came to see us. We thought they didn't care what happened. Even before that, they wouldn't give Dad any work. That's why he had to go build Brother Reuben's church. I don't understand why everyone hates us?"

"Nobody hates you, Beth. It's just that. . ."

His voice trailed off and I didn't know what he was thinking. I wanted to say something about Mom, but I didn't know how to explain everything that happened in a way he'd understand. I got so fidgety I couldn't sit there anymore. I jumped up and ran to the stairs to see if Dad was coming, then I hurried back to the living room. It didn't seem like the Bishop had even noticed I was gone.

I sat down, but my leg started bouncing with agitation. I stood up and yelled, "Mom's going to die if you don't do something. You're the Bishop. Aren't you supposed to help people?"

I started to cry so hard everything got blurry. The Bishop gently pulled me down on the couch. He put his arm around me and said, "Now, now, Elizabeth, don't cry. You're a big girl. You've got to be strong while we work this out."

"I'm sick and tired of being strong. I've been taking care of everybody. It's too hard." I put my head against his chest and sobbed. It hurt so bad, like there was something hard and sharp in my throat. I tried to swallow it, but it was stuck.

I heard the Bishop make a strange gasping sound. I looked over and saw Dad by the stairs. The Bishop jumped up and said, "Oh, my . . . what happened to you, Michael?"

Dad put his hand up to his face and said, "I'm sorry, Bishop. I didn't know you were here. I'm afraid I've taken a beating."

The Bishop hurried over to him. "Who did this to you?"

I ran over and said, "It was Brother Reuben. He went crazy and started beating Dad. Mikey had to hit him in the face with a big stick to make him stop."

"Oh, dear. I had no idea he would go this far. Something's got to be done about that man." The Bishop put his arm around Dad and led him to the couch.

Neither of them spoke for a minute, then the Bishop cleared his throat and said, "Tell me what's going on, Michael."

At first, Dad couldn't seem to speak. He opened his mouth and then closed it and shook his head. The Bishop waited patiently. Finally, Dad started talking in a jerky voice. "I don't know where to . . . I mean, I know I've said and done some things . . . but . . . I need your help, Bishop. I don't know how else to say it. I need help." Tears came to his eyes.

"What exactly do you need?"

"Something's terribly wrong with Sharon. But they can't do the surgery to find out what's causing it unless I show them I can pay for it. I'm afraid I'm going to lose her, Bishop. I've got so much to make up for. Dear God, give me the chance." He put his hands over his face and moaned.

My heart was racing wildly. I wanted to get involved, but I made myself keep quiet. Why couldn't the Bishop just say he'd help her?

Instead, he said, "Don't you have anything left?"

"Nothing . . . except the car. But it's too old to sell. My truck broke down in Southern Utah. I can't even get it home. I don't know how I'm going to work without it. I've got to work."

"That's right. You need to work." The Bishop sadly shook his head. "I warned you, Michael. I tried to tell you about Reuben, but you wouldn't listen."

"I know. I know. I was . . . confused. Can't you understand that?"

"I told you to be careful concerning revelations. You should be listening for the voice of the Holy Spirit, rather than expecting visitations from God. He shook his head at Dad, but there was something in the Bishop's eyes that made me think he really did understand.

I don't think Dad could see that. He hit his fist on his knee. "What I saw was real. As real as anything I've ever experienced in my life. I know you don't believe me, Bishop, but I know what I saw. Don't take that away from me." His eyes were wild, making his face more frightening than it already was.

The Bishop shifted on the couch, moving slightly away from Dad. "I'm afraid if you want help from the Church, you're going to have to reconsider that experience. Do you think if you were following God's word that you and your family would have suffered as you have?"

"What are you saying? That we're being punished? You're all the same. You, Brother Reuben, you give the same message. That's why he said he couldn't help Sharon. He said she was being punished and he couldn't intercede in the wrath of God."

I didn't think the Bishop liked being compared to Brother Reuben. He straightened his tie and cleared his throat. "I think you better rethink your position, Brother Sterling."

Dad's shoulders slumped. "I know, I know. I'm sorry. I should have listened to what you said about Reuben. I should have seen what he was up to."

The Bishop took a deep breath and let it out slowly. "You've done some terrible things, Michael. Maybe you're sorry, but you seem to be holding onto the idea of your vision and blaming most of what's happened on Brother Reuben."

"What do you mean, maybe I'm sorry? I am sorry. I'm so sorry I don't know what to do."

"I can see you feel bad about Sharon and the children, but you must accept responsibility for it. If you can't see that it was your misguided interpretation of things that started the whole chain of events, if you're unwilling to repent for your activities against the Church, then I don't know what I can do for you."

"Activities against the Church? What have I done against the Church?"

"You know full well you've spoken against the living prophet and failed in your duty to your family. And from what you've said, I don't believe you're truly sorry for those things, or that you won't express the same attitudes in the future."

I couldn't believe what the Bishop was saying. Did it mean he wasn't going to help Mom? Was he going to punish her because of what Dad did, just like Brother Reuben wanted to punish her?

I jumped up and yelled, "But what about Mom? She didn't do anything. Why does she have to suffer?"

The Bishop looked at Dad. "Yes, Michael, what about that? What about Sharon?"

"You've got to help her, Bishop."

"But it's not up to me. It's up to you. What are you going to do?"

Dad leaned his head back on the couch and squeezed his eyes shut. "Sharon never believed in my vision. From the beginning she said, 'Why would God talk to you? What's so special about you?' I thought she was insulting me. But maybe she was right, maybe I *am* crazy. Maybe it was something I dreamed up to make myself feel important. But it was so real. I don't know. I just don't know anymore."

Dad was silent for a long time, and then he turned to face the Bishop. "Look, I know I made a huge mistake following Reuben. I know I've harmed my family. But what am I to do with these questions? I can't escape them. I know the Church no longer believes we should practice polygamy, or live by the Law of Consecration. And yet . . . they are divine laws, given to us by God. They are principles that even the Church says we'll live by in the next life. I want to do what's right, that's all I want. Do we believe that Joseph Smith was inspired of God or not? I'm trying to be honest with you, Bishop. These are real questions."

"Michael, you've got to stop this. Put your faith in the living prophet. He's told us what we're to do. Those doctrines you mentioned are not to be practiced at this time. That's all there is to it."

"I wish it was that simple for me."

The Bishop cleared his throat and spoke firmly. "Michael, you are in danger of being excommunicated. Don't you realize that?"

Dad grabbed his arm. "Please, Bishop. You can't do that. You know what it would do to Sharon. She can't handle that stress."

The Bishop shook his head and rubbed his hand over his face. "I don't know what to do, Michael. If you could prove to me that you're truly repentant, maybe we could forgo that. But I'm just not sure you are."

"I am. I really am. I admit I'm still confused, but I want to return to church. I know that's where I'll find the answers to my questions."

"Yes, well . . ."

"Please, Bishop. Can't you at least help Sharon?"

"Yes, we do need to take care of her. She's not to blame for your apostasy. You can tell the hospital we'll arrange to pay for her surgery. We can work out a temporary loan, but you'll be responsible to pay it back. If you repent and get back on track, I'll help you get work so you can do that. But I want you to apologize to the congregation and show them your remorse. I'd prefer to keep this type of thing confidential, but you've caused such a stir in the community I don't know how else to handle it. The members of the Ward need to know you're on the right path again, or I'm not sure they'll hire you even if I suggest it."

"When should I do that?"

"Right away. At testimony meeting tomorrow."

Dad sighed. "Is it really the first of the month?"

"Yes."

"I hardly know what month it is. I feel like I've been in a dream, and now that I'm awake, I've discovered it was really all a terrible nightmare."

The Bishop patted Dad on the back. "So you'll be at testimony meeting tomorrow?"

"Yes. Okay. Thank you, Bishop."

The Bishop got up to leave. Dad followed him to the door and said, "Are you sure we shouldn't wait until my bruises and cuts heal? It might be disturbing to them."

"No. I think it would be best to do it tomorrow."

"All right then. I'll be there."

After the Bishop was gone, Dad stood in the doorway staring into the front yard, as if he was stuck. I pulled him inside and shut the door. "I'm so relieved that the Bishop's going to help us. I wasn't sure he would."

Dad didn't say anything, and he didn't move. I think it was very hard for him to ask the Bishop for help and admit he'd made so many mistakes. I wished there was something I could say to make him feel better, but he really had made a lot of mistakes.

Now that the Bishop was gone, I remembered we'd told Mom we'd be back to see her early in the morning and it was practically noon. I shook his arm. "Come on, Dad. We've got to go see Mom, right now."

That woke him up. "Oh, no. That's right. It's late."

I ran upstairs to get Mikey. I couldn't believe he'd slept through the Bishop's whole visit. But maybe he thought it was his job to do the sleeping for all of us. I shook his arm. "Come on, Mikey. We're going to the hospital to see Mom."

Chapter 34

And they shall make themselves utterly bald for thee, and gird them with sackcloth, and they shall weep for thee with bitterness of heart and bitter wailing.

Holy Bible
Ezekiel 27:31

$\mathcal{D}$ad tried to keep his face hidden as we walked down the hall at the hospital, but everyone still stared at him. The way the florescent lights reflected off his pale skin made the purple bruises and cuts on his face and head stand out in a really terrible way. I started thinking it was Dad's punishment for going against the Church, but if God was punishing him, why had he used an evil person like Brother Reuben to do it? Was that how God worked? I knew God would punish us for our sins, but I'd never really considered how he did it. Did he just make bad things happen? Or let them happen? And what about forgiveness?

When we got up to the third floor, one of the nurses saw Dad and came running out from behind the counter. "Oh, my, Mr. Sterling. What happened to you?"

"It's nothing. Really. I'm okay."

She stood in front of Dad examining his face, but he stepped to the side and said, "Please. I'd like to see my wife."

"You ought to at least have the doctor check that eye. It looks bad."

Dad held out his arm against her and said, "Maybe later. I'd just like to see my wife now."

"Well, all right. But I hope you don't scare her."

"It's okay. I'll tell her what happened."

As the nurse went back behind the counter, she said, "By the way, Mr. Sterling, they'll be doing the exploratory surgery Monday morning at nine. You should be here about seven thirty if you want to see her before she goes in."

"Thank you. We'll be here."

We went in Mom's room. Dad pulled the curtain around us and got a chair for Mikey and me. Then he sat on the edge of the bed and touched Mom's cheek gently with the back of his finger. "Honey, are you awake?"

She opened her eyes, as if she was still half asleep, but when she saw Dad, she gasped and tried to sit up. "Oh, no. What--"

Dad said, "Shhh. Shhh. It's okay. It looks much worse than it is."

She touched his chin and his cheeks and the top of his head, as if he was a little boy who had fallen down and hurt himself. "Oh, my poor darling. What happened to you? Was there an accident?" She looked quickly at Mikey and me.

I shook my head. "It wasn't an accident, Mom. It was Brother Reuben."

She moaned and tried to sit up again. "But why? Why did he do this to you?"

Dad pressed gently on her shoulders to get her to lie back down. "It doesn't matter, darling. It's all over now."

"Did you go see him? Why would you do that?"

I knew it wasn't good for her to get so upset, but I didn't know what to tell her that would make things better. It was a terrible thing that had happened. Nothing could change that.

Dad said, "Shhh, shhh. We won't be seeing him again . . . ever."

Mom's eyes got wild. "What do you mean . . . ever? You didn't--?"

"No, no, nothing like that. Although I'm afraid I wanted to."

"Is that why he hurt you so?"

Dad touched his finger to Mom's lips. "Listen to me. I'm going to be fine. You're the one we have to get fixed up. You understand? When you're better, you'll come home, and we'll start all over."

Then it was Dad who was touching Mom's face, like she was the little girl who was hurt. He brushed back her hair and kissed her forehead and whispered, "I've been awake all night worrying about you. I don't know how I got so far away. I didn't mean to hurt you, honey. You've got to believe that." A sob escaped his throat and tears ran down his cheeks. "I honestly thought I was doing what was right for us. I thought it was what God wanted."

Mom wrapped her arms around him so fiercely it startled me. They cried and hugged for a long time in such a desperate way, I realized they were afraid everything would fly apart if they let go. I didn't want them to let go. I wanted them to hold each other like that, until they remembered who they used to be and how much they loved each other. I wanted to see their forgiveness.

Finally, Dad sat back and gave Mom his hanky, "This can't be good for you. You've got to rest."

"It is good for me. You don't know how good. I've waited so long for this, for you to come home and want to be with us again."

She held him tightly again. After a few minutes, she seemed to remember Mikey and me. She wiped away her tears and said, "Help me up. I want to see the children."

We stood next to the bed, and Mom pulled Mikey close. He let her wipe a smudge off his cheek with her thumb, and then she straightened his shirt. She looked at him so long he started to fidget, so she let him go. He went and stood behind Dad.

Mom looked at me and whispered, "I'm sorry I wasn't stronger for you, Beth. You've been so brave." She took my hand, kissed it, and then held it over her heart, looking deep into my eyes.

An aching pain moved up into my throat, but I forced it back down. If I started to cry, I might never be able to stop. I took a deep breath and held it in until the aching feeling subsided.

Mom must have seen what was going on because she said, "It's been a long hard time, hasn't it, honey? I think it's time for you to get back to being a girl now."

"Oh, Mom. I wish I could do that. But the Bishop said I still have to be strong."

She glanced at Dad. "You talked to the Bishop?"

I said, "He's going to help us, Mom. He came over and told Dad he'd get him some work so he can pay for your surgery, but first he has to ask for forgiveness. He's supposed to do it tomorrow in church."

Mom reached for Dad's hand. "Oh, dear, do you have to do it now? I mean, your face is so bruised and swollen. What will they think?"

Dad touched one of the Band-Aids on his cheek. "That's what I asked, but the Bishop told me to be at testimony meeting tomorrow, so that's what I'll do."

Mom pulled him closer. "I want to be there with you, Michael."

"Don't even think it. The only thing you need to do is stay here and get well. I mean it. I wouldn't have troubled you with all this, but I've been leaving you out of things. I don't want to do that anymore."

He pulled Mikey and me into his hug as the tears ran down his face. "I've missed you all so much. I just hope you can forgive me someday."

I whispered, "We do forgive you, Dad. We're so glad you're home. But you've got to promise you won't ever leave us again."

He squeezed us even tighter. "I promise."

Chapter 35

Satan doth stir up the hearts of the people to contention concerning the points of my doctrine . . .

Doctrine and Covenants
Section 10:63

*W*hen I woke up the next morning, the sun was already shining halfway across the room. Church started at ten thirty. I hurried across the hall to Dad's room and found him still asleep. I shook him. "Dad, Dad, we're going to be late."

He mumbled something and rolled over. I shook him again, harder. "The Bishop's not going to like it if we don't get there on time."

This time he rolled towards me. I gasped when I saw him. His bad eye had swollen completely shut and the good one was only open a slit. How was he going to see to drive?

He blinked several times, trying to clear his vision. "I'm so groggy. What time is it?"

"It's almost ten. You have to get up right now. I'll get Mikey."

When we were both dressed, we found Dad in the bathroom staring at his reflection in the mirror, as if he didn't recognize himself. He started pulling the Band-Aids off of his face.

I said, "Should I get you some salve and some fresh Band-Aids?"

He shook his head.

"Are you sure? If the people see you like that, I don't know what they'll think."

Mikey said, "Yeah, you look like a scary Halloween mask."

Dad looked me straight in the eyes. "Let them experience the full impact of the Lord's punishment, if that's what the Bishop wants. Let's go."

We pulled into the church parking lot, and I could feel the butterflies swirling around in my stomach. I wasn't just nervous for Dad, I was wondering about the other kids. I didn't know what to expect from them. Would they still taunt me about Dad and Brother Reuben?

When we entered the chapel, the people turned to look at Dad. I heard a whoosh of shock ripple across the room. Dad looked straight ahead, and I tried to do the same thing, but it was impossible not to see the judgment on their faces. They seemed like strangers, even though I'd known them my whole life. I wanted to yell, what's wrong with you? Can't you see we're still the same people we've always been? But then I realized that wasn't true. I'd never be the same. I was older and wiser. For some reason that made me sad.

The Bishop went to the podium. He said, "Brother Sterling. You and the children sit down here on the first row. We've saved you a place."

The Bishop seemed nervous as he cleared his throat to try to get everyone's attention. I wondered if he'd always been nervous like that, and I just hadn't noticed it before.

Finally, when the room quieted down, the Bishop asked Brother Sperry to say the opening prayer. When that was over, we sang.

Brightly beams our Father's mercy
from his lighthouse evermore,
but to us he gives the keeping
of the lights along the shore.

Let the lower lights be burning;
send a gleam across the wave.
Some poor fainting, struggling seaman
you may rescue, you may save . . .

I realized the Bishop had picked the song because of Dad; he was the poor struggling seaman the Bishop wanted the church members to save. I looked at their faces to see if there was any sign of forgiveness. Some of them seemed sorry for Mikey and me, but others were frowning. Were they all mad at Dad? I wondered what they would have done if Mom had been sitting beside him. Would they meet her eyes, or would they look away? Would they want to help her? If so, why hadn't they helped us before when we needed it so much?

After the sacrament, the Bishop went back up to the podium and stood there for a minute looking sternly at the congregation. Then, he cleared his throat and spoke. "Brothers and Sisters, you all know the parable of the prodigal son. I ask that you keep that story in mind as we proceed here today. There is one among us who has gone astray and returns to us now seeking forgiveness. Please listen to him with an open mind. Set your judgments aside, that you too may be forgiven when you are in need of it."

He looked at Dad. "Brother Sterling, will you please come forward."

I wasn't sure Dad heard him. He just sat there staring straight ahead. His mouth was moving, but no sound came out. He seemed to be having an argument with himself.

People started to whisper and clear their throats and shift around in their seats. Finally, the Bishop spoke in a loud voice. "Brother Sterling, I believe you have something to say to us."

Dad looked up at the Bishop, as if he was seeing him for the first time. "Yes, I'm, sorry. I guess I do."

"Would you like to come up to the podium where everyone can hear you?"

"No. No, thank you. I'd prefer to remain here . . . if that's alright."

The Bishop nodded, and Dad stood and turned around slowly to face the people. He looked from one side of the room to the other, like he was searching for a friendly face, but he couldn't find one, so he just looked at his feet. Then, he went out into the aisle and fell to his knees. Tears began to roll down his face. The room became deathly quiet. "Oh, Father," he said, looking up toward heaven. "I have done wrong. Even after you gave me Thy counsel, I was led astray and fell before the praise of men. I sought my own importance. I believed I was to be your messenger, but who can speak for Thee, Lord, but Thyself? Who can understand Thy words? Please, Lord, cleanse the conceit from my heart. Touch my mind that I might understand Thy true plan for me. That I may know thy will."

His voice cracked, and he had to stop and wipe his eyes with his hanky. He couldn't seem to think what to say next. He cleared his throat several times. He looked around at the people, but quickly turned his eyes upward again. "Please, Lord. Open the hearts of my brothers and sisters that they might recognize in me their own confusion and in that recognition find compassion to forgive me, and help me. I know I have sinned Lord, but I did not mean to. I wanted only to know and obey Thy will. I wanted only to know the truth of your divine laws. To live them as they were given."

I looked at the people. The ones at the back stretched their necks, and some on the other side of the room were standing so they could see him kneeling in the aisle.

I don't think Dad even noticed. His eyes were still turned toward heaven. "I can't escape my greatest sin, Lord. I have harmed my family. I plead with you not to punish them for my sins." He began to cry. "Please, Lord, bless my wife. Comfort her. Heal her. Bring her home to me and our children." He put his hands over his face and sobbed.

The Bishop waited a few minutes, and then softly told Dad he could sit down.

Dad didn't hear him. He was still kneeling in the aisle, murmuring to himself.

The Bishop looked around. He seemed uncertain about what to do next. Finally, he said, "Brothers and Sisters, do any of you have something to say?"

Sister Gold jumped to her feet. She shook her finger at Dad. "I'm sorry about your wife, Brother Sterling, but it's your fault. I can't imagine how she put up with your shenanigans. It's no wonder she's ill. You should be ashamed of yourself."

She sat down, and Brother Ellison stood up. He was glaring at Dad. "It's hard for me to believe you followed the likes of that man, Reuben. He's a fornicator and an adulterer, and nothing more. Moreover, how do we know you haven't gone down that same road? If you haven't yet, how do we know you won't try it in the future? I don't know if you can be trusted."

Dad moaned and covered his face with his hands.

Brother Taylor jumped up and turned on Brother Ellison. "Now, wait just a minute. He's asked for our forgiveness, hasn't he? Besides, I understand his confusion. Sometimes I wonder why we aren't practicing Celestial Marriage anymore. I mean, the only reason it was banned by the Church was because the U. S. government sent in the army to put an end to it. We all know that."

Sister Gold began shaking her finger at him. "You sound like you're taking his side. Are you crazy? How can any of us think, in this day and age, that a man should have more than one wife? It's ludicrous."

Brother Campbell turned around to face Sister Gold. "There's no question about *if* there will be plural marriage. There will. But it will be in the next life. That's what the prophet tells us."

I was surprised when Todd Morgan got up. I thought he was still on his mission, but he must have come home while we were away. He stood there looking like he was trying to get up his nerve to talk. He was so much younger than the others, I thought it was pretty brave of him to want to give his opinion. He stood there for a long time, and finally blurted out, "How can we have plural marriage in the next life, if we can't do it on earth? I've been studying the Doctrine and Covenants, and some other books, and I mean, marriage is an earthly covenant, isn't it? If we can't marry more than one woman here, we won't have more than one in the next life. And without plural marriage, we can't enjoy the blessings that come from it. I mean . . . we won't be able to become gods."

That caused a real stir. All the men started talking at once, as if they'd been wondering the same thing. But no one seemed to have any answers.

I was shocked. Was it possible that they were all just as confused as Dad was? If so, why didn't they ever say so? From what they were saying, it sounded like they all wanted to be gods. Maybe they'd just been keeping quiet about it, hoping God would take care of things.

What could it mean? It was true that the scriptures said all marriages had to take place on earth. And so did baptism. That's why we had marriage and baptism for the dead, for those people who didn't get to do it while they were alive on earth. But that didn't take care of the problem Todd was talking about. It seemed like the only way a man could get more wives, the way the church wanted them to do it, was to marry them after they were dead. But that seemed too weird.

None of it made any sense, but it did explain why Dad was so confused, and why he wanted God to tell him what the truth was.

I started listening again when Brother Wright stood up and said, "What I'm concerned about is this issue of personal revelation. Is that really a thing of the past? The scriptures clearly say that if a man is righteous, if he prays with an open heart, and if God finds him worthy, then he may be visited by angels, or by Jesus Christ, or by God Himself. I don't know why we have to be suspicious of someone who says it happened to him."

Brother Ellison let out a loud snort and glared at Dad with flashing eyes. "What? You think God has time to talk to fools?"

Dad wrapped his arms around his head and pressed his face against the side of the bench. It made my heart ache. Why couldn't Brother Ellison leave him alone?

I tried to get Dad to come sit next to me on the bench, but he didn't pay any attention. Mikey slid over and tugged on my arm. "I want to go home now, Bethy," he whispered.

By the scared look on his face, I didn't know how long I could keep him there.

The microphone squealed, and the Bishop spoke in a loud voice. "Brothers and Sisters, please!"

A dead silence came over the congregation.

The Bishop looked upset. "Well, Brothers and Sisters, I'm having a hard time with what's happened here today. It's just as I feared. Brother Sterling has had a very bad effect on all of you. It's not for us to question our prophet. He has been called of God, and he knows God's will. He will guide us in righteousness. The scriptures say, if a man seeks wisdom, let him ask of God, but as we can see by Brother Sterling's experience, maybe it's best to leave revelation regarding Church doctrine to the prophet. That way we can benefit from his interpretation and avoid all this personal confusion."

I could still feel tension in the air, but when I looked around, I saw shame on the people's faces. Even the ones who hadn't spoken seemed ashamed of what had taken place.

The Bishop looked at them and shook his head. "I think a good number of you have some soul searching to do."

For a minute, the Bishop looked like he was trying to decide something, then he cleared his throat. "I think you are all aware that Sister Sterling is in the hospital. She is very ill and will be having surgery tomorrow morning. She and the children are the ones who have been injured in all this. I hope you'll include her in your prayers, and that you'll help take care of the family while she's in the hospital."

He nodded towards Mikey and me and said, "The children have had to take on a lot of responsibility. I think it's time we see to them as well. Finally, I hope that you'll forgive Brother Sterling for his confusion. A confusion, which I must say seems to have spread throughout this congregation."

He let out a big sigh and continued, "For now, I think it's important that we make sure Brother Sterling can pay for his wife's surgery. That means he needs work. I expect you can all help with that. If nothing else, we all know he's a great carpenter. Brother Gibson, I know you have a kitchen you've been going to remodel. You might as well get started now. And Brother Metzger, if you're going to raise chickens, like you said, you ought to get started on that coop. By the way, if any of you have a spare truck you can lend Brother Sterling, it would be very helpful. His seems to have broken down."

The Bishop paused and shook his head again. "I hope you've all learned something from this."

He nodded to Sister Henderson, and she hurried to the front of the room with her baton. The Bishop said, "I think the hymn on page nineteen would be appropriate."

We all opened our songbooks and sang:

We thank ye oh God for a prophet,
to guide us in these latter days.
We thank thee for sending the gospel
to lighten our minds with its rays.

We thank thee for every blessing
bestowed by Thy bounteous hand.

We feel it a pleasure to serve thee,
and love to obey Thy command . . .

After the closing prayer, a crowd formed around Dad. Brother Gibson pulled him to his feet and said he wanted to talk to Dad about some things in private, and maybe they could talk about the new kitchen at the same time. Some of the other men shook Dad's hand and offered him work, while the women said they'd be bringing food over that afternoon.

I stood against the wall and watched. It was just like the Bishop said, they were treating him like the prodigal son. Now that it was clear they were going to accept Dad back into the fold, it made me feel a little lonely.

I looked around for Mikey and saw him over by the door with some of his little friends. They were laughing. It looked like Mikey was being accepted back into the fold too. I was the only one who didn't know how to fit back in.

I wondered about Mom. Would she be able to come back to church like nothing had happened? She'd faced the reality of polygamy. So what would she say when people talked about it being practiced in the next life? Would she say it was crazy like Sister Gold said? I thought maybe I should tell her what Todd Morgan said, but I didn't know if that would make her happy, or if it would just fill her with the same disturbing questions I had.

Chapter 36

Behold, with a great plague will the LORD smite thy people,
and thy children, and thy wives, and all thy goods. . .

Holy Bible
2nd Chronicles 21:14

*A*ll the rest of that day, I couldn't stop thinking about what I'd heard in church. How was I supposed to know what was true and what wasn't? If some of God's laws could be changed so easily, then how could I trust any of it? It made me nervous, having such thoughts, but I couldn't keep them away.

That night, I couldn't sleep. I kept thinking about what Todd Morgan had said. "How can we have plural marriage in the next life, if we can't do it on earth?" I suddenly realized I was asking the same questions as Dad had been asking. It gave me a sick feeling in my stomach. But Dad had Joseph Smith, and all the original teachings of the Church, to believe in. Lying there, staring up into the darkness, I realized I didn't have that. I couldn't accept polygamy as a good thing, even if the scriptures said so. Not if it caused hurt and pain, like it had caused Mom. How could God have commanded something like that in the first place?

I wanted to talk to Mom about it, but I didn't want her to know how confused I was when she was still so sick. Wasn't there anyone I could talk to?

That's when I thought of Tommy. I could always talk to Tommy.

But then, I realized he wouldn't understand either. He would just say it was about time I woke up and realized that everything the

Church said was crazy. And it did seem crazy, at least the part about polygamy, and some of the other things like that. It scared me to be doubting things I'd believed all my life. It made me feel like the whole world was shaking, like everything was about to fall apart. I focused on the darkness behind my eyelids and tried to silence my mind.

Then, I heard something. It was a whooshing sound outside the window. Oh, no. Was it the owl again? Was he going to make his deadly cry when Mom was about to go into surgery?

I said, "I don't believe in you, owl." I said it out loud, and then I repeated it again.

I held my breath and listened for a long time. Was it still out there?

I tried to force it to go away with my mind until I remembered it might be the lucky owl. Then I wanted it to stay. It only took me a minute to realize that was ridiculous; I was just believing what I'd read in a book. It was just as crazy as all the other beliefs I'd been thinking about all day. If an owl was out there, so what? It was just a plain old ordinary owl. If it hooted in the night, it was because that's what owls do. I told him to go away and sunk back down in my bed and tried to sleep.

It was so late the next morning when I woke up, I thought that maybe Dad had gone to the hospital by himself. I raced downstairs and looked outside, but the car was still there. I looked all over the house and found him in his study. He was sound asleep at his desk with his head on his arms. I shook him and yelled, "Dad, wake up. We're supposed to be at the hospital."

He lifted his head and tried to focus. That was when I noticed he'd been lying on his blue notebook, the one where he'd written all his questions about becoming a god. It was open, and there was a pen in the middle of it. It scared me to death. Was he thinking about things like polygamy again? I was shocked, but there was nothing I could do about it right now.

I shook him again and yelled, "We're going to miss Mom if you don't hurry."

This time he blinked and jumped out of his chair. "Oh, no. What time is it? Hurry, Beth. Get Mikey. We've got to go."

We hurried out to the car. Dad sped all the way to the busy city streets where he had to slow down. By the time we got to the hospital, the nurse was already rolling Mom to the operating room. We ran down the hall after them and caught up just outside the big double doors. Dad said, "Please, can I have a moment with my wife?"

The nurse stepped aside, and Dad bent down to kiss Mom on the forehead. "Everything's going to be fine, honey. Everyone's praying for you."

Mom could barely open her eyes, but she moaned a little when Dad said, "I love you, sweetheart. Remember, I love you."

I stepped in next to Dad and squeezed her hand. "Mom, the people at church forgave Dad. You don't have to worry about that anymore."

I thought she smiled just a little, but I wasn't sure. Then Dad told me to make room for Mikey.

He said, "Bye, bye, Momma. I hope it won't hurt."

Dad gave Mom another kiss, then the nurse pushed her into the operating room. We stood there staring at the double doors for a few minutes, and then we went down the hall to the waiting room.

Dad sat down and tried to read a magazine, but it seemed like he was just flipping through the pages. He soon gave up and just stared down at the floor. Every once in a while, he'd look up at the clock.

I kept on looking at the clock too. The hands barely seemed to move. Mikey got so fidgety, he finally had to get up and wander around the room, but the room was so small it didn't help him much. He sat down and started kicking his feet up in the air. Then he twisted his fingers into different shapes and made little whistling sounds that made a lady on the other side of the room stare at him.

Dad said, "Keep it down, Michael."

We all needed something to help take our minds off the worry, but there wasn't anything to do. Finally, Mikey turned to Dad and said, "Can't you tell us a story or something?"

"What kind of story?"

Mikey shrugged. "Umm. . . An exciting one . . . about a pirate or a sailor."

Dad cleared his throat and said, "Okay . . . let's see. How about this? Once there was a sailor out on a boat . . . it was somewhere . . . maybe out in the middle of the ocean. It was night and . . . clouds filled the sky, so he didn't even have the stars to guide him. There he was, all alone. It was dark and--"

Mikey said, "He was all by himself in the middle of the ocean?"

"Yes. He was lost. He'd started on a journey to bring back good things for his family, but he'd lost his oars so he couldn't get back home." Dad's eyes got wet, and he started blinking. He looked up at the ceiling and down at the floor. I realized he was thinking about himself. He was the lost man without any oars.

Mikey got impatient. "So, what happened to the sailor?"

Dad put his hand over his eyes and let out a sob.

I whispered. "Dad can't tell a story right now, Mikey."

Mikey started kicking his feet again, swinging them all the way back so that they hit the bottom part of the couch and made a thump.

Dad jumped up. I thought he was going to yell at Mikey, but instead he said, "I'm sorry, I'll be back in a minute." He hurried out of the room.

I shook my head. "Now look what you've done."

"I didn't do nuthin."

"Yes you did. You upset Dad."

"What did I do? I just said for him to tell us a story."

"I know, but I guess he can't think about things like that right now."

"Well, I'm bored. And I'm hungry. Why don't we ever get to eat anymore?"

"Maybe you should close your eyes and try to imagine a story in your own mind."

He tried it, but I don't think he was making up a story. After a few minutes, he curled up next to me on the couch. I didn't know if he fell asleep, or if he was just pretending.

When Dad came back, his eyes were all red. I didn't ask him what was wrong, because I already knew. He was thinking about Mom and all the things he'd done to hurt her. I wanted to say something to comfort him, but I knew it was something that was going to take a long time to heal.

He sat back down, and we continued to wait. The time was going so slow I could hardly stand it. I didn't think it was fair that people had to wait in a place like that while something bad was happening to somebody they loved. The longer we waited, the more scared I got, and the more my imagination went wild thinking of all the things that could go wrong. What could they be doing to her in there? Why was it taking so long?

I tried to distract myself by thinking about how things would be when Mom got home from the hospital, but it didn't work. Instead, I started going over the whole thing again, trying to make sense of it in a new way. If the Church hadn't changed the rules about polygamy in the first place, would Mom have been willing to do it? Would she have just grown up thinking it was what God wanted? And what about me? Would I think it was okay if that's what I had learned when I was young? I didn't know. I couldn't put my mind in that place. I had been told all my life that polygamy was wrong. It was against the law, even if Joseph Smith and Brigham Young did do it.

As I sat there, I began to wonder if I even believed in God anymore. I knew I still needed Him. I needed Him to heal Mom, and I needed Him to help us get back to being a happy family again. But could He really decide what the doctors would find when they looked inside Mom? What if they looked too soon before God had decided if He was going to help? What would they find?

I didn't know how long I'd been sitting there lost in my thoughts, when the doctor came in. He sat down next to Dad and said, "In a way, it's what we were hoping for. I mean, it's not cancer. But there were ulcers in her colon, and that's not good. She's got colitis. She's going to have to be careful what she eats, and it's very important for her to avoid any kind of stress. Otherwise, she'll probably have more of these episodes. And that could lead to cancer."

I couldn't concentrate after he said that word, cancer. It was such a terrible word. I knew what it meant, and the only thing that kept me from bursting into tears was that he'd said she didn't have it yet. Not yet? Did that mean God hadn't decided yet? If it all depended on how much stress she had, it seemed more like it was up to Dad and Mikey and me than it was up to God.

I wanted to grab the doctor's arm and make him tell me exactly what we had to do to keep Mom from being stressed, but I knew it wasn't really that simple. It had to do with her too, and whether or not she could think about things in a different way. Maybe I could help her do that. If I could get clear about things myself.

I heard Dad say, "Is she . . . awake? Can I see her?"

The doctor shook his head. "Better give her another half hour or so to recover. She came through it very well. But I'd like to keep her here for a while. I'll have the nurse come and tell you when she's awake."

"Thank you, doctor. Thank you . . . for everything."

When we went in to see Mom, Dad sat next to her on the bed and held her hand. "Hello, my darling. How do you feel?"

For a minute, she wasn't able to get her mouth working right. Then she mumbled, "Groggy."

Dad kissed her hand. "I can see that, but the doctor says you're going to be just fine now."

Mom smiled a crooked little smile, then closed her eyes. I could see she was sleepy, and I didn't think we should talk to her anymore. Dad must have thought that too because he said, "Come on, kids. Let's let her rest. It's the best thing for her now." He kissed her hand one more time and said, "I'll be back soon, my love. You have a good sleep now."

Dad and Mikey left the room, but I stayed for just a second to look at Mom and try to settle it with myself that she really was okay. She was so little she hardly made a bump beneath the blanket. It was hard to believe she'd gotten so small in such a short time. Would she ever be strong and healthy again? I picked up her hand and softly kissed it just like Dad did. I whispered, "We love you, Mom. We'll be waiting for you at home." Then, I tiptoed out of the room.

Chapter 37

. . . little children do have words given unto them many times, which confound the wise and the learned.

Doctrine and Covenants
Alma 32:23

$\mathcal{O}$n a Saturday morning, after Mom had been in the hospital for nearly two weeks, Dad came in my room and said, "I'm going to go get your mother."

"I'll get Mikey."

"No, Beth. I'm going alone. I need to give her my full attention."

"But Dad, I can sit with her in the back seat while you drive."

"It's better if I go alone. We'll be home before you know it."

After he left, I wandered around the house straightening things up so everything would be nice for Mom when she got home. When I finished, I tried to think if there was anything else I needed to do. That's when I remembered Dad's blue notebook. I had to make sure she didn't see that and get stressed, and I wanted to see what he'd been writing.

I raced downstairs to his study. At first, I couldn't find it. I looked everywhere, in the desk and on the bookshelf, and in the closet. Then I thought maybe Dad hid things the same way I did. I went back to the middle desk drawer and reached way back until I felt the notebook. I pulled it out and sat down in Dad's chair.

For a minute, I just held the notebook against my chest, not sure I really I wanted to know what was inside. Then I slowly opened it and flipped to the last page where he had written his latest words:

- How can I take my wife and children to the Celestial Kingdom if plural marriage is forbidden? The prophet says we will live the law in the next life, but a temple marriage can only be performed on earth, so how can a man abide by God's eternal law, if the prerequisites are not allowed on earth?

- How can I become a god, if I cannot live according to the laws of the Eternal Father? That is the purpose of life, isn't it? The reason I exist is to progress to that ultimate goal. Am I strong enough to overcome the burdens and temptations of my physical existence to reach that goal? I fear I am not. I fear I am doomed.

It was exactly what I was afraid of. Dad was still asking himself the same old questions. Would he get involved in polygamy again? If he did, it would destroy Mom. It made me so angry, I banged the book down on the desk. I felt like tearing the pages out and burning them. Why did he want to give up everything on earth for something in the next life, something he couldn't even be sure of? But maybe he really wouldn't do it. Maybe he wasn't strong enough to go against everyone in the Church, especially now that he didn't have Brother Reuben telling him it was the right thing. I hoped it wasn't true that polygamy was the only way for him to get to heaven, and I hoped he could still be a god, if that's what he really wanted. Most of all I hoped he wouldn't hurt Mom anymore.

I put the notebook back where I'd found it and left the study. I started walking fast all around the house, trying to think how to keep him from doing anything to upset Mom. But what could I say? The doctor had already warned him about the stress, and the Bishop had warned him about questioning the prophet, but he was still doing it. I started to get that old tight feeling in my chest.

I heard the car in the driveway. I hurried out to the carport just as Dad was getting out of the car. I couldn't keep myself from giving him a dirty look.

He looked surprised. "What's that for? Is something wrong?"

"I hope not." That's all I said. I didn't want to talk about it in front of Mom.

I swung open the car door, still feeling a little short of breath. "Welcome home, Mom. I'm really happy you're here."

She gave me a little smile. "I'm happy too, honey. Are you okay?"

I forced a smile. "Yeah, I'm okay."

"That's good."

Dad said, "Come on, Beth. Let me get her in the house. You can talk once we're inside." He helped Mom out of the car, while I ran to open the front door. He took her straight upstairs and put her to bed.

Mikey came in their bedroom, and we both stood there looking at her. I saw a shadow of pain in her eyes that made them dull, and I didn't think it was just the pain from her surgery. I could only hope it would go away in time, once she got used to us all being home together again.

I said, "Do you need anything, Mom? Do you want something to drink, or maybe some Jell-O or something?"

"I wouldn't mind a glass of water, honey. Did you make Jell-O?" Her voice was weak.

"No, some of the ladies in the Ward brought it over. They brought a lot of other stuff too. If you're hungry, I can get you something."

"No. Not right now."

I ran downstairs for the water. When I came back up, Dad had taken off his shoes and was lying next to Mom. He let Mikey and me stay with them for a while, but when she started to doze off, he whispered, "I'll stay with her while she rests. You kids find something to do with yourselves."

I followed Mikey to our bedroom. He sat on the floor and immediately started playing with his erector set, as if I wasn't even there.

That was okay with me. I had things to think about, and I knew just where I wanted to go to do it. I hurried downstairs, put on my jacket, and went out into the backyard. As I hurried through the plum trees, I realized it was the same time of year as when Dad had his vision. The water would be roaring down at the creek, but I didn't care. I wanted to go there anyway. I wanted to be back where everything started. I wanted to face the roaring water, and this time not be afraid. I wanted to find out once and for all if a person really could talk to God.

I ran along the trail through the sagebrush, almost afraid that someone would try to stop me. But there was no one around. There were clouds of fog drifting through the gray branches of the scrub oak, and the old wet leaves on the ground smelled musty, just like they did that day a year ago. My heart raced as I thought about Dad out in the roaring water with the light shining down on his face.

I stopped and held my stomach for a minute to stop its churning. I felt afraid, but I knew that something was waiting for me down at the creek, something I needed to know in order to move on.

As I dropped down into the trees and into the fog, I heard the sound of the water. It was the same terrifying roar as that day Dad had his revelation. The fear moved up into my throat, but I kept on going.

Finally, I made my way through the last of the scrub oak and saw the thundering river. It was wilder than I'd ever seen it before. It was swirling every which way, spilling over the dam so high you could hardly tell there was a dam under there. Broken trees crashed up against the cement walls next to the dam and bounced back out, getting caught in a whirlpool, spinning around and around until they finally broke loose and sailed over the dam. Some of the trees got caught in a big pile near the washed-out bank. For some reason, I felt an urgent need to free the trees, to help them over the dam and send them on their way.

I got down as close as I could and tried to pull the trees loose. But they were too big, and their roots and limbs were all tangled together. I pulled and pulled at them, but I wasn't strong enough to set them free.

I stood up and watched more trees coming to add to the ones already spinning. Suddenly, I realized my family was just like those trees. We'd been spinning around and around, each of us caught up in an eddy of our own beliefs. But those beliefs didn't really belong to us, they were given to us by somebody else. They weren't things we'd found out on our own.

I didn't want to be like those trees anymore. I didn't want to be stuck, going nowhere, waiting for someone else to tell me what to do. I wanted to sail over the dam and float along the top of the raging river all the way out to the Great Salt Lake.

I forced myself to sit down at the edge of the dam. I was so close to the roaring water, it vibrated through my whole body. But I wasn't scared anymore. I felt as if the power of the water had entered me and made me strong. I stood up and called out, "God. Are you there? Are you listening to me?"

My whole body trembled as I waited for an answer, and then, the fog separated and the sunlight came blazing down on me. It was so brilliant, it nearly took my breath away.

I stood there listening and watching the light, wondering if God would talk to me. I waited for a long time, but there was no voice. There was no angel, or anything. There was just the sun breaking through the fog. Nothing more, and nothing less. It was beautiful, but it wasn't God.

I realized I had learned something that would change my whole life. From then on, I wasn't going to accept other people's version of the truth. It might mean the other kids wouldn't like me; maybe nobody would like me. It didn't matter. I was going to read books and learn as much as I could about everything. I would listen carefully to what people said, but then I would decide the truth for myself.

8151164R0

Made in the USA
Lexington, KY
11 January 2011